Spanish
in 30 days

Course Book

by Carmen R. de Königbauer and Harda Kuwer

Spanish

in 30 days

Course Book

by Carmen R. de Königbauer and Harda Kuwer

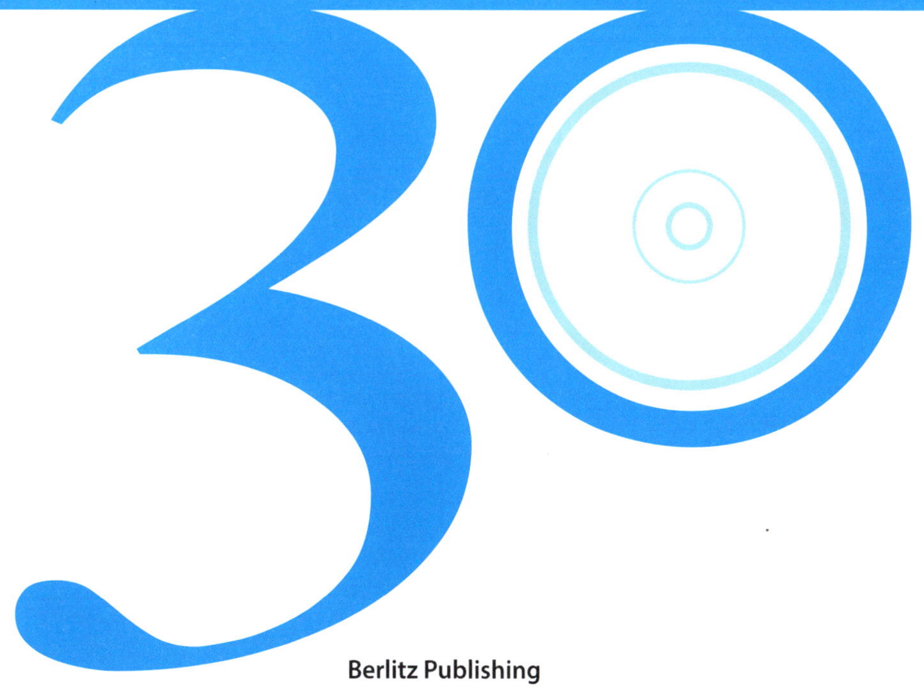

Berlitz Publishing
New York London Singapore

Contacting the Editors

Every effort has been made to provide accurate information in this publication, but changes are inevitable. The publisher cannot be responsible for any resulting loss, inconvenience or injury. We would appreciate it if readers would call our attention to any errors or outdated information. Please contact us at: comments@berlitzpublishing.com

Original edition: 2001 by Langenscheidt KG, Berlin and Munich

Second edition: 2014
Printed in China

Senior Commissioning Editor: Kate Drynan
Design: Beverley Speight
Picture research: Beverley Speight
Spanish editor: Vanessa Martínez Pérez

Cover photos: ©APA Greg Wrona, APA Greg Gladman

Interior photos: © istockphoto p21,37,45,54,64,74,90,106,130,147,155,163,172,180,206,215,222,245, 252; APA Greg Gladman p 83,114, 121,138,198,237; APA Peter Stuckings p15; APA Ming Tang Evans p28; APA Corrie Wingate p98; APA Britta Jaschinski p230; APA Bev Speight p190.

Distribution

Worldwide
APA Publications GmbH & Co. Verlag KG
(Singapore branch)
7030 Ang Mo Kio Ave 5
08-65 Northstar @ AMK, Singapore 569880
Email: apasin@singnet.com.sg

US
Ingram Publisher Services
One Ingram Blvd, PO Box 3006
La Vergne, TN 37086-1986
Email: ips@ingramcontent.com

UK and Ireland
Dorling Kindersley Ltd
(a Penguin Company)
80 Strand, London, WC2R 0RL, UK
Email: sales@uk.dk.com

Australia
Woodslane
10 Apollo St
Warriewood, NSW 2102
Email: info@woodslane.com.au

Contents

How to Use this Book

Spanish in 30 Days is a self-study course which will provide you with a basic knowledge of everyday Spanish in a very short time. The course is divided into 30 short, manageable daily lessons. This book will familiarize you with the main grammatical structures of Spanish and provide you with a good command of essential vocabulary. In 30 days you will acquire both an active and a passive understanding of the language, enabling you to function effectively in day-to-day life.

Each chapter is an episode in a journey that takes place over 30 days, from your arrival to your final departure, with the main focus on typical, day-to-day situations. Each day has the same pattern: first, there is a short intro into what you will learn as well as some country and culture information about Spain. You will then have a text in Spanish – generally a dialogue – followed by a grammar section and a number of exercises to help reinforce what you have learned. At the end of each lesson you will find a list of vocabulary. The quick grammar and vocabulary tests, together with the answer key at the back of the book, will enable you to check your progress.

The audio CD contains all the dialogues from the book. These are marked by a CD symbol. Days 1 to 10 are spoken twice: the first time, quickly and fluently so that you get used to hearing everyday Spanish and, the second time, slowly and more clearly. From day 11 onwards you'll be advanced enough to follow the Spanish text, which will now be spoken only once, in the faster speech of everyday language.

Spanish Pronunciation

There are variations between the Spanish spoken in Spain and that spoken in the Americas – although each is easily understood by the other.

Consonants

Letter	Approximate pronunciation	Example
b	1) as in English	*bueno*
	2) between vowels as in English, but softer	*bebida*
c	1) before e and i, like ***th*** in thin; in Latin America, like ***s*** in sit	*centro*
	2) otherwise like ***k*** in kit	*como*
ch	as in English	*mucho*
d	1) as in English dog, but less decisive	*donde*
	2) between vowels and at the end of a word, like ***th*** in this	*usted*
g	1) before e and i, like ***ch*** in Scottish loch	*urgente*
	2) otherwise, like ***g*** in get	*ninguno*
h	always silent	*hombre*
j	like ***ch*** in Scottish loch	*bajo*
ll	like ***lli*** in million	*lleno*
ñ	like ***ni*** in onion	*señor*
qu	like ***k*** in kick	*quince*

r	more strongly trilled (like a Scottish ***r***), especially at the beginning of a word	***río***
rr	strongly trilled	***arriba***
s	1) like ***s*** in same	***vista***
	2) before b, d, g, l, m, n, like ***s*** in rose	***mismo***
v	like ***b*** in bad, but softer	***viejo***
z	like ***th*** in thin in Latin America, like ***s*** in sit	***brazo***

Letters ***f, k, l, m, n, p, t, x*** and ***y*** are pronounced as in English.

Vowels

Letter	Approximate pronunciation	Example
a	in length, between ***a*** in English pat, and ***a*** in English bar	***gracias***
e	1) like ***e*** in get	***puedo***
	2) in a syllable ending in a vowel like ***e*** in they	***me***
i	like ***ee*** in feet	***sí***
o	like ***o*** in got	***dos***
u	1) like ***oo*** in food	***una***
	2) silent after g in words like ***guerra, guiso,*** except where marked ü, as in ***antigüedad***	
y	only a vowel when alone at the end of a word, like ***ee*** in feet	***y***

Note: In words ending with a vowel, **-n** or **-s**, the next to last syllable is stressed, e.g. ***mañana***; in words ending in a consonant, the last syllable is stressed, e.g. ***señor***; the acute accent **(´)** is used in Spanish to indicate a syllable is stressed, not a change in sound, e.g. ***río***.

Note that some Spanish words have more than one meaning. In these cases, the acute accent is used to distinguish between them, e.g. ***él*** (he) and ***el*** (the); ***sí*** (yes) and ***si*** (if); ***tú*** (you) and ***tu*** (your).

The Alphabet

The Spanish alphabet is the same as the English, with the addition of the tilde (accent) on the letter ***ñ***.

A	ah
B	beh
C	theh
	seh (in Latin America)
D	deh
E	eh
F	ehfeh
G	kheh
H	ahcheh
I	ee
J	khotah
K	kah
L	ehleh
M	emeh
N	ennneh
Ñ	enyeh
O	oh
P	peh
Q	koo
R	erreh
S	ehseh
T	teh
U	oo
V	oobheh
	beh (in Latin America)
W	dobleh beh
X	ekees
Y	ee-greeyega
Z	theta
	setah (in Latin America)

Numbers

0	**cero** *theh•roh*
1	**uno** *oo•noh*
2	**dos** *dohs*
3	**tres** *trehs*
4	**cuatro** *kwah•troh*
5	**cinco** *theen•koh*
6	**seis** *seyees*
7	**siete** *seeyeh•teh*
8	**ocho** *oh•choh*
9	**nueve** *nweh•beh*
10	**diez** *deeyehth*
11	**once** *ohn•theh*
12	**doce** *doh•theh*
13	**trece** *treh•theh*
14	**catorce** *kah•tohr•theh*
15	**quince** *keen•theh*
16	**dieciséis** *deeyeh•thee•seyees*
17	**diecisiete** *deeyeh•thee•seeyeh•teh*
18	**dieciocho** *deeyeh•thee•oh•choh*
19	**diecinueve** *deeyeh•thee•nweh•beh*
20	**veinte** *beyeen•teh*
21	**veintiuno** *beyeen•tee•oo•noh*
22	**veintidós** *beyeen•tee•dohs*

30	**treinta** *treyeen•tah*
31	**treinta y uno** *treyeen•tah ee oo•noh*
40	**cuarenta** *kwah•rehn•tah*
50	**cincuenta** *theen•kwehn•tah*
60	**sesenta** *seh•sehn•tah*
70	**setenta** *seh•tehn•tah*
80	**ochenta** *oh•chehn•tah*
90	**noventa** *noh•behn•tah*
100	**cien** *theeyehn*
101	**ciento uno** *theeyehn•toh oo•noh*
200	**doscientos** *dohs•theeyehn•tohs*
500	**quinientos** *kee•neeyehn•tohs*
1,000	**mil** *meel*
10,000	**diez mil** *deeyehth meel*
1,000,000	**un millón** *oon mee•yohn*

Days

Monday **lunes** *loo•nehs*

Tuesday **martes** *mahr•tehs*

Wednesday **miércoles** *meeyehr•koh•lehs*

Thursday **jueves** *khweh•behs*

Friday **viernes** *beeyehr•nehs*

Saturday **sábado** *sah•bah•doh*

Sunday **domingo** *doh•meen•goh*

Months

January **enero** *eh•neh•roh*

February **febrero** *feh•breh•roh*

March **marzo** *mahr•thoh*

April **abril** *ah•breel*

May **mayo** *mah•yoh*

June **junio** *khoo•neeyoh*

July **julio** *khoo•leeyoh*

August **agosto** *ah•gohs•toh*

September **septiembre** *sehp•teeyehm•breh*

October **octubre** *ohk•too•breh*

November **noviembre** *noh•beeyehm•breh*

December **diciembre** *dee•theeyehm•breh*

Seasons

spring **la primavera** *lah pree•mah•beh•rah*

summer **el verano** *ehl beh•rah•noh*

fall **el otoño** *ehl oh•toh•nyoh*

winter **el invierno** *ehl een•beeyehr•noh*

day: 1

On the plane

Welcome to Spain! Day 1marks your arrival in Spain. You will learn the present tense of the verb *ser* (to be) as well as some regular verbs and personal pronouns. You will be able to make simple sentences and ask questions. You will also start to build your vocabulary and pick up some important language and cultural tips.

COFFEE...

When ordering coffee, you won't be ordering just ***un café*** *- you'll most likely need to specify!*

café solo *= small, strong, black coffee (like espresso)*
café con leche *= large milk coffee that is not the same as coffee with milk*
café cortado *= small coffee with a little milk*
carajillo *= espresso with a dash of brandy, whisky or cognac*

Spanish conversation: En el avión

Azafata:	**¿Habla usted español?**
Karen:	**Sí, un poco.**
Azafata:	**¿Qué toma usted?**
Karen:	**Un café, por favor.**
Azafata:	**¿Con leche y azúcar?**
Karen:	**Sólo con leche, gracias…**
	¡Oh, perdón!
Pasajero:	**No es nada, no es nada… Yo soy de Madrid.**
Karen:	**¡Ah! ¡Usted es español!**
Pasajero:	**Sí. ¿Viaja usted a España como turista?**
Karen:	**No, no viajo como turista sino como au pair para un año.**
Pasajero:	**¡Qué interesante! ¿A qué ciudad viaja usted?**
Karen:	**A Madrid.**
Pasajero:	**¡Perdón! Yo soy José Pérez, soy profesor.**
Karen:	**Yo soy Karen Muller, soy enfermera.**

English conversation: On the plane

Flight attendant:	**Do you speak Spanish?**
Karen:	**Yes, a little.**
Flight attendant:	**What would you like to drink?**
Karen:	**Coffee please.**
Flight attendant:	**With milk and sugar?**
Karen:	**Just milk, thanks…**
	Oh, I'm sorry.
Passenger:	**It's alright, nothing happened… I'm from Madrid.**
Karen:	**Ah, …You're Spanish!**
Passenger:	**Yes. Are you travelling to Spain as a tourist?**
Karen:	**No, I am not going there as a tourist but as an au pair for a year.**
Passenger:	**How interesting! Which city are you going to?**
Karen:	**To Madrid.**
Passenger:	**I'm sorry! I am José Pérez. I'm a teacher.**
Karen:	**I'm Karen Muller. I'm a nurse.**

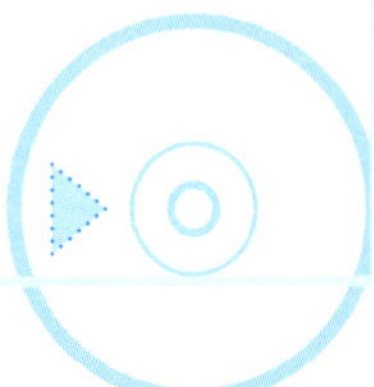

Grammar

Regular verbs ending in *-ar*

The infinitive of Spanish verbs ends in **-ar**, **-er** or **-ir**. Below you will learn how to form verbs ending in **-ar**. In Spanish, the verb ending specifies the person (I, you...) and the tense (in this case, the present tense).

viajar (to travel)			
viaj*o*	I travel	**viaj*amos***	we travel
viaj*as*	you travel	**viaj*áis***	you *(pl.)* travel
viaj*a*	he, she travels	**viaj*an***	they travel

Personal pronouns

(yo) **viajo**	I travel
(tú) **viajas**	you travel
(él, ella, usted) **viaja**	he, she travels/you travel
(nosotros, -as) **viajamos**	we travel
(vosotros, -as) **viajáis**	you *(pl.)* travel
(ellos, ellas, ustedes) **viajan**	they travel/you *(pl.)* travel

Note:
Nosotros, **vosotros** and **ellos** have a feminine form ending in **-as**. **Usted (Ud.)** and **ustedes (Uds.)** are the formal forms of address. The informal form used for friends, children and relatives is **tú**. **Vosotros/as** is not used in Latin America where the plural form of you is expressed by **ustedes** regardless of formality. Unlike in English, these pronouns are used only for emphasis, contrast or to avoid confusion.

Verbs: ser (to be)

Ser is used to identify people/objects with noun phrases and to describe the natural characteristics of a person/object (for more on this, see page 31).

Soy **José Pérez.**	I am José Pérez.
Eres **profesor.**	You are a teacher.
Es **domingo.**	It is Sunday.
Somos **españoles.**	We are Spanish.
Sois **simpáticos.**	You are nice.
Son **de Madrid.**	They are from Madrid.

Simple sentences

Sentence structures are much the same as in English:

Yo soy de Madrid.	I am from Madrid.
Usted es americana.	You are American.

Questions and commands

Sentence structures are much the same as in English:

¿Es Ud. de Boston?	Are you from Boston?
¿Viaja Ud. a España?	Are you traveling to Spain?

Note:
Questions and exclamations open and close with punctuation marks (¿…?) (¡…!).

Negatives

The negation **no** always precedes the verb in Spanish.

***No viajo* como turista.**	I am **not traveling** as a tourist.
***No tomo* café.**	I am **not having** coffee.

Exercises

Exercise 1

Fill in the correct verb form.

1 José (viajar) .... a Madrid.

2 Ella (tomar) .... café con leche.

3 Karen y José (hablar) .... español.

4 Usted (estudiar).. francés.

5 Nosotros (hablar) .... italiano.

6 Tú (entrar) .... en el bar.

7 Ellas (tomar)... el avión.

Exercise 2

Fill in the correct form of ser.

1 Tú .... arquitecto.

2 José .... profesor.

3 Él .... italiano.

4 Pedro .... ingeniero.

5 Vosotras .... simpáticas.

6 Ellos .... españoles.

7 La leche .... blanca.

Exercise 3

Put the sentences from exercise 1 into the negative.

1 ....

2 ....

3 ....

4 ....

5 ....

6 ....

7 ....

Exercise 4

Translate the following text into Spanish:

He is from Barcelona. He is Spanish.

I am from England. Are you traveling as a tourist? Are you traveling to Spain?

Do you take milk and sugar? No, just milk, thank you.

....

....

....

....

I am Paul. I am a teacher and am learning Spanish. How interesting!

....

....

Vocabulary

Below is a list of vocabulary encountered in this chapter.

a	*to*
adiós	*goodbye*
América	*America*
americano, -a	*American*
año *m*	*year*
aquí	*here*
arquitecto *m*	*architect*
avión *m*	*airplane*
azafata *f*	*flight attendant*
azúcar *m*	*sugar*
bar *m*	*bar*
blanco, -a	*white*
Boston	*Boston*
café *m*	*coffee*
ciudad *f*	*city, town*
como	*as, like*
con	*with*
de	*from*
de nada	*you're welcome*
día *m*	*day*
domingo *m*	*Sunday*
en	*in*
enfermera *f*	*nurse*
entrar	*to enter*
España *f*	*Spain*
español/ -a	*Spanish; Spaniard/ Spanish woman*
estudiar	*to learn, study*
gracias	*thank you*
hablar	*to speak*
ingeniero *m*	*engineer*
inglés, -a	*English; Englishman/ woman*
Inglaterra	*England*
interesante	*interesting*
italiano, -a	*Italian*
leche *f*	*milk*
muchas gracias	*many thanks*
no pasa nada	*it's alright, nothing happened*
no	*no*
no hay de que	*Don't mention it!*
país *m*	*country*
pasajero *m*	*passenger*
perdón	*sorry, excuse me*
poco, -a	*little*
por favor	*please*
profesor *m*	*teacher*
qué	*how, which*
¡Qué interesante!	*How interesting!*
¿Qué?	*What?*
ser	*to be*
sí	*yes*
simpático, -a	*nice*
sino	*but, otherwise*
sólo	*only*
tomar	*to take, drink*
turista *m/f*	*tourist*
un	*one*
un poco	*a little*
un, -a	*one*
usted	*you (formal)*
viajar	*to travel*
y	*and*

day: 2

At the airport

Day 2 sees you arrive at the airport. You will learn the present tense of the verb *estar* (another verb meaning to be). You will learn about articles - how to distinguish between masculine and feminine words, how to make plurals and learn how to use adjectives. You will also pick up some more vocabulary and useful cultural tips.

¿SEÑORITA? ¿SEÑORITO?

Señorita *is not only used as a polite name for an unmarried woman, young or old, but it is also the standard term for a female teacher. A waitress will also respond to* ***señorita****.*

The masculine ***señorito****, on the other hand, is more of a reference to the male offspring of rich land owners in Andalusia and often carries the negative connotation of "spoilt brat". Instead, use* ***señor****.*

Spanish conversation: En el aeropuerto

En el control de pasaportes:

Policía:	**¡Buenos días!**
Karen:	**¡Buenos días!**
Policía:	**El pasaporte, por favor.**
Karen:	**Sí, aquí.**
Policía:	**Por aquí, por favor.**

En la cinta de equipaje:

Pasajero:	**¿Es todo su equipaje?**
Karen:	**Una maleta grande y un bolso.**
Pasajero:	**Es mucho. ¡Claro, para un año en Madrid!**
Karen:	**Ah, sí… […] ¿Dónde está mi pasaporte? ¡No está en el bolso!… ¡Oh, aquí está!**
Pasajero:	**Señorita Muller, aquí está mi tarjeta.**
Karen:	**Muchas gracias, Señor Pérez… Ah, allí está mi maleta.**
Pasajero:	**¿Dónde está mi equipaje?**
Karen:	**Allí está mi bolso.**
Pasajero:	**¿Está completo su equipaje?**
Karen:	**Sí… ¿Y su maleta?**
Pasajero:	**¡Allí está!**

English conversation: At the airport

At passport control:

Policeman:	**Good morning!**
Karen:	**Good morning!**
Policeman:	**Your passport please.**
Karen:	**Yes, here it is.**
Policeman:	**This way, please.**

At baggage claim:

Passenger:	**Is that all your luggage?**
Karen:	**A big suitcase and a bag.**
Passenger:	**That's a lot. Of course, it's for one year in Madrid.**
Karen:	**Yes, … Where is my passport? It's not in my bag!… Ah, here it is… !**
Passenger:	**Ms. Muller, here is my business card.**
Karen:	**Many thanks Mr. Pérez… Ah, there's my suitcase.**
Passenger:	**Where is my luggage?**

Karen: There is my bag.
Passenger: Do you have all your luggage?
Karen: Yes… and your suitcase?
Passenger: There it is!

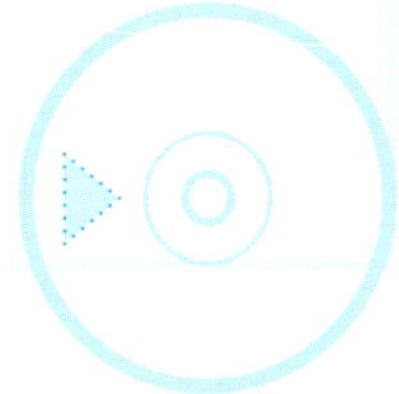

Grammar

Verbs: estar (to be, to be located)

Estoy en Madrid.	I am in Madrid.
Estás de viaje.	You are traveling.
Está enfermo, -a.	He/she is ill.
Estamos listos.	We are ready.
Estáis tristes.	You are sad.
Están aquí.	They are here.

Note:
Estar, in distinction to ser, is used to indicate a state, where something/someone is located and for dates (for more on ser, refer back to page 17).

The definite/indefinite articles

In Spanish, the definite article **the** has 4 forms, depending on whether the noun is masculine, feminine, singular or plural: el (m), la (f), los (m pl), las (f pl). In English, **the** does not change.
The indefinite article **a**, **an** or **some** also has 4 forms in Spanish, depending on whether the noun is masculine, feminine, singular or plural: un (m), unos (m pl), una (f pl), unas (f pl).

definite article		indefinite article	
el pasajero	the passenger	los pasajeros	the passengers
un libro	a book	unos libros	some/a few books
la azafata	the flight attendant	las azafatas	the flight attendants
una tarjeta	a business card	unas tarjetas	some/a few business cards

As a general rule, masculine nouns end in -o, feminine nouns in -a.
However, there are some exceptions that you will need to learn!
el día – the day, la mano – the hand, el/la turista – the tourist (can be *masculine and feminine*).

Note:
The neutral article **lo** is used when forming nouns from adjectives or verbs: **lo bueno** the good; **a lo lejos** in the distance.

Adjectives

Most adjectives have two endings: **-o** when used with a masculine noun and **-a** when used with a feminine noun:

el* pasajero simpátic*o	the nice passenger
la* azafata español*a	the Spanish flight attendant

Adjectives ending in **-e**, **-l** and **-n** have only **one form** for **both genders**, e.g.

el* cielo azu*l	the blue sky
la* maleta azu*l	the blue suitcase

The plural is formed as with nouns by adding **-s** or **-es**:

las* maletas pequeñ*as	the small suitcases
los* libros azul*es	the blue books

Note:
The adjective agrees with the noun to which it relates in gender and number.

Plural nouns

The plural of nouns is formed by adding **-s** to words ending in a **vowel**:

el café	**los café*s***
la señorit*a*	**las señoritas**

or with **-es** when the word ends in a **consonant**:

el españo*l*	**los español*es***
la ciuda*d*	**las ciudad*es***

Exercises

Exercise 1

Fill in the correct form of estar.

1 ¿Dónde (estar) .... la azafata?
2 ¿Cómo (estar) .... Uds.?
3 ¿Dónde (estar) .... vosotros?
4 ¿Dónde (estar) .... ellos?
5 La maleta (estar) .... allí.
6 El café (estar) .... caliente.

Exercise 2

Fill in the correct articles and verb forms.

1 Yo (tomar) .... el café.
2 El avión (ser)........................... grande.
3 El pasajero (ser)....................... simpático.
4 El bolso (ser)........................... grande.
5 Las maletas (pesar) .... mucho.
6 ¿(Ser) Ud. .... au pair?
7 España (ser) .... un país grande.
8 La señorita (saludar) ....

Exercise 3

Form the plural.

el pasaporte... una azafata.................................
el equipaje... un pasajero...............................
la maleta.. una tarjeta................................
la aduana... un bolso....................................
el diccionario.. un libro.....................................

Exercise 4

Complete the endings of the adjectives below.

1 Las manos están suci.........

2 Los bolsos son grand.........

3 Sois muy simpátic.........

4 El libro es interesant.........

5 La leche es blanc.........

6 La azafata es amabl.........

Exercise 5

Match the adjectives with the nouns and add the indefinite article.

e.g. ***una azafata simpática***

grande – simpático – dulce – pesado – rubio

.... maleta ....

.... café ....

.... pasajero ....

.... aviones ....

.... aduanero ....

Vocabulary

Below is a list of vocabulary encountered in this chapter.

aduana *f*	*customs*
aduanero *m*	*customs officer*
aeropuerto *m*	*airport*
allí	*there*
amable	*friendly*
azul	*blue*
bolso *m*	*bag*
bueno	*of course, good*
¡Buenos días!	*Good morning! (until 12 noon)*
¡Buenas tardes!	*Good afternoon! (until 8 p.m.)*
¡Buenas noches!	*Good evening/night! (after dinner)*
cielo *m*	*sky*
cinta *f*	*belt*
cinta *f* **de equipaje**	*baggage claim*
completo, -a	*complete*
control *m*	*control*
control *m* **de pasaportes**	*passport control*
declarar	*to declare*
¿Dónde?	*Where?*
dulce	*sweet*
enfermo, -a	*ill, sick*
equipaje *m*	*luggage*
estar	*to be*
grande	*large, big*
¡Hola!	*Hello!*
Hola, ¿qué tal?	*Hello, how are you?*
Hola, ¿qué hay?	*Hi, what's up?*
interesante	*interesting*
libro *m*	*book*
listo, -a	*ready*
maleta *f*	*suitcase*
mano *f*	*hand*
mi	*my*
mucho, -a	*much, many*
necesario, -a	*necessary*
necesitar	*to need*
para	*for*
pasaporte *m*	*passport*
pequeño, -a	*small, little*
pesado,-a	*heavy*
pesar	*to weigh*
policía *m*	*policeman*
por aquí	*this way*
ropa *f*	*clothing*
rubio, -a	*blond*
saludar	*to greet*
su	*your (formal)*
sucio, -a	*dirty*
tarjeta *f*	*business card*
todo	*everything*
triste	*sad*
viaje *m*	*journey*

day: 3

The city

Day 3 takes you into the city. You will learn the essential irregular verb *ir* (to go) and you will learn the difference between *ser* and *estar* (both meaning to be!). You will also become familiar with numbers 0 to 30 and continue to build your vocabulary.

TAXI!

The sticker ***SP*** *at the front and rear bumper of taxis is not an abbreviation for Spain, it means* ***"Servicio Público"****, public transport.*

It is advisable to only take cabs with this sticker as the fares charged by private "taxi drivers" can be excessive. A surcharge for rides to and from the airport is standard. For tips, it's acceptable to simply round up the fare.

Spanish conversation: Ir a la ciudad

Pasajero:	**¿Cómo va al centro?**
Karen:	**Voy en taxi, es cómodo y práctico. ¿Y Ud.?**
Pasajero:	**Voy en autobús hasta la Plaza de Colón, que está en el centro y luego en metro.**
Karen:	**Bueno, Sr. Pérez, hasta otro día.**
Pasajero:	**Adiós, Srta. Muller, mucha suerte con la familia.**
Karen:	**Gracias, adiós.**

Karen va a la Oficina de Información.

Karen:	**Por favor, ¿dónde tomo el taxi para el centro?**
Empleada:	**Allí por la puerta grande a la izquierda y luego a la derecha.**
Karen:	**¿Está lejos?**
Empleada:	**No, está cerca.**
Karen:	**Muchas gracias.**
Empleada:	**De nada.**

Karen toma un taxi al centro.

Karen:	**Al centro, por favor.**
Taxista:	**Sí, señorita. ¿Adónde va Ud. exactamente?**
Karen:	**Aquí está la dirección. Es Paseo de la Castellana n.º 6.**
Taxista:	**Está bien.**
Karen:	**Hay mucho tráfico por aquí.**
Taxista:	**Ahora estamos en el Paseo de la Castellana.**
Karen:	**¿Cuánto es?**
Taxista:	**Son 25 euros.**
Karen:	**Es barato.**

Karen paga.

Karen:	**Gracias, adiós.**

English conversation: The drive to the city

Passenger: **How are you getting to the city?**
Karen: **I'm taking a taxi; that's comfortable and practical. And what about you?**
Passenger: **I'm taking the bus to the Plaza de Colón, which is in the city centre, and then I'll take the subway.**
Karen: **Well, Mr. Pérez, bye for now.**
Passenger: **Goodbye, Ms. Muller, good luck with the family.**
Karen: **Thank you, goodbye.**

Karen goes to the information office.

Karen: **Where can I get a taxi to the city, please?**
Employee: **Over there, through the big door to the left and then right.**
Karen: **Is it far?**
Employee: **No, it's close.**
Karen: **Many thanks.**
Employee: **You're welcome.**

Karen takes the taxi to the city.

Karen: **To the city center please.**
Taxi driver: **Yes, miss. Where exactly do you want to go?**
Karen: **Here is the address. It's Paseo de la Castellana No. 6.**
Taxi driver: **Very well.**
Karen: **There's a lot of traffic here.**
Taxi driver: **We are now in Paseo de la Castellana.**
Karen: **How much is it?**
Taxi driver: **That'll be 25 euros.**
Karen: **That's cheap.**

Karen pays.

Karen: **Thank you, goodbye.**

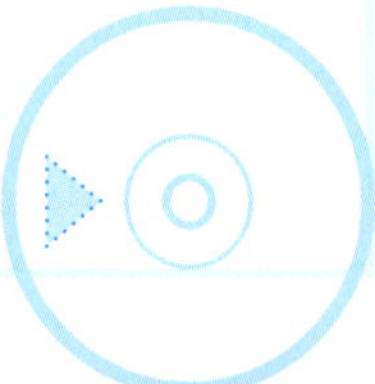

Grammar

Verbs: ir (to go)

voy	I go	vamos	we go
vas	you go *(sing. form)*	vais	you *(pl.)* go
va	he/she goes	van	they go/you *(Ud.)*

Please note:

Voy a pie. = I go on foot.

but

Voy en coche. = I go by car.

Ser and estar

Ser is used to express something **permanent** such as times and numbers (hours, days, quantities) or someone's background and profession.

Es la una de la tarde	It's one o'clock in the afternoon
Soy ingeniero	I am an engineer
Hoy *es* lunes	It's Monday today

Estar is used to describe something **passing** or **transitory**, such as a temporary location or a temporary condition.

Está en la calle	He is on the street
Está enfermo	He is ill

Note the different meanings:

La puerta *es* grande.	La puerta *está* abierta
The door is big	The door is open
Karen *es* de Boston	Karen *está* en Madrid
Karen is from Boston	Karen is (now) in Madrid

Nouns are always preceded by ser

Karen *es* enfermera	José *es* profesor

hay

The impersonal verb form hay means "there is, there are". Note that hay never changes its form, regardless of whether or not it refers to the singular or plural.

Hay mucho tráfico	There is a lot of traffic
Hay dos personas	There are two people

Adjectives

Adjectives can be positioned **before** and **after** the noun. Normally the adjective follows the noun.

la puerta *grande*	the big door

Where it precedes a noun it expresses a valuation.

la *famosa* cerveza	the famous beer (praising)
la cerveza *famosa*	(a neutral statement that the beer is famous)

Numerals and quantities precede the noun:

hay *mucho* tráfico	**son *tres* personas**

Numbers: 0 to 30

0	**cero**	**11**	**once**	**22**	**veintidós**
1	**uno**	**12**	**doce**	**23**	**veintitrés**
2	**dos**	**13**	**trece**	**24**	**veinticuatro**
3	**tres**	**14**	**catorce**	**25**	**veinticinco**
4	**cuatro**	**15**	**quince**	**26**	**veintiséis**
5	**cinco**	**16**	**dieciséis**	**27**	**veintisiete**
6	**seis**	**17**	**diecisiete**	**28**	**veintiocho**
7	**siete**	**18**	**dieciocho**	**29**	**veintinueve**
8	**ocho**	**19**	**diecinueve**	**30**	**treinta**
9	**nueve**	**20**	**veinte**		
10	**diez**	**21**	**veintiuno**		

Exercises

Exercise 1

Fill in the correct form of **ir**.

1 (Yo) .... a casa.

2 (Nosotros) .... a la Plaza de Colón.

3 El coche .... a la derecha.

4 .... (ustedes) a Inglaterra?

5 Hoy (nosotros) .... a la playa.

Exercise 2

Ser or **estar**?

Karen Muller .... enfermera. Ella .... de Estados Unidos. .... americana. .... de Boston, pero .... en Madrid con una familia. La familia García .... simpática. La Sra. García .... madrileña. Los niños .... en casa. Ellos .... niños cariñosos.

Exercise 3

Ser or **estar**?

1 ¿De dónde .... Uds.? .... de Madrid.

2 Tú .... de Barcelona, ¿verdad? Sí, (yo) .... de Barcelona.

3 ¿Dónde .... Juan? Él .... en Granada.

Exercise 4

Place the adjectives in their correct position before or after the noun.

gente/mucha ....

la lengua/francesa ....

los turistas/franceses ....

ruido/tanto ....

hoteles/buenos ....

la semana/última...

azafatas/pocas ....

pasajeros/tres ....

Exercise 5

Did you notice how a combines with ir to specify the direction (where one is going) while en is used to describe the means of transport?

Choose either: ¿Vamos en…? or ¿Vamos a…?

Vamos .... autobús

Vamos .... Granada

Vamos .... tren

Vamos .... barco

Vamos .... avión

Vamos .... Madrid

Exercise 6

Translate the following text into Spanish:

Karen takes her luggage and goes to the city center. That's 25 euros. Karen pays. At the Paseo de la Castellana No. 6 she gets off (bajar). There are a lot of people in the center. Here is the address. Where is the house?

....

....

....

....

....

....

....

Vocabulary

Below is a list of vocabulary encountered in this chapter.

¿Adónde?	*Where to?*
a la derecha	*to/on the right*
a la izquierda	*to/on the left*
ahora	*now*
autobús *m*	*bus*
bajar	*to get off*
barato, -a	*cheap*
barco *m*	*boat, ship*
bueno, -a	*good*
calle *f*	*street*
cariñoso, -a	*affectionate*
casa *f*	*house*
centro *m*	*city centre*
cerca	*close*
cerveza *f*	*beer*
ciudad *f*	*city*
coche *m*	*car*
¿Cómo?	*How?*
cómodo, -a	*comfortable*
cuánto, -a	*how much*
¿Cuánto es?	*How much does it cost?*
¿De dónde?	*From where?*
derecha	*right*
dirección *f*	*address*
donde	*where*
empleada *f*	*employee*
enfermo, -a	*sick, ill*
está bien	*OK*
Estados Unidos	*United States*
euro *m*	*euro (€)*
exactamente	*exactly*
excelente	*excellent*
extranjera *f*	*foreigner*
extranjero *m*	*foreigner*
fabricar	*to produce*
familia *f*	*family*
famoso, -a	*famous*
gente *f*	*people*
hasta	*until*
hasta otro día	*until later, bye for now*
hay	*there is/are*
hotel *m*	*hotel*
hoy	*today*
Inglaterra *f*	*England*
ir	*to go, drive*
izquierda	*left*
jerez *m*	*sherry*
lejos	*far*
lengua *f*	*language*
luego	*afterwards*
lunes *m*	*Monday*
madrileño, -a	*inhabitant of Madrid, from Madrid*
metro *m*	*subway*
niña *f*	*girl*
niño *m*	*boy*
niños *m pl*	*children*
nuestro, -a	*our*
oficina *f*	*office*
oficina *f* **de información**	*information bureau/office*
otro, -a	*other*
pagar	*to pay*
para	*for, to*
pero	*but*
persona *f*	*person*

pie *m*	*foot*
playa *f*	*beach*
plaza *f*	*square*
por	*through*
práctico, -a	*practical*
puerta *f*	*door*
ruido *m*	*noise*
semana *f*	*week*
suerte *f*	*happiness*
tanto, -a	*so much*
tarde *f*	*afternoon*
taxi *m*	*taxi*
tráfico *m*	*traffic*
tren *m*	*train*
último, -a	*last*
verdad *f*	*truth*
¿Verdad?	*Right?*
vino *m*	*wine*

day: 4

Meeting the family

Day 4 talks about the family. You will learn regular verbs ending in *-ir*, how to use *se habla* to make impersonal statements and possessive determiners. You will also learn how to compare and describe things. Finally, you will learn about Spanish family traditions.

SPANISH NAMES...

In Spain, married women retain both of their surnames, the first of which is from their father and the second from their mother, e.g. ***Carmen Galván Torres*** *marries* ***José García Ginestar****. Their daughter* ***Lucía*** *will be called:* ***Lucía García Galván****. If Carmen is addressed as* ***Sra. de García****, the* ***"de"*** *is not a title of nobility but merely indicates that Carmen is the wife of Mr. García. The titles* ***Don*** *and/or* ***Doña*** *are used to express respect when addressing an older person or someone with authority such as in* ***Don Alfonso*** *or* ***Doña María****.*

Spanish conversation: Encuentro con la familia

Karen toca el timbre, la Sra. Carmen García abre la puerta.

Karen: **Buenas tardes señora yo soy Karen Muller.**
Carmen: **Bienvenida señorita Karen. Mucho gusto. Yo soy Carmen de García.**
Karen: **Encantada Sra. de García.**
Carmen: **¿Está cansada?**
Karen: **Sí, un poco.**
Carmen: **Oh, aquí está mi marido, Pedro García.**
Pedro: **Encantado bienvenida a nuestra casa.**
Karen: **Mucho gusto, Sr. García.**
Carmen: **Aquí está Lucía.**
Lucía: **¡Hola, Karen!**
Karen: **Encantada… y ¿quién eres tú?**
David: **Soy David.**
Karen: **¡Qué alto eres!**
David: **Lucía es más alta que yo. Y papá es el más alto.**
Carmen: **¿Toma un café con nosotros?**
Karen: **Gracias, con gusto.**
David: **Mamá, la señorita Karen es muy amable.**

English conversation: Meeting the family

Karen rings the doorbell, Mrs. Carmen de García opens the door.

Karen: **Good afternoon, I am Karen Muller.**
Carmen: **Welcome, Karen. Nice to meet you. I'm Carmen de García.**
Karen: **Nice to meet you too, Mrs. de García.**
Carmen: **Are you tired?**
Karen: **Yes, a little.**
Carmen: **Oh, this is my husband, Pedro García.**
Pedro: **Nice to meet you, welcome to our house.**
Karen: **It's a pleasure to meet you too, Mr. García.**
Carmen: **This is Lucía.**
Lucía: **Hi, Karen.**
Karen: **Nice to meet you… and who are you?**
David: **I am David.**
Karen: **How tall you are!**
David: **Lucía is taller than me and dad is the tallest.**
Carmen: **Will you have coffee with us?**
Karen: **Thank you, I'd love to.**
David: **Mum, Karen is very nice.**

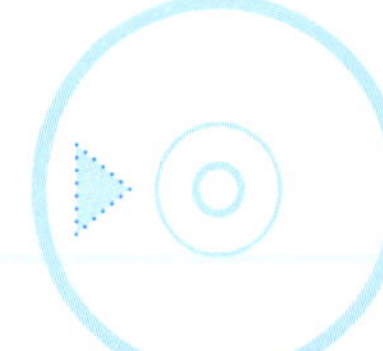

Grammar

Regular verbs ending in *-ir*

abrir (to open)	
abr*o* la puerta	I open the door
abr*es* una botella	you open a bottle
abr*e* el libro	he/she opens the book
abr*imos* una caja	we open a box
abr*ís* la puerta	you open the door
abr*en* el libro	they open the book

The impersonal form: *se habla*

se + **3rd person singular** or **plural** (depending on the object) = **one, you**

se habl*a* español	one speaks Spanish, Spanish is spoken
¿Qué lenguas *se* habl*an* en España?	Which languages do you speak in Spain? or Which languages are spoken in Spain?

Possessive determiners

The possessive determiner (my, your, his, etc.) always **precedes** the noun in Spanish.

singular		plural	
mi	my	mis	my
tu	your	tus	your
su	his, her, your *(polite)*	sus	his, her, your *(polite)*
nuestro, -a	our	nuestros, -as	our
vuestro, -a	your	vuestros, -as	your
su	their, your *(polite)*	sus	their, your *(polite)*

e.g. mi coche my car - mis coches my cars
su maleta his suitacase - sus maletas his suitcases

As you have seen above, su can refer to a number of different people. For instance, su maleta could be his, her, your (polite), their or your (pl. polite) suitcase.
To clarify who is being referred to with su, you can use de + **possessive determiner/noun**.
For example:

su coche: el coche *de mi hermano*	=	my brother's car
su coche: el coche de Ud.	=	your (polite) car

Comparative and superlative

más/menos + adjective + que = more/less… than

Lucía es *más alta que* David	= Lucía is taller than David
La maleta es *menos bonita que* el bolso	= The suitcase is not as nice as the bag

tan + adjective + como = as much/ the same… as

Carmen es *tan alta como* Karen	= Carmen is as tall as Karen

el/la/lo más + adjective = the most/the least

Papá es *el más alto*	= Dad is the tallest

adjective + -ísimo/s, ísima/s = absolute superlative

El monte es *altísimo*	= The mountain is huge
La cucaracha es *pequeñísima*	= The cockroach is tiny

más de precedes **numbers** and **times**

Tengo *más de veinte* euros	= I have more than 20 euros

no más que before numbers = **only**.
No quedan *más que* tres alumnos = There are only three pupils (students) left

Adjectives with irregular comparative/superlative forms			
bueno	mejor	el/la mejor	good, better, the best
malo	peor	el/la peor	bad, worse, the worst
grande	mayor	el/la mayor	big, bigger, the biggest
pequeño	menor	el/la menor	small, smaller, the smallest

Definite article with *señor*, *señora* and *señorita*

La señora García abre la puerta	Mrs. García opens the door
El señor López no está en casa	Mr López is not at home
¿Dónde vive *la señorita* Ramírez?	Where does Miss Ramírez live?

Note: The definite article precedes señor, señora and señorita except when addressing someone, e.g. ¡Buenos días señorita García!

Exercises

Exercise 1

Fill in the verb forms.

	vosotros	usted	tú	ellas
1 hablar	....	....	....	....
2 escribir	....	....	....	....
3 ser	....	....	....	....
4 bailar	....	....	....	....
5 abrir	....	....	....	....

Exercise 2

Form sentences with se.

1 En España (hablar) español. ....

2 El flamenco (bailar) en Andalucía. ....

3 La puerta (abrir) automáticamente. ....

4 En el centro de Madrid (tomar) el metro. ....

Exercise 3

Fill in the possessive determiners.

1 (Tú) .... maleta es nueva.

2 (Nosotros) .... padres están de viaje.

3 El coche es de (yo) .... abuelo.

4 (Ud.) .... amigo es amable.

5 Hablo con (vosotros) .... hermanos.

6 (Vosotros) .... casa es más grande que (nosotros) .... chalet.

7 Aquí están (Uds.) .... llaves.

8 ¿Jugáis con (nosotros) .... amigos?

Exercise 4

Fill in the correct types of comparative.

1 La tierra es .... grande .... la luna.

2 Los Alpes son .... altos .... los Pirineos.

3 La Plaza de España es .... moderna .... la Plaza de Colón.

4 Las películas alemanas son buenas, pero las francesas son .... de todas.

5 El Retiro es .... parque .... famoso de Madrid.

Exercise 5

Write out these numbers in Spanish: 14, 29, 15, 9, 1, 4, 25, 21, 19, 30

....

....

....

....

....

Exercise 6

Complete these sentences.

1 La hija de mi marido es mi ....

2 El padre de mi hija es mi ....

3 Mi hija es la .... de mi madre.

4 Mi hijo y mi hija son mis ....

5 Mi madre es la .... de mi marido.

6 La mujer de mi hermano es mi ....

Vocabulary

Below is a list of vocabulary encountered in this chapter.

abrir *to open*
abuelo *m* *grandfather*
abuela *f* *grandmother*
abuelos *m pl* *grandparents*
Alpes *m pl* *the Alps*
alto, -a *big, tall, high*
alumno *m* *pupil/student*
amigo *m* *friend*
Andalucía *f* *Andalusia*
automáticamente *automatically*
bailar *to dance*
bicicleta *f* *bicycle*
bienvenido, -a *welcome*
bonito, -a *pretty, beautiful*
botella *f* *bottle*
cansado, -a *tired*
chalet *m* *detached house*
cónyuge *spouse*
con mucho gusto *nice to meet you, my pleasure*
cucaracha *f* *cockroach*
cuñado *m* *brother-in-law*
cuñada *f* *sister-in-law*
difícil *difficult*
encantado, -a *nice to meet you*
encuentro *m* *meeting*
esposa *f* *wife*
esposo *m* *husband*
escribir *to write*
fácil *easy*
familia *f* *family*
hijo *m* *son*
hija *f* *daughter*
hijos *m pl* *children*
hermano *m* *brother*
hermana *f* *sister*
jugar *to play*
lengua *f* *language*
llave *f* *key*
luna *f* *moon*
malo, -a *bad*
madre *f* *mother*
marido *m* *husband*
más *more*
mi *my*
moderno, -a *modern*
monte *m* *mountain*
mucho, -a *much*
mujer *f* *woman, wife*
muy *very*
nieto *m* *grandson*
nieta *f* *granddaughter*
nietos *m pl* *grandchildren*
nombre *m* *name*
nuestro, -a *our*
nuevo, -a *new*
padre *m* *father*
parque *m* *park*
película *f* *film*
Pirineos *m pl* *the Pyrenees*
primo *m* *cousin*
prima *f* *cousin*
puerta *f* *door*
quedar *to stay*
¿Quién? *Who?*
sobrino *m* *nephew*

sobrina *f*	*niece*
suegro *m*	*father-in-law*
suegra *f*	*mother-in-law*
tío *m*	*uncle*
tía *f*	*aunt*
tíos *m pl*	*uncles and aunts*
tierra *f*	*earth*
timbre *m*	*doorbell*
tocar	*to play (an instrument)*
tocar el timbre	*to ring the doorbell*
vivir	*to live*

day: 5

At home

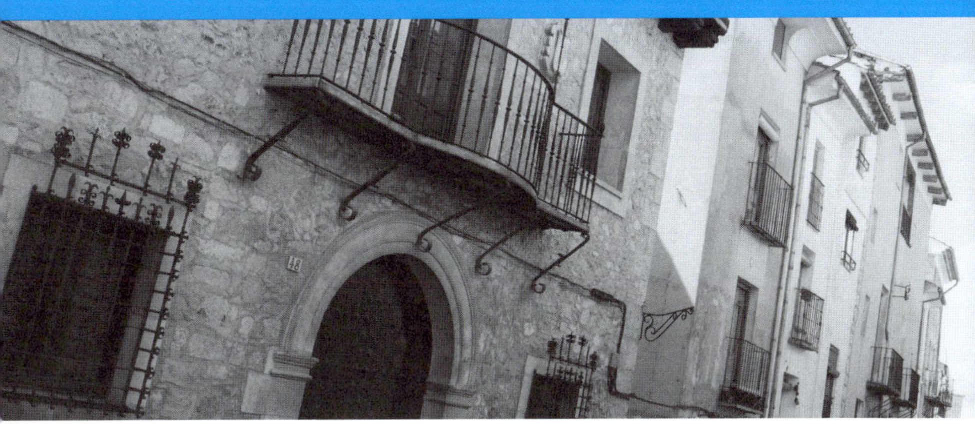

Day 5 teaches you how to describe things. You will learn how to use regular verbs ending in *-er* as well as how the irregular verbs *tener* (to have), *venir* (to come) and *tener que* (to have to) are congugated. The exercises will help you to absorb all of this new information.

APARTMENTS IN SPAIN...

If you are invited to someone's flat in Spain, make sure that you know either the name that appears on the buzzer or the apartment number as you will not always find their name on the list - especially if they are only renting. The number will also be used if someone gives you their address, e.g. **Calle Alonso 6, 4° dcha A**, *means that the person lives on 6 Alonso Street, 4th floor in apartment A on the right.*

Spanish conversation: En casa

Carmen:	**Nuestro piso es grande. Tiene tres dormitorios, una cocina, una sala de estar y comedor, dos baños, un aseo y un vestíbulo. Aquí en España las cocinas son más grandes porque a veces comemos en ellas… ¿Viene? Esta es su habitación, por la mañana entra el sol. Y aquello es su baño.**
Karen:	**¡Qué guay! Es todo bastante grande.**
Carmen:	**El barrio en el que vivimos es tranquilo. Estamos cerca de la Plaza de Colón y de la estación del metro.**
Karen:	**¿Está lejos el Parque del Retiro?**
Carmen:	**No, en absoluto. Hay también un autobús que pasa por la puerta de casa.**
Karen:	**¡Qué bien! ¿Y la parada dónde está?**
Carmen:	**Allí enfrente. En la esquina.**

Lucía entra en la habitación de Karen con su conejo.

Lucía:	**¡Mira, Karen! Es mi conejo Nicolás.**
Karen:	**¡Ah, un conejo! ¡Qué mono!**
Lucía:	**Nicolás come pan, zanahorias, pero también come las cosas.**
Karen:	**¡Mira, Lucía!**

Karen saca algo de su bolso.

Lucía:	**¡Oh, qué bonito!, un oso de felpa.**
Karen:	**Es Franz, es mi mascota.**
Lucía:	**¿Es Franz un nombre alemán?**
Karen:	**Sí, como Francisco en español.**
Lucía:	**¿Me regalarás el oso el día de mi santo?**
Karen:	**A ver.**
Carmen:	**Karen, ¿está contenta con su habitación?**
Karen:	**Sí…**

English conversation: At home

Carmen:	**Our flat (apartment) is large. It has three bedrooms, a kitchen, a living room and dining room, two bathrooms, one toilet and a hallway. Here in Spain the kitchens are larger because we sometimes eat in the kitchen. Are you coming? This is your room. This room gets the sun in the morning. And there is your bathroom.**
Karen:	**Wow, that's great! It's really quite spacious.**
Carmen:	**The neighbourhood we live in is quiet. We are close to the Plaza de Colón and the subway station.**
Karen:	**Is Retiro Park far from here?**
Carmen:	**No, not at all. There is also a bus that passes right by our front door.**
Karen:	**How nice! And the bus stop? Where is it?**
Carmen:	**Over there on the other side. At the corner.**

Lucía comes into Karen's room with her rabbit.

Lucía:	**Look, Karen! This is my rabbit Nicolás.**
Karen:	**A rabbit! How cute!**
Lucía:	**Nicolás eats bread, carrots, but also chews on my stuff.**
Karen:	**Look here, Lucía!**

Karen takes something from her bag.

Lucía:	**How nice! A teddybear.**
Karen:	**That's Franz, my mascot.**
Lucía:	**Is Franz a German name?**
Karen:	**Yes, like Francisco in Spanish.**
Lucía:	**Will you give me the teddybear as a present on my name day?**
Karen:	**We'll see.**
Carmen:	**Karen, do you like your room?**
Karen:	**Yes…**

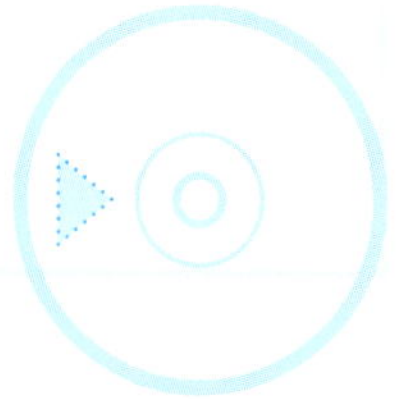

Grammar

Regular verbs ending in *-er*

comer (to eat)	
Com*o* pan.	I eat bread.
com*es*	you eat
com*e*	he, she eats, you (form.) eat
com*emos*	we eat
com*éis*	you eat
com*en*	they, you (form.) eat

Irregular verbs

tener (to have)		venir (to come)	
tengo	I have	*vengo*	I come
t*ie*nes	you have	v*ie*nes	you come
t*ie*ne	he, she has	v*ie*ne	he, she, it comes
tenemos	we have	venimos	we come
tenéis	you have	venís	you come
t*ie*nen	they have	v*ie*nen	they come

Some irregular verbs add a **-g** in the first person.
Please note that in **¿Tiene Ud. coche?** (Do you have a car?) there is no article after **tener**.
An article is not necessary if it refers to objects one does not normally have more than one of!

Tengo 30 años	I am 30 years old
Tienen frío	They are cold
Tenemos sueño	We are tired
tener que + infinitive = have to, must	
Tengo que ir a casa	I must go home

hay and estar	
Hay expresses **whether** something exists; **estar** specifies **where** something is located:	
***En* la mesa *hay* un periódico**	There is a newspaper on the table
El periódico *está en* la mesa	The newspaper is on the table

Combining *de/a* + definite article *el*

de + el = del	
la parada *del* autobús	the bus stop
a + el = al	
Vamos *al* cine	We're going to the cinema

Exercises

Exercise 1

Decide whether to use: ser, estar, tener or hay.

1 El cielo .... azul.

2 En el cielo .... nubes.

3 En el bar .... 10 personas.

4 La familia .... en el bar.

5 Madrid .... en el centro del país.

6 David .... 7 años.

7 Ellos .... en Madrid.

8 Carmen .... de España.

9 Ella .... un coche negro.

10 Pedro .... en casa.

11 La casa .... cerca de la plaza.

12 .... muchas rebajas ahora.

Exercise 2

Hay or estar?

1 .... muchas personas en el teatro.

2 El parque .... a dos kilómetros de aquí.

3 Junto al río .... una carretera.

4 La parada .... enfrente de la puerta.

5 En la habitación .... un conejo.

6 El osito de peluche .... en el bolso.

7 ¿.................. lejos el parque?

8 ¿Dónde .... una estación de metro?

9 ¿Dónde .... la cocina?

10 .... poca gente en la calle.

Exercise 3

Select: el, los, un, una, unos, unas, del or al.

1 En la plaza hay .... casa.

2 Va .... dormitorio.

3 .... conejos son roedores.

4 No van .... cine sino .... teatro.

5 .... profesor es .... hombre amable.

6 .... bolso .... aduanero es pesado.

7 En el avión hay .... azafatas.

8 .... chicos .... instituto van a Madrid.

Exercise 4

Which translations are incorrect?

1 de nada
- a for nothing
- b you're welcome

2 mucho gusto
- a my pleasure
- b tastes good

3 muy encantado
- a all the best
- b nice to meet you

4 qué bien
- a how nice
- b thank you

5 muchas gracias
- a best regards
- b many thanks

6 hasta la vista
- a goodbye
- b good night

1 .... 2 .... 3 .... 4 .... 5 .... 6 ....

Exercise 5

You are looking for a flat and you see the following classified ad. Choose which answers are right and which are wrong writing Sí or No beside each statement below.

Se alquila

Madrid, Ventas. Habitación amueblada, confortable y soleada con ducha, ascensor, teléfono, calefacción, 35 M2, 300 euros/mes. Tel. 425 08 24.

1 Es una habitación con baño ....

2 Tiene 35 M2 ....

3 No tiene calefacción ....

4 Tiene ascensor ....

5 No tiene muebles ....

6 Tienes que pagar 300 euros/mes ....

7 No tiene ventanas ....

Exercise 6

Fill in the correct verb forms.

1 ¿(tomar Uds.) .... mucha cerveza?

2 ¿(comer vosotros) .... en casa?

3 ¿(beber tú) .... vino?

4 (vivir nosotros) .... en una calle tranquila.

5 (tener yo) .... sed.

6 El autobús (pasar) .... por la puerta.

7 (abrir Ud.) .... la ventana.

8 (Ella hablar) .... mucho.

Vocabulary

Below is a list of vocabulary encountered in this chapter.

a veces	*sometimes*
a ver	*we'll see*
algo	*something*
alquilar	*to rent*
amueblado, -a	*furnished*
aquello	*that (thing)*
ascensor *m*	*lift /elevator*
aseo *m*	*toilet*
azul	*blue*
baño *m*	*bathroom*
barrio *m*	*neighbourhood*
bastante	*rather*
beber	*to drink*
bonito, -a	*pretty*
calefacción *f*	*heating*
carretera *f*	*street*
chico *m*	*boy*
cine *m*	*cinema*
cocina *f*	*kitchen*
comedor	*dining room*
comer	*to eat*
conejo *m*	*rabbit*
confortable	*comfortable*
contento,-a	*content*
cosa *f*	*thing*
día *m* **del santo**	*name day*
dormitorio *m*	*bedroom*
ducha *f*	*shower*
en absoluto	*not at all*
enfrente	*opposite*
entrar	*to enter*
esquina *f*	*corner*
estación *f* **del metro**	*subway station*
frío *m*	*cold*
¡Guay! *(colloquial)*	*Great!*
habitación *f*	*room*
hambre *f*	*hunger*
instituto *m*	*institute*
junto, -a	*next to*
kilómetro *m*	*kilometre*
mañana *f*	*morning, tomorrow*
mascota *f*	*mascot*
mes *m*	*month*
mesa *f*	*table*
mirar	*to see*
mono, -a	*cute*
mueble *m*	*piece of furniture*
negro, -a	*black*
nube *f*	*cloud*
oso *m*	*bear*
osito de peluche	*teddybear*
oso *m* **de felpa**	*teddybear*
pan *m*	*bread*
parada *f*	*(bus) stop*
pasar	*to pass (by), drive (by)*
periódico *m*	*newspaper*
piso *m*	*flat/apartment*
rebaja *f*	*discount*
regalar	*to give (present)*
río *m*	*river*
roedor *m*	*rodent*
sacar	*to take out*
sala de estar	*living room*

sed *f* *thirst*
sol *m* *sun*
soleado, -a *sunny*
sueño *m* *sleep*
también *also, too, as well*
teatro *m* *theatre*
teléfono *m* *telephone*
tener *to have*
tranquilo, -a *quiet*
venir *to come*
ventana *f* *window*
ver *to see*
vestíbulo *m* *hallway*
ya veremos *we'll see*
zanahoria *f* *carrot*

day:6

Family life

Day 6 discusses daily life. You will learn stem-changing verbs such as *poder* (can/to be able to) and you will learn how to describe your day using reflexive verbs, as well as how to tell the time.

MEALTIMES...

*In Spain **el desayuno** (breakfast) is usually eaten belween 7:00 and 9:00 a.m. Many people will have a coffee, toast and cakes with jam. **La comida** (lunch) is usually around 2:00 or 3:00 p.m. and generally consists of three dishes: one vegetable, one rice and some meat or fish followed by fruit or something sweet for dessert. **La cena** (dinner) takes place between 9:00p.m. and10:00 p.m. and might consist of **tortilla** or a similar dish. Wine often accompanies the main meal, followed by coffee. Bread is a staple with every meal.*

Spanish conversation: La vida familiar

Carmen:	**Hoy me quedo en casa. Pasaremos todo el día juntas, cocinaremos…**
Karen:	**Pero si no sé…**
Carmen:	**¡No importa! Ya nos las arreglaremos. Tiene que trabajar en casa todos los días hasta las dos de la tarde. Luego puede ir a sus clases de español.**
Karen:	**Muy bien.**
Carmen:	**Por la mañana nos levantamos a las 7.00, solemos desayunar a las 7.30 y a las 8.00 los niños van al colegio. Yo luego me voy al trabajo.**
Karen:	**¿Dónde trabaja Ud.?**
Carmen:	**Trabajo en una agencia de viajes.**
Karen:	**¿Su marido no se va de casa?**
Carmen:	**Depende… Como es pintor necesita la inspiracion para poder trabajar.**
Karen:	**¡Ah, comprendo!**
Carmen:	**Para pintar se va al estudio. Hay también mañanas cuando va de paseo.**
Karen:	**¿Qué trabajo tengo por las mañanas?**
Carmen:	**Ud. tiene que preparar el desayuno para toda la familia. Después hay que arreglar las camas, ir de compras y preparar el almuerzo para todos. No queda tiempo para aburrirse. En su tiempo libre puede mirar la tele, leer libros, escuchar música…**
Karen:	**Y ¿qué tengo que comprar?**
Carmen:	**No es un problema. Aquí está la lista.**

English conversation: Family life

Carmen:	**I am staying home today. We'll spend the whole day together, we'll cook…**
Karen:	**But I can't…**
Carmen:	**Doesn't matter! We'll manage. You'll have to do the housework every day until 2 p.m. Then you can go to your Spanish classes.**
Karen:	**Good.**
Carmen:	**We get up at 7 o'clock in the morning, we usually have breakfast at 7:30, at 8 o'clock the children go to school. I go to work afterwards.**
Karen:	**Where do you work?**
Carmen:	**I work in a travel agency.**
Karen:	**Your husband doesn't leave the house?**
Carmen:	**It depends… As he is an artist, he needs inspiration to be able to work.**
Karen:	**Ah, I understand!**
Carmen:	**He goes to the studio to paint, but there are also mornings when he goes for a walk.**
Karen:	**What do I have to do in the morning?**
Carmen:	**You have to prepare breakfast for the whole family. Then there are beds to be made up, shopping to be done and lunch to be prepared for everybody. There'll be no time to be bored. In your spare time you can watch TV, read books, listen to music…**
Karen:	**And what do I have to buy?**
Carmen:	**Here is the list!**

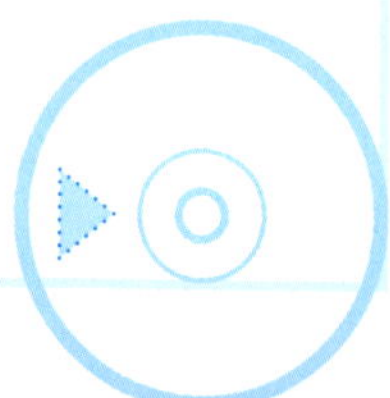

Grammar

Stem changing verbs: *o* to *ue*

poder (to be able/can)		soler (to usually do)	
p*ue*do	I can	s*ue*lo	I usually
p*ue*des	you can	s*ue*les	you usually
p*ue*de	he/she can	s*ue*le	he/she usually
podemos	we can	solemos	we usually
podéis	you can	soléis	you usually
p*ue*den	they can	s*ue*len	they usually

When the stem of these verbs is stressed, the **o** in the stem changes to **ue**.

Reflexive verbs

lavarse (to wash oneself)	
me lavo	I wash myself
te lavas	you wash yourself
se lava	he/she washes himself/herself
nos lavamos	we wash ourselves
os laváis	you wash yourselves
se lavan	they wash themselves

The reflexive pronoun (**me**, **te**, **se**, etc.) is attached to verbs in the infinitive:

no tienes que aburrir*te*	you need not bore yourself
hay que lavar*se*	one has to wash oneself

Some verbs that are reflexive in Spanish are not reflexive in English:
quedarse (to stay), **levantarse** (to get up), **llamarse** (to be called)

Note the changes in meaning when a verb is made reflexive below:

ir	to go	**irse**	to go away
quedar	to meet up, to be left over	**quedarse atrás**	to stay behind
llamar	to call	**llamarse**	to be called
levantar	to lift	**levantarse**	to get up

todo	**all, everyone, whole, full, entire**
todo, -a + definite article + noun = whole/wholly	
todo el día	the entire day
toda la familia	the whole family

todos, -as + definite article + noun = every (one), all

todos los días	every day
todas las mañanas	every morning, all mornings

Telling the time

¿Qué hora es?	What time is it?
¿A qué hora?	At what time?
Es la una/Son las dos	It is one o'clock/two o'clock
en punto	one o'clock/two o'clock sharp
y cinco	five past one/five past two
y cuarto	a quarter past one/past two
y media	half past one/half past two
menos cuarto	quarter to one/quarter to two
menos veinticinco	25 minutes to one/to two
a la una menos cuarto	at a quarter to one
a las ocho en punto	at eight o'clock sharp
a mediodía	at noon, 12:00 a.m.
a medianoche	at midnight, 12:00 p.m.
a eso de las cinco	at about five
a las cinco más o menos	around five o'clock

a specifies an exact time, **por** is used for time spans:

a las cinco de la tarde at five o'clock in the afternoon

por la tarde in the afternoon

In Spanish, you say **es la una**. For all other times you use the plural **son**: **son las dos**, **tres**, etc.

Exercises

Exercise 1

How much did you understand? Tick the appropriate column.

	Sí	No
1 En España el desayuno es una comida fuerte.	....	....
2 Se suele tomar vino con la comida.	....	....
3 Se merienda a las 11.00 de la mañana.	....	....
4 La comida tiene sólo un plato.	....	....
5 En España se cena a las 7.30 de la tarde.	....	....
6 Los españoles desayunan huevos, jamón y tortilla.	....	....
7 Se merienda bocadillos y fruta.	....	....
8 La cena es floja.	....	....
9 Como postre se come fruta y platos dulces.	....	....
10 Carne o pescado es un plato del mediodía.	....	....

Exercise 2

Insert the reflexive verb form.

1 ¿Cómo .... llamas? .... llamo Vicente.

2 ¿No .... aburre en la escuela?

3 .... quedamos en casa.

4 .... van de paseo.

5 ¿.............. laváis todas las mañanas?

6 .... levantas a las ocho y media.

7 Hay que peinar .... por las mañanas.

Exercise 3

todo el, **toda la**, **todos los** or **todas las**?

1 Me quedo en casa .... día.

2 ¿Sabes cantar .... canciones?

3 Voy al trabajo .... mañanas.

4 Vamos de vacaciones .... años.

5 Solemos ir de paseo .... tardes.

6 No puedo trabajar .... vida.

7 No .... españoles bailan flamenco.

8 En .... cielo se pueden ver aviones.

Exercise 4

Match the times in numbers. Then write out the remaining times in words.

Note that in Spain the 24-hour clock is used in airports, train stations, etc.

a 1.30 b 17.15 c 4.45 d 7.00 e 1.00 f 11.55 g 10.05 h 12.35 i 15.20 j 22.00

.... la una menos veinticinco

.... las diez de la noche

.... las siete en punto

.... las doce menos cinco

.... las cinco y cuarto de la tarde

....

....

....

....

....

Exercise 5

Fill in the verbs in the 1st person singular.

1 (poder) No .... ir a clase.

2 (estar) ....en el bar de la esquina.

3 (ir) Por la mañana .... a la parada del autobús.

4 (soler) Por las tardes .... ir de paseo.

5 (tener) .... mucha hambre y sed.

6 (quedarse) Si .... en casa no tengo inspiraciones.

7 (venir) ....del colegio.

8 (ser) No.............................. de Madrid sino de Nueva York.

9 (comer) .... zanahorias y pan.

10 (arreglar) Por la mañana .... las camas.

Exercise 6

Rewrite this dialogue using the formal usted in the 3rd person singular.

– ¿Puedes ir a la agencia de viajes, por favor?

....

– Sí, ¿puedes decirme dónde está?

....

– Tienes que ir hasta la esquina, cruzas la calle y tomas el paseo a la derecha. Y estás allí enfrente.

....

....

– Muy bien, gracias por tu explicación.

....

Vocabulary

Below is a list of vocabulary encountered in this chapter.

a eso de	*at about (time)*	**fuerte**	*strong, substantial*
aburrirse	*to be bored*	**gato** *m*	*cat*
agencia *f* **de viajes**	*travel agency*	**hacer la compra**	*to do the grocery shopping*
arreglar	*to order*	**hora** *f*	*hour*
arreglarse	*to get by, manage*	**hoy**	*today*
arroz *m*	*rice*	**huevo** *m*	*egg*
bocadillo *m*	*sandwich*	**importar**	*to be important*
cama *f*	*bed*	**inspiración** *f*	*inspiration*
canción *f*	*song*	**ir de compras**	*to go shopping*
cantar	*to sing*	**irse**	*to go away*
carne *f*	*meat*	**jamón** *m*	*ham*
cena *f*	*supper*	**junto, -a**	*together*
cenar	*to have supper*	**lavarse**	*to wash oneself*
clase *f*	*class*	**leer**	*to read*
cocinar	*to cook*	**levantarse**	*to get up*
colegio *m*	*school*	**libre**	*free*
comida *f*	*lunch*	**lista** *f*	*list*
compra *f*	*shopping*	**llamarse**	*to be called*
comprar	*to buy*	**magdalena** *f*	*sponge cupcakes*
comprender	*to understand*	**más o menos**	*about, approximately, more or less*
consistir de	*to consist of*		
cuarto *m*	*quarter*	**medianoche** *f*	*midnight*
depende	*it depends*	**medio, -a**	*half*
desayunar	*to have breakfast*	**mediodía** *m*	*midday, noon*
desayuno *m*	*breakfast*	**merendar (-ie-)**	*to have a snack in the evening*
después	*afterwards*		
dulce *m*	*sweet(s), pastry*	**merienda** *f*	*evening meal*
escuchar	*to listen*	**mermelada** *f*	*jam*
estudio *m*	*studio*	**música** *f*	*music*
familiar	*family (adj.)*	**necesitar**	*need*
flojo, -a	*light*	**noche** *f*	*evening, night*
fruta *f*	*fruit*	**pan** *m*	*bread*

para	*so that, therefore, so*	**soler (-ue-)**	*to usually do*
pasar	*to spend*	**tele(visión)** *f*	*TV*
paseo *m*	*walk*	**tiempo** *m*	*time*
peinarse	*to comb one's hair*	**tiempo** *m* **libre**	*spare/leisure time*
pescado *m*	*fish (dish)*	**todo el día**	*the whole day*
pintar	*to paint*	**todos, -as**	*all, whole*
pintor *m*	*painter*	**tomarse tiempo**	*to take one's time*
plato *m*	*dish, course*	**tortilla** *f*	*Spanish omelet*
poder	*to be able, can*	**tostada** *f*	*toast*
postre *m*	*dessert*	**trabajar**	*to work*
preparar	*to prepare*	**trabajo** *m*	*work*
problema *m*	*problem*	**vacaciones** *f pl*	*vacation*
quedarse	*to stay*	**verduras** *f pl*	*vegetables*
queso *m*	*cheese*	**vida** *f*	*life*
saber	*to know, to be able*	**ya**	*already*
sé	*I can, know how*		

day: 7

In the kitchen

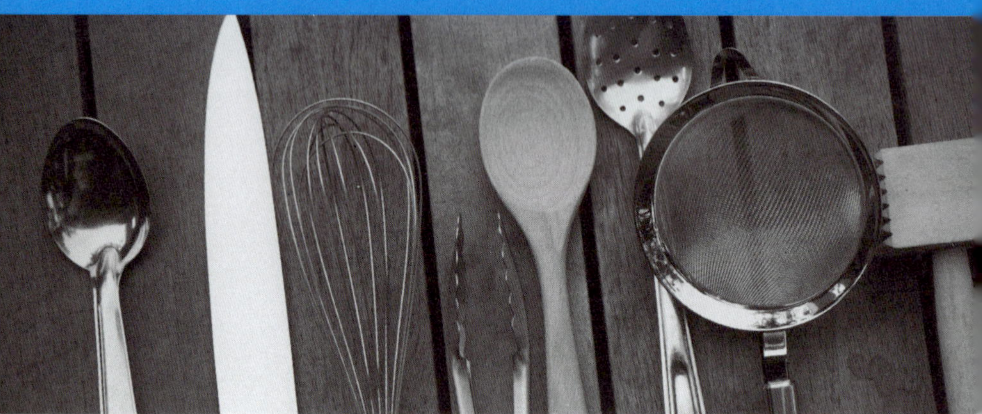

Day 7 covers essential verbs *saber* (to know) and *hacer* (to do/make), as well as how to say this and that, etc. You will also build up some more vocabulary and learn about Spanish cuisine.

REGIONAL SPECIALITIES...

Some wonderful dishes worth trying include: ***gazpacho andaluz*** *– a cold tomato soup, common to Andalusia. In Madrid, try* ***cocido madrileño*** *(a stew) and while in Castile, try the* ***asados de cordero o cabrito*** *(lamb or goat roasts) or* ***cochinillo*** *(roast suckling pig). In Catalonia try* ***conejo al alioli*** *(roasted rabbit with garlic mayonnaise) and* ***zarzuela*** *(stewed fish). The* ***fabada asturiana*** *is a stew made from white beans, peppers, sausages and bacon, typical to Asturias. In Galicia, enjoy fresh* ***mariscos y pescados*** *(seafood and fish). For sweet tooths, try* ***ensaimada*** *pastries from Mallorca and* ***churros****, sweet, deep-fried fritters.*

Spanish conversation: En la cocina

Carmen: **Karen, ¿sabe cocinar?**
Karen: **No sé cocinar. Bueno, depende… Puedo preparar ensaladas…**
Carmen: **¡No importa! Podemos cocinar juntas.**
Karen: **Sí, esto me gusta.**
Carmen: **Aquí están los artefactos que necesita un ama de casa para poder cocinar. Esto es una sartén y éstas son cazuelas de diferentes tamaños… Aquí están los platos, y las tazas y allí los vasos y los cubiertos: los tenedores, los cuchillos y las cucharas.**
Karen: **¿Qué es esto?**
Carmen: **Eso es un porrón. Se echa vino y se pone sobre la mesa. Y ahora hacemos un plato típico de España, la paella.**
Karen: **Muy bien. ¿Cómo se hace?**
Carmen: **Necesitamos arroz, carne de pollo, judías verdes, cebollas, tomates, ajo, un poco de jerez, sal y azafrán y unas cucharadas de aceite de oliva. Hay paellas diferentes, ¿sabe? Se hacen con los ingredientes típicos de la región, pero siempre con arroz.**
Karen: **¿Se come a menudo la paella en España?**
Carmen: **No, la paella es un plato para ocasiones un poco excepcionales. Se suele cocinar en una paellera a fuego lento… ¿Puede preparar un postre?**
Karen: **¡Esto es una buena idea!**
Carmen: **¿Qué tipo de postre es?**
Karen: **Es una sorpresa.**
Carmen: **¡Qué bueno! Estoy muy curiosa, ¡se me hace la boca agua!**

English conversation: In the kitchen

Carmen: **Karen, do you know how to cook?**
Karen: **I can't cook, well it depends… I can make salads…**
Carmen: **It's not important! We can cook together.**
Karen: **Yes, I'd like that.**
Carmen: **Here are the tools a housewife needs for cooking. This is a frying pan and these are various sizes of casseroles… Here are the plates and the cups and there are the glasses and the cutlery: the forks, the knives and the spoons.**
Karen: **What's that?**
Carmen: **That's a "porron". You pour wine into it and put it on the table. And**

	now we'll prepare a typical Spanish dish, paella.
Karen:	Great! How do you make it?
Carmen:	We need rice, chicken meat, green beans, onions, tomatoes, garlic, a little sherry, salt and saffron and a few tablespoons of olive oil. There are different types of paella, you know? They are prepared with ingredients typical of the region, but rice is always in it.
Karen:	Do you often eat paella in Spain?
Carmen:	No, paella is more a meal for special occasions. It is usually cooked in a paella pan on low heat… Can you prepare dessert?
Karen:	That's a good idea!
Carmen:	What kind of dessert is it going to be?
Karen:	It's a surprise.
Carmen:	Great! I'm really curious. My mouth is watering already!

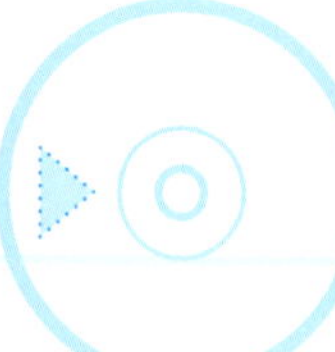

Grammar

Verbs

saber (to know)	
Sé cocinar	I can cook
Sabes leer	You can read
Sabe cantar	He/she can sing
Sabemos español	We know Spanish
Sabéis esto de memoria	You know this by heart
Saben dónde está	They know where he is

Unlike the term **poder**, the verb **saber** + infinitive refers to an innate or acquired ability. The addition of a small accent, however, makes a major difference:

Sé español	I know Spanish
Se habla español	One speaks Spanish/Spanish is spoken

hacer	to make, do	poner	to put, place
Two other verbs with **-g-** in the first person singular are **hacer** (to make, do) and **poner** (to place, put):			
ha*g*o	**hacemos**	**pon*g*o**	**ponemos**
haces	**hacéis**	**pones**	**ponéis**
hace	**hacen**	**pone**	**ponen**

Useful phrases:

Hace buen tiempo	The weather is nice
Pongo la mesa	I lay the table

Demonstrative pronouns

esto **this** (temporally or spatially close to the speaker)

Este **libro de** ***aquí*** **es de Ud.**	This book here belongs to you
estos **libros**	these books (here)
esta **flor**	this flower (here)
estas **flores**	these flowers (here)
esto	this (here)

eso **that** (temporally or spatially further away from the speaker and close to the person who is being addressed)

Ese **libro de ahí es de Ud.**	That book there belongs to you
esos **libros**	those books (there)
esa **flor**	that flower (there)
esas **flores**	those flowers (there)
eso	that (there)

aquello **that there** (furthest away in both time and distance)

Aquel **libro de** ***allí*** **es de Ud.**	That book there belongs to you
aquellos **libros**	those books (there)
aquella **flor**	that flower (there)
aquellas **flores**	those flowers (there)
aquello	that (there)

Este **es mi oso de felpa**	This is my teddy bear

¿Qué es esto?	What is this?

el instead of *la*

el ama **de casa** ***moderna***	the modern housewife
las amas **de casa** ***modernas***	the modern housewives

Feminine nouns beginning with a stressed **a-/ha-** take the definite article **el** in the singular.

Exercises

Exercise 1

Fill in the correct form of saber.

1 El no .... dónde están ellos.

2 (Yo) no .... cocinar.

3 ¿...................... (vosotros) por qué no viene?

4 (Ellas) .... mucho español.

5 ¿Ud. .... cómo ir al centro?

6 ¿ .... tú el camino?

7 Tienes que .... tocar la guitarra.

8 Preguntan si (nosotros) .... preparar postres.

Exercise 2

Select the correct demonstrative pronoun.

1	Es mi amigo, el hombre	**a** este	**b** aquéllo	**c** esta
2	Los años 50: ¡..... tiempos son interesantes!	**a** aquellos	**b** esos	**c** estos
3	No voy a ..... lugar, me quedo aquí.	**a** esta	**b** eso	**c** aquel
4	..... año viajo a Madrid.	**a** este	**b** esa	**c** aquella
5	Entre todas las chicas ..... es la más bonita.	**a** este	**b** la aquélla	**c** esta

1 .... **2** .... **3** .... **4** .... **5** ....

Exercise 3

Select the correct definite article.

1 .... coche

2 .... hambre

3 .... cama

4 .... Alpes

5 .... tarde

6 .... azafata

7 .... viaje

8 .... domingo

9 .... agua

10 .... día

Exercise 4

Conjugate these verbs following the example below.

e.g. **poner** **pongo** **ponéis** **pones** **ponemos**

1 comer ....

2 estar ....

3 hacer ....

4 ir ....

5 ser ....

6 saber ....

7 venir ....

8 tener ....

9 preparar ....

10 abrir ....

Exercise 5

Fill in the correct form of the verbs in brackets.

Yo (hacer) .... muchos viajes. No (ir) .... a ciudades sino al campo. (Alquilar) .... un chalet y (disfrutar) .... de la vida. (Ponerse) .... el traje más bonito y (tener) .... fiestas. A mis fiestas (venir) .... mucha gente. Todos (bailar) .... y (cantar) .... Mis fiestas (ser) .... las mejores fiestas del año.

Exercise 6

Translate the text below into Spanish.

Good afternoon, Mrs. García. I'm from Valencia. I am a little tired. My suitcases are heavy. Is your husband at home? Many thanks for the coffee. What, you know how to cook paella? At what time do we eat dinner? At 10 in the evening? I am going for a short walk.

....

....

....

....

....

....

Vocabulary

Below is a list of vocabulary encountered in this chapter.

a fuego lento *on low heat*
(el) agua *f* *water*
a menudo *often*
abierto *open*
aceite *m* *oil*
aceite *m* **de oliva** *olive oil*
ajo *m* *garlic*
(el) ama *f* **de casa** *housewife*
arroz *m* *rice*
azafrán *m* *saffron*
carne *f* **de pollo** *chicken meat*
campo *m* *country(side)*
cazuela *f* *casserole (dish)*
cebolla *f* *onion*
cocinar *to cook*
cubierto *m* *cutlery*
cuchara *f* *spoon*
cucharada *f* *tablespoonful*
cuchillo *m* *knife*
curioso, -a *curious, interested*
de memoria *by heart*
depende *it depends*
diferente *different*
disfrutar de *to savour*
echar *to pour*
ensalada *f* *salad*
excepcional *exceptional*
fiesta *f* *feast, party*
flor *f* *flower*

fuego *m*	*fire*	**preparar**	*to prepare*
gustar	*to enjoy, like*	**región** *f*	*region*
hacer	*to do, make*	**saber**	*to know how, be able to*
hacer autostop	*to hitchhike*	**sal** *f*	*salt*
herramienta *m*	*tool*	**salchicha** *f*	*sausage*
idea *f*	*idea*	**sartén** *f*	*frying pan*
ingrediente *m*	*ingredient*	**siempre**	*always*
judías *f pl* **verdes**	*green beans*	**sorpresa** *f*	*surprise*
		tamaño *m*	*size*
me	*me*	**tampoco**	*neither, not either*
ocasión *f*	*occasion*	**taza** *f*	*cup*
paella *f*	*paella (Spanish rice dish)*	**tenedor** *m*	*fork*
paellera *f*	*paella pan*	**típico, -a**	*typical*
para	*in order to, for*	**tipo** *m*	*type, kind*
plato *m*	*plate*	**tomate** *m*	*tomato*
pollo *m*	*chicken*	**traje** *m*	*suit*
poner	*to place, put*	**un poco**	*a little, some*
porrón *m*	*decanter (wine jar)*	**vaso** *m*	*glass*
postre *m*	*dessert*		

Test 1

Work your way around the board. Each correct answer will take you to the next question until you have completed the exercise. Enjoy!

1
Choose one of the two possible solutions. Then go to the square showing the number of the solution you think is correct.

2
Juan es un chico....
español ▶ 8
español ▶ 21

3
¡Muy bien!
David... en el coche.
es ▶ 16
está ▶ 14

8
¡Falso!
Volver al n.º 2

9
¡Muy bien!
¿Vamos... cine?
a el ▶ 6
al ▶ 17

10
¡Falso!
Volver al n.º 21

11
¡Falso!
Volver al n.º 13

16
¡Falso!
Volver al n.º 3

17
¡Fantástico!
... problema es grande.
El ▶ 3
La ▶ 25

18
¡Falso!
Volver al n.º 27

19
¡Falso!
Volver al n.º 4

24
¡Muy bien!
Aquí termina el test.

25
¡Falso!
Volver al n.º 17

26
¡Qué bien!
Este año yo... a Perú.
voy ▶ 24
vas ▶ 29

27
¡Muy bien!
Yo no... cocinar.
sabo ▶ 18
sé ▶ 7

4

¡Muy bien!
Ella va… coche.

con ▶ 19
en ▶ 9

5

¡Falso!

Volver al n.º 7

6

¡Falso!

Volver al n.º 9

7

¡Bien! ¿Dónde… la estación?

hay ▶ 5
está ▶ 13

12

¡Muy bien! El coche… en el garaje.

hay ▶ 22
está ▶ 27

13

¡Correcto!
Se… italiano y alemán.

habla ▶ 26
hablan ▶ 11

14

¡Fantástico!
Los niños… en la cocina.

están ▶ 12
son ▶ 28

15

¡Falso!

Volver al n.º 30

20

¡Falso!

Volver al n.º 23

21

¡Muy bien!
¿… te llamas?

Qué ▶ 10
Cómo ▶ 30

22

¡Falso!

Volver al n.º 12

23

¡Fantástico!
Antonio… alto.

es ▶ 4
está ▶ 20

28

¡Falso!

Volver al n.º 14

29

¡Falso!

Volver al n.º 26

30

¡Correcto!
¿Están ellos… Madrid?

a ▶ 15
en ▶ 23

day: 8

Shopping

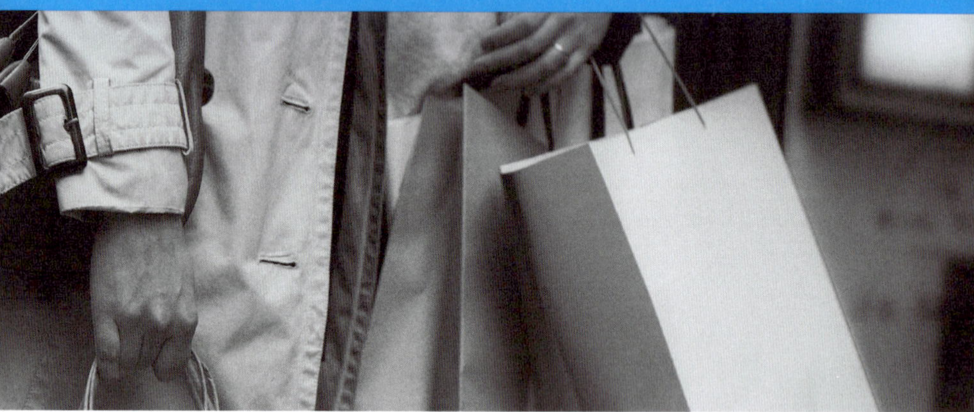

Day 8 covers more stem-changing verbs (*e* to *ie*), object pronouns (direct and indirect) and numbers. You will learn about shopping in Spain and further build your vocabulary and knowledge of Spain and Spanish culture.

OPENING HOURS…

In Spain most shops and supermarkets are open every day except Sundays. The standard opening hours are from 10:00 a.m. to 2:00 p.m. and from 5:00 p.m. to 8:00 p.m. A number of large department stores are open throughout the day from 10:00 a.m. to 9:00 p.m. and for reduced hours on Sundays.

Spanish conversation: De Compras

Dependiente:	**Buenos días, ¿qué le pongo?**
Karen:	**Hola, buenos días. Un kilo de ese bistec, por favor.**
Dependiente:	**Muy bien. ¿Algo más?**
Karen:	**¿A cómo está este jamón?**
Dependiente:	**¿El serrano? A 24 euros el kilo.**
Karen:	**Entonces me pone 200 gramos de jamón y 300 gramos de queso manchego, por favor.**
Dependiente:	**¿300 gramos del manchego joven?**
Karen:	**No lo sé, ¿puedo probar un poquito?**
Dependiente:	**Sí, claro, aquí tiene un trozo.**
Karen:	**¡Huy, está rico! Lo tomo.**
Dependiente:	**Aquí tiene, ¿quiere algo más?**
Karen:	**Un cuarto de kilo de chorizo.**
Dependiente:	**Lo siento, pero no me queda. ¿Desea alguna cosa más?**
Karen:	**No, nada más, gracias.**

Karen mira la lista de la compra y habla sola:

	¿Qué más necesito?… Dos litros de leche, un paquete de harina, una lata de sardinas, una botella de aceite y aceitunas verdes. Además tomates, huevos… y zanahorias para Nicolás.
Karen:	**¡Hola!, ¿cuánto cuesta el kilo de tomates?**
Empleada:	**Noventa y nueve céntimos, estos tomates son buenísimos.**
Karen:	**Están duros, ¿verdad? Un kilo, por favor.**
Empleada:	**¿Puede ser un poquito más?**
Karen:	**Sí, pero no mucho.**
Empleada:	**Las patatas y zanahorias están en oferta esta semana.**
Karen:	**Oh…, medio kilo de zanahorias. Por favor, ¿dónde están los huevos?**
Empleada:	**Allí a la derecha, son de gallinas de corral. ¿Es todo?**
Karen:	**Sí, eso es todo, gracias.**

English conversation: Shopping

Shop assistant:	**Good afternoon. What would you like?**
Karen:	**Hi, good afternoon. One kilo of steak, please.**
Shop assistant:	**Good, anything else?**
Karen:	**How much is the ham?**
Shop assistant:	**The cured ham? 24 euros per kilo.**
Karen:	**Give me 200 grams of the ham then and 300 grams of the Manchego cheese, please.**
Shop assistant:	**300 grams of the young Manchego?**
Karen:	**I don't know. Can I try a little?**
Shop assistant:	**Yes sure, here, take a piece.**
Karen:	**Mhmm, that tastes delicious. I'll take it.**
Shop assistant:	**Here you are. Would you like anything else?**
Karen:	**A quarter kilo of spicy sausage.**
Shop assistant:	**I am sorry, but I don't have any left. Anything else you would like?**
Karen:	**No, nothing more, thank you.**

Karen looks at her shopping list and mumbles to herself:

	What else do I need?... Two litres of milk, one bag of flour, one tin of sardines, one bottle of oil and green olives. Also tomatoes, eggs... and carrots for Nicolás.
Karen:	**Hi, how much is a kilo of tomatoes?**
Shop assistant:	**99 cents, these tomatoes are exceptionally good.**
Karen:	**They're firm, right? One kilo please.**
Shop assistant:	**Can it be a little more?**
Karen:	**Yes, but not too much.**
Shop assistant:	**Potatoes and carrots are on special offer this week.**
Karen:	**I see, ... half a kilo of carrots. Where are the eggs, please?**
Shop assistant:	**Over there on the right, they are free-range. Is that all?**
Karen:	**Yes, that's all, thank you.**

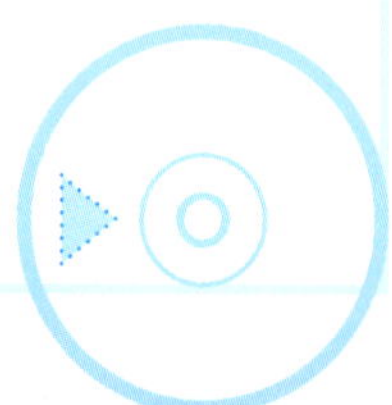

Grammar

Verbs whose stem changes from *e* to *ie*

querer (to like, want, love)		empezar (to start)	
qu*ie*ro	I want	emp*ie*zo	I start
qu*ie*res	you want	emp*ie*zas	you start
qu*ie*re	he/she wants	emp*ie*za	he/she starts
queremos	we want	empezamos	we start
queréis	you want	empezáis	you (pl.) start
qu*ie*ren	we want	emp*ie*zan	we start

Where the stem of these verbs is stressed the **e** of the stem changes to **ie**.

Direct and indirect object pronouns

indirect		direct	
me	I	*me (a mí)*	(to) me
te	you	*te (a ti)*	(to) you
le	him/her/it	*lo, la (a él/ella/usted)*	(to) him/her/it
nos	us	*nos (a nosotros/nosotras)*	(to) us
os	you *(pl.)*	*os (a vosotros/vosotras)*	(to) you *(pl.)*
les	them	*los, las (a ellos/ellas/ustedes)*	(to) them

Note that the direct and indirect object pronoun forms are the same for the 1st and 2nd person singular (**me**, **te**) and plural (**nos**, **os**).

The **indirect object pronoun** answers the question *for whom?* or *to whom?*

Pablo le da las llaves.	Pablo gives **him** the keys.
Puedes preguntar*les*.	You can ask **them**.

The **direct object pronoun** answers the question *what?* or *whom?*

Quiero comer el pan.	I want to eat **the bread**.
Quiero comerlo or **Lo quiero comer.**	I want to eat **it**.

The pronouns of the 3rd person singular and plural apply to both **people** and **objects**.
In Spainish **lo** is often replaced with **le**:

***le/lo* veo**	I see (it/him)

medio – otro	
medio kilo de queso	half a kilo of cheese
media docena de huevos	half a dozen eggs
otro pan	another/one more loaf of bread
otra botella de leche	another/one more bottle of milk

However: ***un* cuarto de kilo de chorizo** a quarter of a kilo of chorizo
Note: there is no indefinite article before **medio** and **otro**

Numbers 31 to 2000

31	**treinta y uno, -a**	**200**	**doscientos, -as**
32	**treinta y dos**	**300**	**trescientos, -as**
40	**cuarenta**	**400**	**cuatrocientos, -as**
50	**cincuenta**	**500**	**quinientos, -as**
60	**sesenta**	**600**	**seiscientos, -as**
70	**setenta**	**700**	**setecientos, -as**
80	**ochenta**	**800**	**ochocientos, -as**
90	**noventa**	**900**	**novecientos, -as**
100	**cien, ciento**	**1000**	**mil**
102	**ciento dos**	**2000**	**dos mil**

y is inserted only between tens and single digits:
e.g. **treinta *y* cinco** (35) **but** **ciento dos** (102)
Before nouns **ciento** becomes **cien**
e.g. ***cien* libros** - one hundred books

Multiples of **ciento** agree with the gender of the noun:
seiscient*as* cos*as* (600 things)
trescient*os* libr*os* (300 books)

Note:
Numbers with **more than four digits** can have a period [full stop] instead of a comma as you would use in English or else, more commonly these days, just a space.
15,280 (UK/US) = **15.280** or **15 280** (Spain)

Note that **monetary amounts use a comma** instead of a period [full stop].
$1.20 (US)/£1.20 (UK) = **€1,20** (Spain)

Exercises

Exercise 1

Fill in the verb forms. **nosotros** **usted** **tú** **ellas**

1 querer ....

2 almorzar ....

3 sentir ....

4 comprar ....

5 empezar ....

6 soler ....

Exercise 2

Tick the person and indicate singular or plural for the pronouns in each sentence.

	1st pers.	2nd pers.	3rd pers. sg. pl.
1 *Te* duchas todos los días.	....	....	....
2 No puedo mirar*las*.	....	....	....
3 *Se* lava con agua caliente.	....	....	....
4 *Me* levanto a las siete.	....	....	....
5 ¿Quién *nos* quiere?	....	....	....
6 *Lo* compro para mi madre.	....	....	....
7 No sé qué preguntar*os*.	....	....	....
8 ¿Sabes *tú* dónde están?	....	....	....
9 ¿Qué *le* pongo?	....	....	....
10 *Les* cantan una canción.	....	....	....

Exercise 3

Answer the questions using the following example as a guide.

¿Quién compra las zanahorias? Yo *las* compro.

1 ¿Quién abre la ventana? ....

2 ¿Quién hace el trabajo? ....

3 ¿Quién come patatas? ....

4 ¿Quién escribe los libros? ....

5 ¿Quién nos quiere? ....

6 ¿Quién compra la cerveza? ....

7 ¿Quién pone la mesa? ....

8 ¿Quién toma los cigarrillos? ....

Exercise 4

Replace the nouns with the appropriate pronouns.

1 (El periódico) .... compro.

2 (La lengua) no .... habla Ud. bien.

3 (La bicicleta) .... falta una rueda.

4 Tenéis que saludar .... (la azafata).

5 Podéis preguntar .... (las chicas) qué hora es.

6 (El flamenco) no .... baila.

7 No .... alquiláis (las habitaciones).

8 (El pollo) puedes poner .... un poco de sal.

9 (Las enfermeras) .... llaman.

10 (Julia) .... cantamos algunas canciones.

Exercise 5

Select the correct answer.

1 250 is written:
- **a** dos cien cincuenta
- **b** doscientos cincuenta
- **c** doscientos cincuenta

2 701 is written:
- **a** siete cientos uno
- **b** setecientos y uno
- **c** setecientos uno

3 50 is written:
- **a** cincuenta
- **b** quinientos
- **c** quince

4 522 is written:
- **a** quinientos veinte y dos
- **b** quinientos veintidós
- **c** cincuentaveintidós

1......... **2**......... **3**......... **4**.........

Exercise 6

Translate the following text into Spanish.

Half a kilo of tomatoes, please, 2 liters of milk, one loaf of bread, a quarter kilo of carrots, half a dozen eggs, another bottle of milk and two jars of jam.

....

....

....

....

....

....

Vocabulary

Below is a list of vocabulary encountered in this chapter.

¿A cómo está?	*How much is it?*
¿Algo más?	*Anything else?*
aceitunas *f pl*	*olives*
además	*furthermore*
alguno, -a	*some(one)*
alquilar	*to rent, let*
bistec *m*	*(beef) steak*
céntimo *m*	*cent*
chorizo *m*	*spicy sausage*
corral *m*	*chicken farm*
costar (-ue-)	*to cost*
dependiente *m/f*	*shop assistant*
desear	*to wish*
duro, -a	*hard, firm*
empezar (-ie-)	*to start*
en oferta *f*	*on special offer*
entonces	*then*
gallina *f*	*chicken*
gallinas *f pl* **de corral**	*free-range chickens*
gramo *m*	*gram*
harina *f*	*flour*
jamón *m* **serrano**	*cured ham*
joven	*young*
kilo *m*	*kilo(gramme)*
lata *f*	*can, tin*
lo siento	*I am sorry*
manchego	*Manchego (cheese)*
paquete *m*	*packet, bag*
patata *f*	*potato*
probar (-ue-)	*to try out*
querer (-ie-)	*to want, like, love*
rico, -a	*tasty, rich, delicious*
sardina *f*	*sardine*
sentir (-ie-)	*to regret*
solo, -a	*alone*
tierno	*young (cheese)*
trozo *m*	*piece*
un poquito	*a little*
una barra de pan	*a loaf of bread*
una rebanada de pan	*a slice of bread*
un paquete de cigarrillos	*a packet of cigarettes*
un ramo de flores	*a bunch of flowers*
una tableta de chocolate	*a chocolate bar*
un tarro de mermelada	*a jar of jam*
un tubo de mayonesa	*a tube of mayonnaise*
una caja de cerillas	*a box of matches*
una docena de huevos	*a dozen eggs*
una loncha de jamón	*a slice of ham*

day:9

Trains

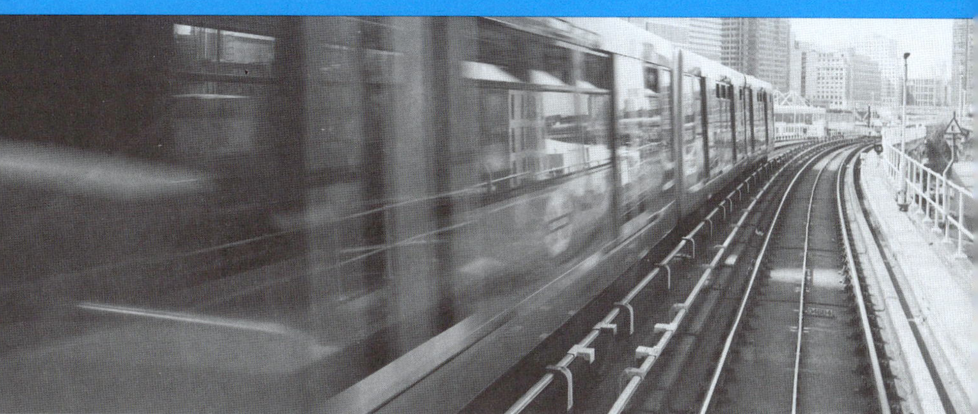

Day 9 introduces the immediate future using *ir + a + infinitive*. You will learn how to use *hay que* (to say you have to do something) and *para* (in order to/to). You will also learn the ordinal numbers (first, second, etc.) and learn about traveling through Spain by train.

RAIL TRAVEL...

The bigger Spanish cities usually have more than one train station. ***Atocha*** *in Madrid serves the trains to the south and east while the* ***Chamartín*** *station provides train links to the north and west of Spain.*

RENFE *is the name of the state-run Spanish railway company. Its ticket offices are located at the stations or in central locations in the city. A surcharge is charged for trips on the premium trains* ***TER*** *and* ***Talgo*** *as well as the* ***AVE****, which is the high-speed rail link. Train journeys within Spain are relatively cheap. Look out for* ***días azules*** *– blue days for discounted fares.*

Spanish conversation: En la estación central

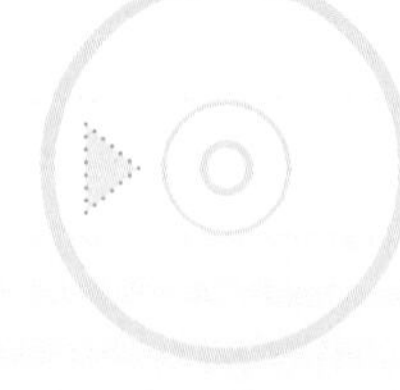

Karen:	**Mañana voy a ir en tren a Toledo.**
Pedro:	**¿Cuánto tiempo va a quedarse?**
Karen:	**Sólo un día, voy ida y vuelta. Voy a sacar el billete en la ventanilla de venta de billetes de RENFE.**

En la estación.

Pasajero:	**Puede pasar Ud. primero, señorita. Yo tardo un rato.**
Karen:	**Muy amable, gracias.**
Empleado:	**Buenas tardes, ¿adónde va Ud. señorita?**
Karen:	**Buenas tardes, deseo sacar un billete para Toledo, por favor.**
Empleado:	**¿Ida y vuelta?**
Karen:	**Sí, segunda clase, no fumadores.**
Empleado:	**¿Para cuándo lo desea?**
Karen:	**Para mañana.**
Empleado:	**¿Para qué hora?**
Karen:	**Perdón, Ud. me hace muchas preguntas, ¿hay que saber el día y la hora?**
Empleado:	**Sí, en España los billetes de tren hay que comprarlos para un día concreto y una hora exacta.**
Karen:	**Ah, entonces... para el tren de las 8.00 de la mañana. ¿Puedo reservar un asiento junto a la ventanilla?**
Empleado:	**Sí, todavía quedan asientos libres.**
Karen:	**¿Hay que hacer transbordo?**
Empleado:	**El rápido de las 7.00 es un tren directo.**
Karen:	**¿Desde qué andén sale el tren, por favor?**
Empleado:	**El tren para Toledo parte del andén n.º 8, es el último andén de la derecha.**

El próximo día en el tren.

Karen:	**Perdón, señor, tengo una reserva para este asiento.**
Señor:	**Oh... lo siento mucho. Mi asiento es el no. 6.**
Karen:	**El tren lleva retraso, ¿verdad?**
Señor:	**Sí, lleva 15 minutos de retraso.**
Karen:	**¿Le molesta si abro la ventanilla? Hace mucho calor en este departamento, y hasta Toledo vamos a tardar un rato.**

English conversation: At the main train station

Karen:	**Tomorrow I'm taking the train to Toledo.**
Pedro:	**How long are you going for?**
Karen:	**Just one day. I'll go there and come back. I'll buy the ticket at the RENFE ticket counter.**

At the station.

Passenger:	**You can go first, miss. I'll need a little more time.**
Karen:	**That's very kind of you, thank you.**
Rail employee:	**Good afternoon. Where are you going?**
Karen:	**Good afternoon, I'd like to buy a ticket to Toledo, please.**
Rail employee:	**Round-trip?**
Karen:	**Yes, second class, non-smoking.**
Rail employee:	**For which day?**
Karen:	**For tomorrow.**
Rail employee:	**At what time?**
Karen:	**Excuse me, you are asking a lot of questions. Does one have to know the day and the time?**
Rail employee:	**Yes, in Spain you have to buy your train ticket for a definite day and a specific time of day.**
Karen:	**Well then… for the train at 8 o'clock in the morning. Can I reserve a seat by the window?**
Rail employee:	**Yes, there are still some vacant seats.**
Karen:	**Will I have to change trains?**
Rail employee:	**The express train at 7 o'clock is a direct train.**
Karen:	**From which platform does the train leave, please?**
Rail employee:	**The train to Toledo leaves at platform 8, it's the last platform on the right.**

The next day on the train.

Karen:	**Excuse me, sir, I have a reservation for this seat.**
Man:	**Oh, … I am sorry. My seat is number 6.**
Karen:	**The train is late, isn't it?**
Man:	**Yes, it's 15 minutes late.**
Karen:	**Do you mind if I open the window? It is very hot in this compartment and it will be quite a while before we get to Toledo.**

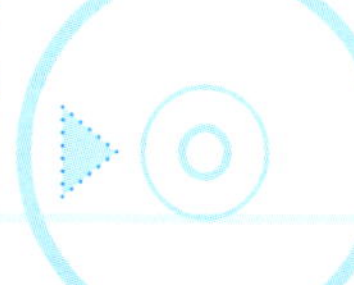

Grammar

Immediate future with *ir + a* – to be going to

ir + a+ infinitive = going to do something	
Voy a **sacar el billete.**	I'm going to buy the ticket.
Vas a **ir al cine.**	You're going to go to the cinema.
Va a **hacer una paella.**	He/she's going to make paella.
Vamos a **levantarnos.**	We are going to get up.
Vais a **lavaros.**	You are going to wash yourself.
Van a **irse.**	They are going to leave.

hay que + infinitive = one has to, you have to

Tener que is used rarely in the impersonal form; instead of **se tiene que** one normally uses the impersonal **hay que**:

hay que tener suerte	you have to have luck

para

Para is used to specify an objective, designation or purpose:

el tren *para* Toledo	the train to Toledo
una reserva *para* este asiento	a reservation for this seat

para viajar = in order to travel or when defining a date:	
el billete *para* mañana	the ticket for tomorrow

Ordinal numbers

1. **primero, -a**	5. **quinto, -a**	9. **noveno, -a**
2. **segundo, -a**	6. **sexto, -a**	10. **décimo, -a**
3. **tercero, -a**	7. **séptimo, -a**	
4. **cuarto, -a**	8. **octavo, -a**	

Ordinal numbers over and above 10 are uncommon. Instead, cardinal numbers are attached to the noun:

el piso *once*	the eleventh floor
el día *quince*	the fifteenth day

When specifying a date, ordinal numbers are used only for the first day of the month:

el primero de agosto or **el uno de agosto but el dos de agosto**

When used before masculine nouns, **primero** and **tercero** drop the **o**:

el *primer* piso	the first floor	**el *tercer* hijo**	the third son

Ordinal numbers are also used for fractions:

un *cuarto*	a quarter	**un *quinto***	a fifth	**la *tercera***	a third

Exercises

Exercise 1

Rewrite the sentences with ir + a following the examples below.

e.g. **No lo hacemos: No vamos a hacerlo.**

e.g. **Compro pan: Voy a comprar pan.**

1 No lo hago ahora: ....

2 Tocas la guitarra: ....

3 Van en coche a Madrid: ....

4 No lo escribimos: ....

5 Vas a la calle: ....

6 Tienes que llamarle: ....

7 Pilar no estudia español: ....

8 No encuentro el libro: ....

9 Empezáis temprano: ....

Exercise 2

1 ¿Para qué compras el billete?	**a** Para poder hablar español.
2 ¿Para qué te vas a la estación?	**b** Para ir de paseo.
3 ¿Para qué tomas un taxi?	**c** Para comprar un billete.
4 ¿Para cuándo tienes el tren?	**d** Para ir a Toledo.
5 ¿Para quién compras zanahorias?	**e** Para ir al centro.
6 ¿Para qué estudias español?	**f** Para mañana.
7 ¿Para qué sales?	**g** Para Nicolás.

1......... **2**......... **3**......... **4**......... **5**......... **6**......... **7**.........

Exercise 3

Insert y where required.

1 Dos ..... mil ..... tres ..... cientos ..... cincuenta ..... tres. (2353)

2 Diez ..... mil ..... dos ..... cientos ..... siete. (10 207)

3 Ocho ..... cientos ..... ocho. (808)

4 Mil ..... quince. (1015)

5 Treinta ..... mil ..... quinientos ..... setenta ..... cinco. (30 575)

Exercise 4

Write out the numbers.

Vivimos en el 4° piso: Vivimos en el cuarto piso.

1 Alfonso XIII, rey de España: ....

2 Siempre llego 1°: ....

3 Hoy es el 3° día de la semana: ....

4 Quiero 1/2 litro de leche: ....

5 Juan Carlos I de Borbón: ....

6 Subimos a la 10° planta: ....

7 Compro 1/4 kilo de tomates: ....

8 Estamos en el 7° mes del año: ....

Exercise 5

Fill in a, para, en or de.

1 El profesor es .... Madrid.

2 Esos libros son .... Pilar.

3 La casa está .... el centro.

4 Necesito leche .... el café.

5 Tengo que ir .... casa.

6 Mañana vamos .... teatro.

7 El tren sale .... las ocho.

8 El bolso es .... cuero.

9 La familia García vive .... Barcelona.

10 El ramo de flores está .... la mesa.

Vocabulary

Below is a list of vocabulary encountered in this chapter.

andén *m*	*platform*	**planta** *f*	*floor*
asiento *m*	*seat*	**pregunta** *f*	*question*
billete *m*	*ticket*	**primero, -a**	*first*
billete *m* **de tren**	*train ticket*	**próximo, -a**	*next*
calor *m*	*heat*	**rato** *m*	*moment*
clase *f*	*class*	**RENFE** *f* **(Red Nacional de Ferrocarriles Españoles)**	*state-run Spanish railway company*
coche *m*	*train compartment*	**reserva** *f*	*reservation*
concreto,-a	*concrete*	**reservar**	*to book, make a reservation*
cuero *m*	*leather*	**rey** *m*	*king*
desear	*to want, wish*	**sacar**	*to take out; buy*
directo, -a	*direct*	**salir**	*to depart*
encontrar (-ue-)	*to find*	**segundo, -a**	*second*
estación *f*	*station*	**subir**	*to board*
exacto, -a	*exact*	**tardar**	*to last*
fumador *m*	*smoker*	**tardar un rato**	*to take a little longer*
hace mucho calor	*it's very hot*	**temprano, -a**	*early*
hacer transbordo	*to change trains*	**todavía**	*still*
hasta	*until*	**(tren) rápido** *m*	*express train*
ida *f*	*one way*	**vagón** *m*	*train compartment*
ida y vuelta	*round-trip*	**venta** *f*	*sale*
llevar retraso	*to be delayed*	**ventanilla** *f* **de venta de billetes**	*ticket counter*
molestar	*to disturb/mind*	**vuelta** *f*	*return journey*
no fumadores	*non-smoking*		
¿Para cuándo?	*For when?*		
¿Para qué hora?	*For what time?*		
¿Para qué?	*For what?*		
¿Para quién?	*For whom?*		
partir	*to depart, leave*		
pasar	*to pass through*		

day: 10

The tourist

Day 10 talks about the tourism industry in Spain. You will learn how to form more stem-changing verbs (*c* to *zc*), and discover how to use *por* and *para*. You will continue to build your vocabulary and discover more about Spanish culture.

ALCÁZAR…

Alcázar *is the name for Spanish palaces, castles and fortifications that were built after the invasion by the Moors in 711 A.D. and which were built in the Moorish style. This architecture is characterized by its brick construction and multiple inner courtyards. The most famous* ***Alcázares*** *are those of Toledo, Seville and Segovia.*

Spanish conversation: En la información turística

Karen: **Buenos días, quisiera visitar Toledo y necesito un plano de la ciudad, por favor.**

Empleada: **¿Es la primera vez que está en Toledo?**

Karen: **Sí, no conozco la ciudad. ¿Qué lugares turísticos puedo visitar?**

Empleada: **Bueno, la Catedral de Toledo, la casa de El Greco, el Alcázar, puede dar un paseo por la parte antigua de la ciudad, por la calle de Cervantes, por el paseo del Carmen, y a mediodía puede ir al restaurante Aurelia para probar uno de nuestros platos típicos, por ejemplo perdices a la toledana…**

Karen: **Es sólo una excursión de un día. ¿Tiene una visita con guía?**

Empleada: **Sí, tenemos visitas con guía cada dos horas.**

Karen: **Pues, eso a mí me interesa mucho.**

Carlos: **Perdón, señorita, a mí también me interesa una visita con guía. ¿Me puede ofrecer algo?**

Empleada: **Bueno, en esta época del año esto no es un problema. A menudo también organizan excursiones los hoteles…**

Carlos: **Sí, es verdad, pero a mí me gusta ir por mi cuenta. Eso de ir en grupo es un rollo.**

Karen: **Pero… de vez en cuando es divertido, ¿no le parece?**

Carlos: **Bueno, yo tomo rara vez algo en grupo… Bueno, casi nunca. Señorita, ¿a qué hora comienza la visita con guía?**

Empleada: **Nuestro autobús sale siempre a las 9.30 de la mañana. Es un grupo español.**

Carlos: **Para mí usted habla muy bien el castellano… Bueno, de vez en cuando parece tener un acento… Habla un poco diferente.**

Empleada: **Señores, el autobús de las 9.30 está para partir.**

English conversation: At the tourist office

Karen:	**Good morning, I would like to see Toledo and need a map of the town, please.**
Employee:	**Is this your first time in Toledo?**
Karen:	**Yes, I don't know the town. What kind of tourist attractions can I visit?**
Employee:	**Well, the Cathedral of Toledo, the house of El Greco, the Alcázar, you can go for a walk through the old part of the town, Cervantes Street, through the Paseo del Carmen, and at noon you can go to Aurelia Restaurant to try one of our typical dishes, for example quail Toledo style…**
Karen:	**It's only a day trip. Do you have a guided tour?**
Employee:	**Yes, we offer guided tours every two hours.**
Karen:	**Well, I would be very interested in that.**
Carlos:	**Excuse me, I would be very interested in a guided tour as well. What can you offer me?**
Employee:	**Well, that's not a problem at this time of the year. The hotels also often organize excursions…**
Carlos:	**Yes, right, but I like going on my own. Going in groups is boring.**
Karen:	**But… from time to time it can be fun, don't you think?**
Carlos:	**Well, I rarely do things in a group… actually almost never. What time does the guided tour start?**
Employee:	**Our bus always leaves at 9:30 in the morning. It's a Spanish group.**
Carlos:	**I think you speak Spanish very well… OK, sometimes you seem to have an accent…you sound a little different.**
Employee:	**Ladies and gentlemen, the 9:30 bus is ready to leave.**

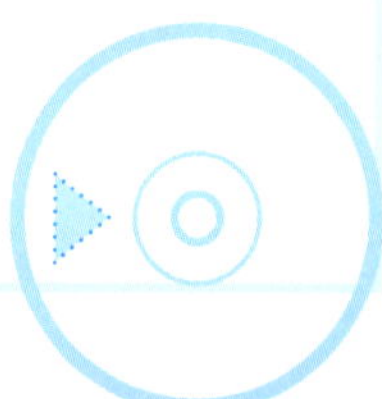

Grammar

Stem-changing verbs: *c to zc*

conocer (to know, get to know)		parecer (to appear)	
conozco	I know	parezco	I appear
conoces	you know	pareces	you appear
conoce	he/she/it knows	parece	he/she/it appears
conocemos	we know	parecemos	we appear
conocéis	you (pl) know	parecéis	you (pl) appear
conocen	they know	parecen	they appear

In the first person singular the c is preceded by a z.

Object pronouns after prepositions

The following **object pronouns** come after prepositions such as a, de, para, por:

mí	me, to me
ti	you, to you
él, ella, ello, Ud.	him/her, to him/to her, to you *(formal)*
nosotros	us
vosotros	you (pl)
ellos, ellas, Uds.	them, to them, you, to you *(formal)*

Las flores son *para ti*.	The flowers are for you.
Esto es *por ti*.	That is because of you.

The Spanish play it safe here by repeating pronouns:
a mí, a ti etc. are used for **emphasis** and are always **supplemented** by me, te etc.

A mí me interesa.	I am interested in it.
A ellos les ofrecen vino.	They offer them wine.

Quisiera (would like)

quisiera + infinitive = I would like to

Quisiera visitar la ciudad.	I would like to visit the city.

estar + para + infinitive = about to be doing something

El autobús *está para partir*.	The bus is about to leave.

por	
cause or reason	
Gracias *por* tu ayuda.	Thank you **for** your help.
approximate time	
por la mañana	**in the** morning
purchase price	
por 200 euros	**for** 200 euros
approximate location + movement	
por la ciudad	**through** the city
means of communication	
por teléfono	**over** the telephone

Note the following expressions: **por fin** = at last; **¡Por Dios!** = For God's sake!

Exercises

Exercise 1

Write out the correct form of the verbs.

1 Los niños (parecer) .... tener hambre.

2 Ud. (poder) .... dormir.

3 Yo no lo (conocer) ....

4 Me (parecer) .... muy caro.

5 ¿No (querer, tú) .... ir con nosotros?

6 Hay que (trabajar) .... todos los días.

7 ¿(Tú) (conocer) .... el camino?

Exercise 2

Emphasize the object in the following statements.

1 .... me saluda todas las mañanas.

2 .... nos visita todos los días.

3 .... les preguntan muchas cosas.

4 ....os compran libros interesantes.

5 .... las invitan a un bar.

6 .... les gusta bailar.

7 .... te invitan a la fiesta.

Exercise 3

Fill in the appropriate object pronoun.

1 Es para (usted) ....

2 Es para (yo) ....

3 Es para (nosotros) ....

4 Es para (ellas) ....

5 Es para (tú) ....

6 Es para (ustedes) ....

Exercise 4

Translate the following text into Spanish.

I'd like a piece of cheese, please. I'd like to visit the old part of the town. I'd like to try it. Can I go? I'd like to study Spanish. I can speak Spanish.

....

....

....

....

....

Exercise 5

Por or para?

1 El supermercado está cerrado .... la tarde.

2 Vamos a Madrid .... visitar la ciudad.

3 No trabajan .... las mañanas.

4 Compro un billete .... Toledo.

5 Necesitamos pescado .... la cena.

6 Vamos a la playa .... tomar el sol.

7 Me llama .... teléfono .... invitarme a su fiesta.

Exercise 6

Put in the appropriate verb form.

Inma (ser) .... enfermera y Paco (estudiar) .... informática. Los dos (ser) .... buenos amigos. (Conocerse) .... bien. (Encontrarse) .... a menudo para ir al cine o al teatro. Inma (trabajar) .... cerca de la calle donde (vivir) .... Paco. Por las tardes (soler) .... ir de paseo. (Estudiar) .... inglés porque (querer) .... ir a Estados Unidos.

Vocabulary

Below is a list of vocabulary encountered in this chapter.

a menudo	*often*
acento *m*	*accent*
algo es un rollo	*something is boring*
antiguo, -a	*old*
ayuda *f*	*help*
cada	*every*
cada dos horas	*every two hours*
caro, -a	*expensive*
casi nunca	*almost never*
castellano *m*	*Castilian*
catedral *f*	*cathedral*
comenzar	*to start, begin*
conocer	*to know, get to know*
cuenta *f*	*account*
de vez en cuando	*from time to time*
diferente	*different*
divertido, -a	*funny, entertaining*
dormir	*to sleep*
encontrarse	*to meet*
época *f* **del año**	*season*
estudiar	*to study, learn*
excursión *f*	*excursion*
grupo *m*	*group*
guía *m*	*(travel) guide*
hotel *m*	*hotel*
información *f*	*information*
informática *f*	*information technology*
la primera vez	*(for) the first time*
lo hago por mi cuenta	*I'll do it on my own*
lugar *m*	*place*
¿No le parece?	*Don't you think?*
ofrecer	*to offer*
organizar	*to organize*
parecer	*to appear, seem*
parte *f*	*part*
perdiz *f*	*quail*
plano *m* **de la ciudad**	*street map, map of the city*
por Dios	*for God's sake*
por fin	*at last; finally*
porque	*because*
problema *m*	*problem*
quisiera	*I'd like to*
rara vez	*seldom, rarely*
turístico, -a	*touristic*
verdad *f*	*truth*
vía *f* **aérea**	*by air*
visita *f*	*visit*
visitar	*to visit*
siempre	*always*
casi siempre	*almost always*
a menudo	*often*
a veces	*sometimes*
de vez en cuando	*occasionally, from time to time*
rara vez	*rarely*
casi nunca	*almost never*
nunca	*never*

day: 11

Romance

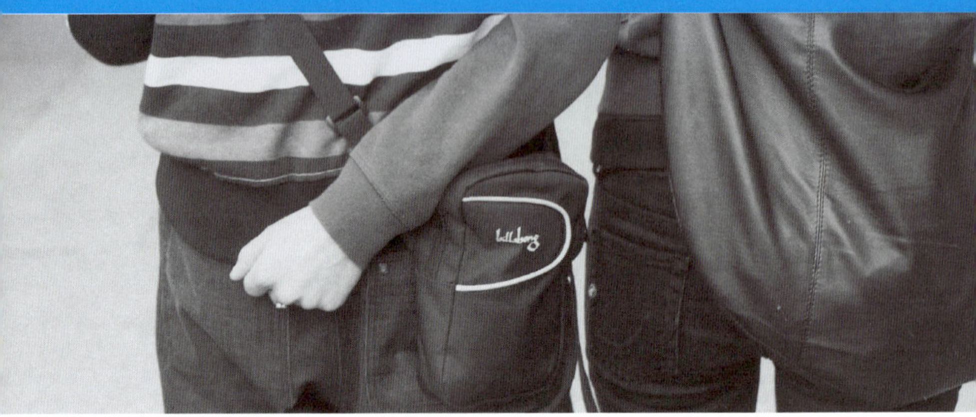

Day 11 talks about romance. You will learn the verbs *dar* (to give) and *salir* (to go out). You will be able to practice all of the new grammar rules presented in this chapter and you will pick up useful colloquial expressions and further build your vocabulary.

¿VALE?

When making a phone call, the standard way to answer the phone is with ***¡Diga!*** *and/or* ***¡Dígame!*** *(Tell me). You will also hear* ***perdone*** *and* ***disculpe*** *which are both polite ways to say "excuse me". Another useful expression is* ***vale*** *(okay/alright) which can be used in place of* ***sí*** *(yes).*

Spanish conversation: La primera cita de Karen

Lucía: **Karen, ¿quién es ese chico de Toledo?**
Karen: **Se llama Carlos Martini, es argentino, y da clases de tenis. Quiere salir conmigo.**
Lucía: **¿Contigo?... huy. ¿Es guapo?**
Karen: **Sí, es interesante y guapo.**

Suena el teléfono.

Pedro: **¡Dígame!**
Carlos: **Oiga, por favor, ¿está Karen en casa?**
Pedro: **¿De parte de quién?**
Carlos: **De Carlos Martini.**
Pedro: **Sí, un momento. Karen, es para Ud.**
Karen: **Hola, ¿quién habla?**
Carlos: **Soy yo, Carlos.**
Karen: **Ah... Hola Carlos. ¿Cómo estás?**
Carlos: **Bien, gracias. ¿Y tú?**
Karen: **Gracias, muy bien.**
Carlos: **¿Qué vas a hacer esta tarde? ¿Tienes ganas de salir conmigo?**
Karen: **Esta tarde voy a ir a la escuela.**
Carlos: **Después de tus clases podemos encontrarnos, ¿no?**
Karen: **Sí, vale. ¿Qué vamos a hacer?**
Carlos: **¿Conoces el café Triana que está cerca de la universidad?**
Karen: **Sí, lo conozco.**
Carlos: **¿Por qué no nos encontramos allí?**
Karen: **¿A qué hora?**
Carlos: **¿Te parece bien a las 7.00 de la tarde?**
Karen: **Está bien, a las 7.00. Voy a estar delante de la puerta.**

Karen llega a las 7.15 al café Triana. Carlos la espera.

Karen: **Perdón Carlos... llego tarde. No es mi culpa, es culpa del autobús. A esta hora hay un tráfico increíble. Lo siento mucho.**
Carlos: **Bueno, los hombres estamos acostumbrados a esperar a las mujeres...**

English conversation: Karen's first date

Lucía:	**Karen, who is this guy from Toledo?**
Karen:	**His name is Carlos Martini, he is Argentinian and gives tennis lessons. He wants to go out with me.**
Lucía:	**With you?… Wow. Is he handsome?**
Karen:	**Yes, he is interesting and good-looking.**

The telephone rings.

Pedro:	**Hello!**
Carlos:	**(Tell me, please.) Is Karen at home?**
Pedro:	**Who is speaking?**
Carlos:	**Carlos Martini.**
Pedro:	**Yes, one moment… Karen, it's for you.**
Karen:	**Hello, who's speaking?**
Carlos:	**It's me, Carlos.**
Karen:	**Ah… hi Carlos, how are you?**
Carlos:	**Fine, thanks, and you?**
Karen:	**Thank you, very well.**
Carlos:	**What are you doing this afternoon? Would you like to go out with me?**
Karen:	**I have school this afternoon.**
Carlos:	**We could meet after your classes, couldn't we?**
Karen:	**Yes, OK. What are we going to do?**
Carlos:	**Do you know Café Triana, near the university?**
Karen:	**Yes, I know it.**
Carlos:	**Why don't we meet there?**
Karen:	**At what time?**
Carlos:	**Is 7:00 in the evening OK for you?**
Karen:	**7 o'clock is fine. I'll be in front of the door.**

Karen arrives at Café Triana at 7:15 p.m. Carlos is waiting for her.

Karen:	**I'm sorry Carlos… I'm late. It's not my fault, it's the bus' fault. The traffic at this time of day is incredible. I am really sorry.**
Carlos:	**It's OK, us men are used to waiting for women…**

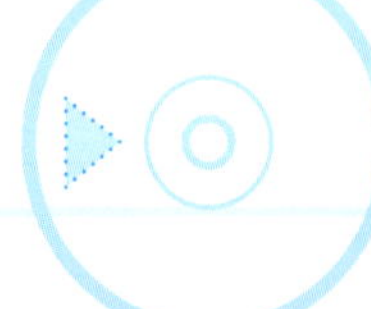

Grammar

Verbs

dar (to give)			
doy	I give	damos	we give
das	you give	dais	you give
da	he/she gives, you *(formal)* give	dan	they/you *(formal)* give

Note: the irregular verb dar is conjugated just like ir (see Day 4).

salir (to leave, go out)			
salgo	I go out	salimos al teatro	we go out to the theatre
sales a la calle	you go out in the street	salís de casa	we leave the house
sale a bailar	he/she goes out dancing	salen todas las noches	they go out every night

Only in combination with mi, ti and sí does the preposition con (with) take a **special form**.

con + mi = conmigo with me

con + ti = contigo with you

con + sí = consigo with him-/herself, oneself

With all other personal pronouns con remains **unchanged**:

con él, con ella, con Uds.

a with a direct object

If the **direct object** is a person, it is always preceded by a

Esperamos *a las mujeres*.	We wait for the women.
Conozco *al señor García*.	I know Mr. García.
but	
Compra el periódico.	He buys the newspaper.

Tener normally has **no** a

Tienes una madre simpática.	You have a nice mother.

We Spaniards…

If the speaker includes himself in the subject of his statement, the verb will be in the 1st person plural instead of the 3rd:

los hombres est*amos* acostumbrados…	we men are used to…
but	
los hombres están acostumbrados…	(the) men are used to…

Exercises

Exercise 1

Select the appropriate combinations.

		a	b	c
1	¿Viene solo o ..... ?	**a** con ti	**b** con tú	**c** contigo
2	Tenemos clases	**a** con ella	**b** conella	**c** con sí
3	Habla	**a** con sí	**b** consigo misma	**c** con lo
4	Ana pregunta	**a** portigo	**b** por ti	**c** por tú
5	Hago un postre	**a** para ella	**b** para la	**c** parasí
6	¿Quieres salir esta tarde ..... ?	**a** con mi	**b** conmigo	**c** con me

1 .... **2** .... **3** .... **4** .... **5** .... **6** ....

Exercise 2

Insert a where necessary.

1. ¿Conoces .... mi padre?
2. Tengo .... un hermano y .... dos hermanas.
3. ¿Conoces .... esta calle?
4. La madre quiere mucho .... su hija.
5. No conozco .... este señor.
6. Visitamos .... la ciudad de Toledo.
7. Compran .... un plano de la ciudad.
8. Carlos espera .... Karen.
9. Eso .... mí me interesa mucho.

Exercise 3

Say it in Spanish.

We Spaniards love life. We enjoy the feasts and we savour the sherry. This is how we Spaniards are. Do you know Spaniards?

....

....

....

....

Exercise 4

Complete the sentences by inserting the appropriate verb in the present tense.

hacer, estar, parecer, ir, salir, dar, tener, poner, conocer, saber

1 Yo le .... muy bien.

2 ¿Qué .... (vosotros) todos los días por la mañana?

3 ¿(Nosotros) .... a tomar un café?

4 ¿Cuántos gramos de queso le .... (yo)?

5 Me .... muy bien.

6 (Yo) .... a las cinco y media de la oficina.

7 Los españoles .... acostumbrados al sol.

8 (Ellos) .... ganas de ir a España.

9 (Yo) ....clases de español.

10 No lo .... de verdad.

Exercise 5

Which sentences belong together?

1 ¿Puede esperar un poco?
2 ¿De parte de quién?
3 ¿Quién habla?
4 Hola, ¿cómo estás?
5 ¿A qué hora?
6 ¿Te parece bien?
7 ¿Quieres salir conmigo?
8 ¿Conoces el Café Triana?

a Soy yo.
b Sí, con gusto.
c De Carlos Martini.
d Sí, está bien.
e Muy bien, gracias.
f A las 7.00 en punto.
g Sí, lo conozco.
h Sí, no hay ningún problema.

1 .... **2** .... **3** .... **4** .... **5** .... **6** .... **7** .... **8** ....

Exercise 6

Fill in the corresponding verb forms. **tú** **nosotros** **ustedes**

1 dar ....
2 salir ....
3 ir ....
4 parecer ....
5 conocer ....
6 dormir ....
7 querer ....
8 ser ....

Vocabulary

Below is a list of vocabulary encountered in this chapter.

acostumbrado, -a	*accustomed, used to*
café *m*	*café*
chico *m*	*boy, guy*
cita *f*	*date*
clases *f pl* **de tenis**	*tennis lessons*
culpa *f*	*fault*
dar	*to give*
delante de	*in front of*
¿De parte de quién?	*literally: From who? (here:) Who's speaking?*
¡Dígame!	*literally: Tell me! (when answering the phone)*
disculpe	*excuse me*
escuela *f*	*school*
esperar	*to wait*
estar-acostumbrado a alguna cosa	*to be used to something*
gana *f*	*wish, desire*
guapo, -a	*handsome, good-looking*
hombre *m*	*man, human being*
increíble	*incredible*
llegar	*to arrive*
llego tarde	*I am late*
¡Lo siento mucho!	*I am so sorry!*
Lo siento	*I'm sorry*
momento *m*	*moment*
mujer *f*	*woman*
no es posible!	*not possible!*
¡Oiga!	*Listen!*
¡Perdón!	*sorry!*
perdone	*excuse me*
¿Por qué no?	*Why not?*
¡Qué lástima!	*What a shame!*
salir	*to go out, leave*
sonar	*to ring, sound*
tener ganas de	*to want to*
¿Te parece bien?	*Does that sound good?*
universidad *f*	*university*

day: 12

A trip to Madrid

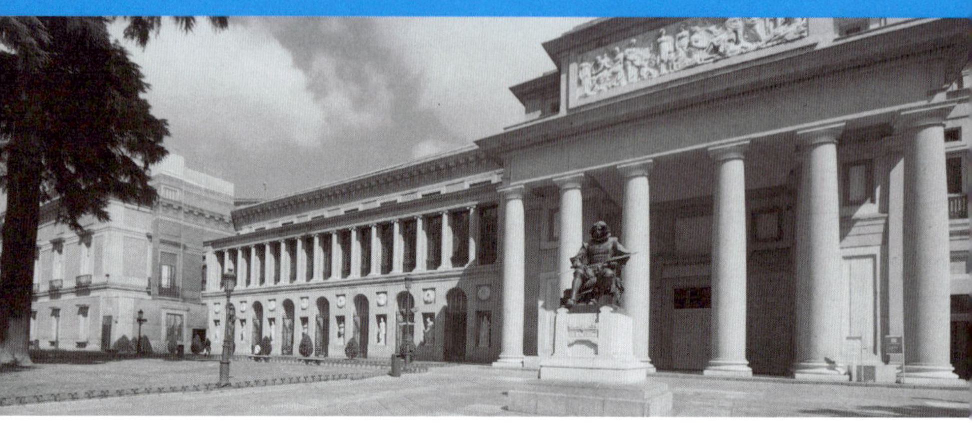

Day 12 introduces the past tense. You will also learn the verb *ver* (to see) and how to make exclamations. This chapter also features some interesting tips about *tapas* as well and you will be able to build up your vocabulary on sightseeing.

TAPAS...

Tapas *are delicious little snacks that often come when you order a beer* ***(caña)*** *or wine. Depending on the bar, you may get complimentary* ***tapas*** *with each drink, or there may be an extra charge. Most bars will offer* ***tapas*** *such as small fish* ***(boquerones)****, cheese* ***(queso)****, olives* ***(aceitunas)*** *or ham* ***(jamón)****. Other typical alternatives include meatballs* ***(albóndigas)*** *or fried potatoes with a spicy sauce* ***(patatas bravas)****, as well as* ***tortilla****.*

Spanish conversation: Visita a la ciudad

Pedro: **Karen, vamos a hacer una visita a la ciudad. Todavía no ha visitado las partes históricas y famosas de Madrid.**

Karen: **Con mucho gusto. ¿Qué cosas dignas de ver hay aquí?**

Pedro: **Vamos hasta la calle Toledo para visitar la iglesia de San Isidro, para los madrileños es la catedral.**

Karen: **¿De qué época es?**

Pedro: **Es del siglo XVII. San Isidro es el patrón de Madrid.**

En la iglesia.

Karen: **¡Qué preciosa! No he visitado una igual. ¿Adónde vamos?**

Pedro: **Ahora vamos a la plaza de la Cibeles.**

Karen: **¿En qué dirección está?**

Pedro: **En principio, todo recto.**

Karen: **¿Pasamos también por la calle Alcalá?**

Pedro: **Claro. Empieza en la Plaza de la Cibeles. En esta calle están los bancos, las tiendas elegantes y los comercios caros. ¡Atención vamos a cruzar!**

Karen: **¡Qué interesante! Quisiera visitar también el famoso Museo del Prado.**

Pedro: **Estamos cerca de la Plaza Cánovas del Castillo [...], luego pasamos al Prado.**

En el museo.

Pedro: **Estos cuadros reflejan la grandeza e importancia histórica de España. Me encantan. Las obras de Goya son geniales.**

Karen: **¡Qué impresionante! ¿Se pueden tomar fotografías aquí?**

Pedro: **No, está prohibido, lo siento.**

Karen: **¡Qué lástima! ¿Quién ha pintado este cuadro?**

Pedro: **Es de Velázquez, ¿le gusta?**

Karen: **Sí, me impresiona mucho. Estoy un poco cansada, hemos caminado todo el día.**

Pedro: **¿Ha probado ya las tapas madrileñas? Hay un bar cerca de aquí. He comido allí unas tapas excelentes. Podemos ir a probarlas.**

Karen: **¡Vale!, buena idea.**

English conversation: A tour of the city

Pedro:	Karen, let's do a tour of the city today. You still haven't seen the historical and famous parts of Madrid.
Karen:	I'd like that very much. Which sights are there to see?
Pedro:	We'll go as far as the Calle Toledo to visit the church of Saint Isidro, which is the cathedral for the locals of Madrid.
Karen:	From which period is it?
Pedro:	It is from the 17th century. Saint Isidro is the patron saint of Madrid.Inside the church.
Karen:	How magnificent! I have never visited a church like this. Where are we going now?
Pedro:	Now we're going to the Plaza de la Cibeles.
Karen:	In which direction is it?
Pedro:	Basically straight ahead.
Karen:	Will we also pass the Calle Alcalá?
Pedro:	Sure. It starts at the Plaza de la Cibeles. That street is lined with banks, elegant stores and expensive shops. Watch out, we're crossing the street!
Karen:	How interesting! I would also like to visit the famous Prado Museum.
Pedro:	We are near the Plaza Cánovas del Castillo and we'll go to the Prado afterwards.

In the museum.

Pedro:	These paintings reflect the greatness and historical significance of Spain. I love them. Goya's works are those of a genius.
Karen:	How impressive! Can I take pictures here?
Pedro:	No, that's not allowed, I'm sorry.
Karen:	What a shame! Who painted this picture?
Pedro:	That's by Velázquez. Do you like it?
Karen:	Yes, I am very impressed by it. I am a little tired; we've been walking around all day.
Pedro:	Have you already tried Madrid's tapas? There's a bar close by. I've had excellent tapas there. We can go there to try them.
Karen:	OK! That's a good idea.

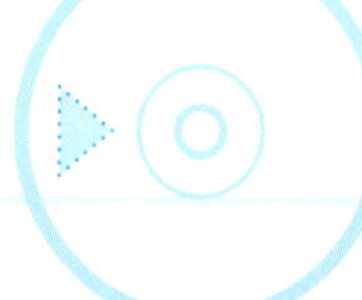

Grammar

Perfect tense

The perfect tense signifies **an action that has been completed**, but which is **closely related to the present**. It is formed by taking the present tense of **haber** (to have) and combining it with the past participle of a verb.

haber (to have)			
he	*I had*	*hemos*	*we had*
has	*you had*	*habéis*	*you (pl) had*
ha	*he/she/it had*	*han*	*they had*

The perfect tense is used with expressions of time: **hoy** (today), **esta mañana** (this morning), **esta semana** (this week), **este año** (this year), **todavía** (still), **ya** (already), **hace poco** (a short while ago).

Note that **haber** + past participle always stay together:

No me *he lavado* hoy.	I didn't wash today.
Hemos llegado.	We have arrived.

The past participle of verbs is formed by taking the infinitive of the verb and dropping the ending as follows: **-ar** becomes **-ado**; **-er** and **-ir** become **-ido**.

hablar (to speak)		comer (to eat)		vivir (to live)	
habl*ado*	spoken	**com*ido***	eaten	**viv*ido***	lived

The past participle **remains unchanged** in the perfect tense:

***He lavado* la ropa.**	I have washed the clothes.

The past participle takes the **gender** and **number** of the **noun** to which it relates:

las lenguas hablad*as*	the spoken languages.

Verbs

ver (to see)			
veo	I see	**vemos**	we see
ves	you see	**veis**	you see
ve	he/she sees, you *(form.)* see	**ven**	they/you *(form.)* see

Conjunction: and

Note that the past participle takes the **gender** and **number** of the **noun** to which it relates:

las lenguas hablad*as*	the spoken languages

Before **i** and **hi** the conjunction **y** (and) changes to **e**

la importancia *y* grandeza	**la grandeza *e* importancia**
es interesante *y* guapo	**es guapo *e* interesante**

Exclamations using *¡Qué!*

¡Qué + adjective (+ verb)!
¡Qué + noun (+ verb)!

¡*Qué* preciosa es!	**¡*Qué* preciosa!**
¡*Qué* interesante es!	**¡*Qué* interesante!**
¡*Qué* hambre tengo!	**¡*Qué* hambre!**

Exercises

Exercise 1

Form the past participle of these verbs.

comer, querer, hablar, caminar, venir, trabajar, dormir, levantar, conocer, visitar

....

....

....

Exercise 2

Write out the past participle of the verbs in italics.

1 Parece interesante, pero es muy *aburrir*. ....

2 *Afeitar* parece más joven. ....

3 Las camas están *arreglar*. ....

4 ¡Está *prohibir* fumar! ....

5 (Ella) Se queda *impresionar*. ....

6 Las canciones *cantar* son preciosas. ....

Exercise 3

Rewrite the sentences in the perfect tense.

Comes mucho. Has comido mucho.

1 Hablas mucho ....

2 No tengo tiempo ....

3 ¿Estás en casa? ....

4 ¿Compras el periódico hoy? ....

5 ¿Arregláis las camas por la mañana? ....

6 Desayunamos muy poco. ....

Exercise 4

Y or e?

En abril voy a estudiar español .... alemán. Para ello voy a ir primero a España .... luego a Alemania. He estudiado ya una vez estas lenguas .... también el francés pero quiero mejorarlas. España .... Alemania son países interesantes .... importantes.

Exercise 5

Rewrite the sentences as in the example.

E.g. La Sra. Goméz es muy buena. ¡Qué buena es la Sra. Goméz!

1 Tengo mucha sed ....

2 Es muy rico ....

3 Esta chica es muy guapa ....

4 Esta mujer está muy enferma ....

5 La iglesia es muy impresionante ....

6 La película es muy interesante ....

7 El jamón está muy caro hoy ....

8 Tengo mucha hambre ....

Exercise 6

Decide which form of to have – haber or tener – fits here.

1 Miguel .... veinte años.

2 En la calle .... mucha gente.

3 ¿.................. (tú) comido ya?

4 ¿.................. (vosotros) comprado tomates?

5 Ud. .... una mujer muy simpática.

6 ¿Por qué no .... (Uds.) venido al café hoy?

7 En la mesa .... un periódico.

8 ¡Qué hambre .... (yo)!

Vocabulary

Below is a list of vocabulary encountered in this chapter.

abril *m*	*April*
afeitar(se)	*to shave (oneself)*
atención *f*	*attention*
banco *m*	*bank*
caminar	*to walk*
comercio *m*	*business, store*
con mucho gusto	*I'd like (that) very much*
cosas *f pl*	*sights/objects*
dignas de ver	*worth seeing*
cruzar	*to cross*
cuadro *m*	*picture*
digno, -a	*worthy*
dirección *f*	*direction*
elegante	*elegant*
en principio	*in principle, actually*
época *f*	*period, era*
fotografía *f*	*photo*
genial	*great, brilliant, fantastic*
grandeza *f*	*greatness*
haber	*to have*
histórico, -a	*historical*
igual	*equal*
importancia *f*	*importance*
impresionante	*impressive*
impresionar	*to impress*
me encantan	*(here:) I love them*
mejorar	*to improve*
museo *m*	*museum*
obra *f*	*work*
pasar	*to pass (by)*
patrón *m*	*patron saint*
precioso, -a	*valuable; magnificent*
prohibido, -a	*forbidden*
¡Qué lástima!	*What a shame!*
reflejar	*to reflect*
siglo *m*	*century*
tapa *f*	*tapa*
tienda *f*	*shop*
todavía no	*not yet*
todo recto	*straight ahead*
tomar fotografías *f*	*to take pictures*
una igual	*one like it*
visitar	*to visit*

day: 13

The restaurant

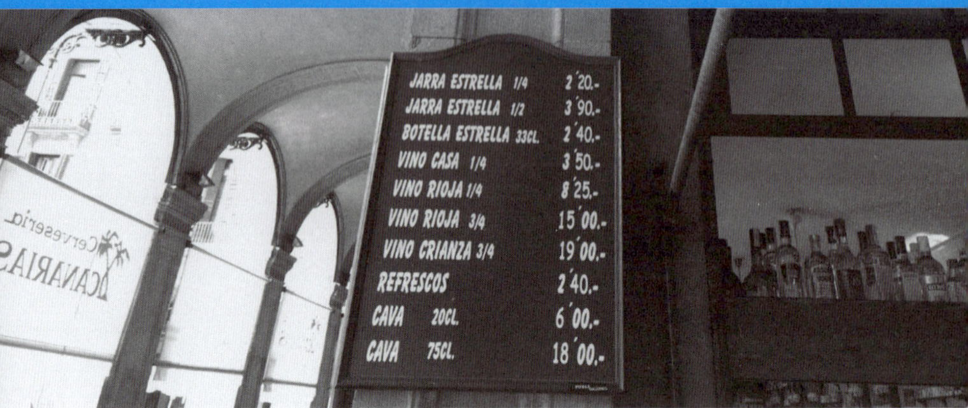

Day 13 introduces more stem-changing verbs (*e* to *i*). You will also learn indefinite pronouns (*alguno*, *nada*, *ninguno*, etc.) and learn about the existence of double negatives! Finally, you will learn how to say what you like (and don't like), and discover all the places where you can go to eat.

WHERE TO EAT...

La cafetería *generally offers cakes, ice cream, sandwiches and shakes.* ***El bar*** *will usually have a variety of* ***tapas*** *and beverages. Meanwhile, if you hear of* ***tascas****, these are typical in Madrid and also serve* ***tapas****.*

El mesón *will specialize in local cuisine and will usually have a rustic appearance.* ***La hostería*** *is a typical restaurant that will have regional dishes on the menu while* ***las tabernas*** *are perfect for a drink and a chat.*

Spanish conversation: En el restaurante

Carlos: **Hemos reservado una mesa para dos personas.**
Camarero: **¿A nombre de quién?**
Carlos: **A nombre de Martini.**
Camarero: **Sí, dos personas… Por aquí, por favor.**
Karen: **¡Qué hambre tengo! No he comido nada esta tarde.**
Carlos: **Yo no he comido tampoco.**
Camarero: **Señores, la carta.**
Después de unos minutos vuelve el camarero.
Camarero: **¿Han decidido ya?… ¿Qué van a tomar?**
Karen: **Los calamares me encantan… Sí, calamares a la romana, y de primero gambas al ajillo, por favor.**
Carlos: **Yo tomo de primero… una crema de espárragos y de segundo una parrillada de pescado.**
Camarero: **¿Y para beber?**
Karen: **Bueno, yo quisiera una sangría.**
Carlos: **Para mí una cerveza de barril, por favor.**
El camarero sirve la comida y las bebidas.
Karen: **¡Ñam, ñam! Me encanta el ajo.**
Carlos: **¡Qué buen aspecto tiene!**
Camarero: **¿Desean Uds. algún postre? ¿Un café…?**
Karen: **Sí, para mí un flan con nata, por favor.**
Carlos: **Un coñac, por favor.**
Camarero: **¿Algún coñac en especial?**
Carlos: **No me apetece ninguno en especial, la marca de la casa. Karen, ¿qué tal has comido?**
Karen: **Nunca he comido tan bien. La comida es buena aquí… ¡Oh, qué tarde es! ¿Pedimos la cuenta?**
Carlos: **Sí. Camarero, la cuenta, por favor.**
El camarero deja la cuenta y se va.
Karen: **Carlos, yo pago mi parte, por favor.**
Carlos: **No, te invito yo.**
Karen: **Pues, muchas gracias… ¿Cuánto se da de propina en España?**
Carlos: **Entre el 5 y 10 por ciento. Dejamos 4 euros, ¿vale?**
Karen: **Está bien.**

English conversation: At the restaurant

Carlos: **We booked a table for two.**
Waiter: **What's the name?**
Carlos: **Martini.**
Waiter: **Yes, a table for two… this way, please.**
Karen: **I am really hungry! I haven't eaten anything this afternoon.**
Carlos: **I haven't eaten anything either.**
Waiter: **Here's the menu.**
The waiter returns after a few minutes.
Waiter: **Have you decided already?…What are you having?**
Karen: **I like squid… yes, squid à la Romana and the garlic prawns as a starter, please.**
Carlos: **I'll have as a starter… the asparagus cream soup and for the second course grilled fish.**
Waiter: **And for drinks?**
Karen: **Well, I'd like sangria.**
Carlos: **And for me a draught beer, please.**
The waiter serves the food and the drinks.
Karen: **Mmm, … I really like garlic.**
Carlos: **That does look good indeed!**
Waiter: **Would you like some dessert? Coffee… ?**
Karen: **Yes, for me caramel pudding with cream, please.**
Carlos: **Brandy, please.**
Waiter: **Any particular brandy?**
Carlos: **No, nothing fancy. The house brand. Karen, how did you like the food?**
Karen: **I have never eaten anything that good. The food is good here… Oh, it's late! Shall we ask for the bill?**
Carlos: **Yes. Waiter, the bill, please.**
The waiter brings the bill and goes away again.
Karen: **Carlos, let me pay my share, please.**
Carlos: **No, this is my treat.**
Karen: **Well then, many thanks. How much of a tip does one leave in Spain?**
Carlos: **Between 5 and 10 percent. We'll leave 4 euros, OK?**
Karen: **That's fine.**

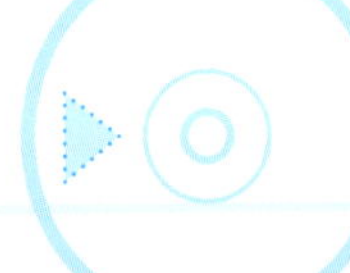

Grammar

Verbs with stem changes: *e* to *i*

servir (to serve)		pedir (to ask for)	
s*i*rvo	I serve	p*i*do	I ask for
s*i*rves	you serve	p*i*des	you ask for
s*i*rve	he/she/it serves	p*i*de	he/she/it asks for
servimos	we serve	pedimos	we ask for
servís	you (pl) serve	pedís	you (pl) ask for
s*i*rven	they serve	p*i*den	they ask for

In this verb group the e of the **stem syllable** becomes i in those verb forms where the stem is stressed.

Indefinite pronouns

algo, alguno, algún/alguna/ alguien, algunos/algunas
something, someone, some/a few
nada, ningún, ninguno/ninguna, ningunos/ningunas, nadie
nothing, not any/none, no one

¿Quiere *algo* más?	**No, *nada* más.**
¿Desean *alguna* cosa más?	**No, *ninguna* más.**
¿Quiere *algún* coñac en especial?	**No, *ninguno* en especial.**
¿Has encontrado a *alguien*?	**No, no he encontrado a *nadie*.**
¿Has comprado *algún* libros?	**No, no he comprado *ninguno*.**

In front of masculine nouns **alguno** becomes **algún** and **ninguno** becomes **ningún**:

***¿Algún* coñac?**	Some cognac?
***Ningún* amigo me ayuda.**	None of my friends help me.

Double negatives

no + verb + **nada** (nothing)
nadie (nobody, no one)
nunca (never)
tampoco (neither)
ninguno, -a (nobody, no one, none)

No… nada, **nadie**, **nunca**, **tampoco**, **ninguno**, **ninguna** enclose the verb:

***No* quiero *nada más*.**	I want nothing more.
***No* habla con *nadie*.**	She speaks to no one.
***No* voy *nunca* a la playa.**	I never go to the beach.
Yo *no* he comido *tampoco*.	I haven't eaten either.
***No* me visita *ningún* amigo.**	None of my friends visit me.

If the verb is **preceded** by **nada**, **nadie**, etc., the 'no' is dropped:

***Nunca* he comido tan bien.**	I have never eaten so well.

bien, mal – bueno, malo

estar + bien/mal **ser + bueno/malo**

bien and **mal** as **adverbs** are used to **define verbs**. They are generally used with **estar**.

bueno and **malo** as **adjectives** are used to **define nouns**. They are generally used with **ser**.

se come bien aquí	one **eats well** here
el *perro es malo*	the **dog** is **bad**

Exercise 1

Right or wrong? Tick the appropriate box.

	Sí	No
1 Las tascas están alrededor de las grandes ciudades.	....	....
2 Si queremos tapas vamos a la cafetería.	....	....
3 La hostería ofrece platos de la región.	....	....
4 Las ventas ofrecen un menú turístico.	....	....
5 El bar ofrece una variedad de tapas y bebidas.	....	....
6 El mesón ofrece una carta variada a precio fijo.	....	....
7 En la taberna siempre hay algo para comer.	....	....
8 En una cafetería se pueden comer bocadillos.	....	....

Exercise 2

Conjugate as in the example.

e.g. **comer** **como** **coméis** **comes** **comemos**

1 ver ....

2 pedir ....

3 salir ....

4 servir ....

Exercise 3

Fill in algo, nada, alguien, algún, alguno, -a, ningún, ninguno, -a, or algunos, -as.

1 ¿Hay .... en la mesa?

2 No conozco a .... hombre como él.

3 No sabe ....

4 .... trenes salen toda la noche.

5 ¿Hay .... parque por aquí?

6 .... de estas casas me gusta.

7 ¿Esperas a .... ?

Exercise 4

Where necessary add no to complete the sentences.

1 .... lo sabe nadie.

2 ¡Tampoco tú .... estás en la escuela!

3 Nada .... es tan importante como tener amigos.

4 .... se acuerda nunca de su familia.

5 .... sabe cocinar.

6 .... pasa nada si no vienes.

Exercise 5

Bien; bueno, -a; mal or malo, -a?

1 El postre es (bien/bueno) ....

2 No estoy (bien/bueno) .... hoy.

3 La película es bastante (mal/mala) ....

4 El traje le está (mal/malo) ....

Vocabulary

Below is a list of vocabulary encountered in this chapter.

acordarse	*to remember*
al ajillo	*roasted with garlic*
alguien	*someone*
alrededor de	*at… around*
apetecer	*to want to*
aprender	*to learn*
así como	*as well as*
aspecto *m*	*look*
barril *m*	*barrel*
batido *m*	*milkshake*
bebida *f*	*drink*
bien	*good, fine*
cafetería *f*	*cafeteria*
calamares *m pl*	*calamari (squid)*
camarero *m*	*waiter*
carta *f*	*menu*
casa *f* **de comidas**	*place to eat*
caza *f*	*hunt*
cerveza *f* **de barril**	*draught beer*
charlar	*to chat*
coñac *m*	*brandy*
copa *f*	*(wine) glass*
crema *f*	*cream soup*
cuenta *f*	*bill*
decorado *m*	*decoration*
dejar	*to leave (behind)*
¿De quién?	*Whose?*
después de	*after*
encantar	*to enjoy, like*
entre	*between*
espárrago *m*	*asparagus*
especial	*special*
especializarse en	*to specialize in*
flan *m*	*caramel pudding*
gamba *f*	*prawn*
helado *m*	*ice cream*
importante	*important*
local	*local*
marca *f*	*brand*
menú *m* **turístico**	*tourist menu*
nadie	*no one, nobody*
nata *f*	*whipped cream*
ninguno, -a	*not one, nobody*
nunca	*never*
pagar	*to pay*
parrillada *f*	*grilled food*
pasar	*to pass (by)*
pastel *m*	*cake*
pedir	*to request*
pescado *m*	*fish (dish)*
por ciento *m*	*percent*
precio *m* **fijo**	*set price*
propina *f*	*tip*
¿Qué tal has comido?	*How did you like the food?*
sangría *f*	*sangria*
sencillo, -a	*simple, plain*
servir	*to serve*
taberna *f*	*(wine) bar*
tasca *f*	*pub*
variado, -a	*various*
variedad *f*	*variety*
volver	*to return*

day: 14

Making friends

Day 14 introduces irregular past participles. You will also learn adverbs and diminutives (how to say something is small). Finally, you will further build your vocabulary and learn more about the Spanish culture and way of life. At the end of this chapter you will also see there is a fun game, try it to see how you are progressing!

KISS KISS...

Spaniards are quick to strike up a conversation and it seems as if the feeling of anonymity, which exists in the western world, has bypassed the Iberian peninsula. Spanish people are open and friendly, and often greet one another with a ***beso*** *(kiss).*

Spanish conversation: Una situación desagradable

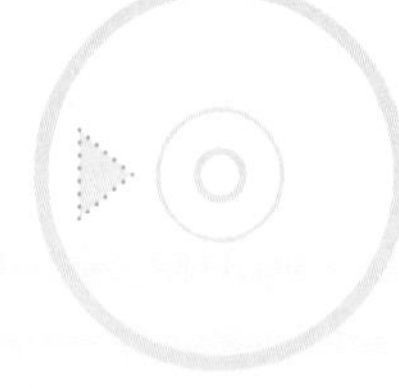

Karen en el parque.

Karen:	**¡Fuera de aquí! ¡Eso no se hace!**
El ama:	**¡Fito, ven aquí! ¡Por Dios! Señorita, lo siento mucho.**
Karen:	**¡Oh, mis pantalones blancos! Son nuevos.**
El ama:	**¡No sé cómo ha podido pasar esto! Fito normalmente es un perrito pacífico. Lo siento de verdad.**
Karen:	**Tranquila, no tiene que preocuparse.**
El ama:	**Desvergonzado, ¿qué has hecho? Con tanta gente se pone naturalmente un poco nervioso. ¿Desea anotar mi número de teléfono? Puede llamarme si tiene problemas con el lavado.**
Karen:	**No, creo que no hace falta.**
El ama:	**¡Tengo que pedirle excusas!**

En casa.

Carmen:	**Lucía, ¿dónde está Karen?**
Lucía:	**Ha salido para dar un paseo por el parque.**
Carmen:	**Pero no me ha dicho absolutamente nada.**
Lucía:	**Ha escrito una nota y la ha puesto sobre la mesa.**
Carmen:	**Pues, no la he visto…**
Lucía:	**¡Mamá! ¡Aquí está Karen! ¡Ya ha vuelto!**
Carmen:	**Karen, pero… ¿qué ha hecho con esos pantalones blancos? ¿Qué ha pasado?**
Karen:	**Un perrito me ha ladrado y saltado en el parque con las patas húmedas.**
Carmen:	**¿No ha sido de nadie?**
Karen:	**Sí, la señora se ha excusado mil veces.**
Lucía:	**Has tenido suerte porque no te ha mordido. Pero, perro que ladra no muerde.**
Karen:	**Generalmente, yo no tengo miedo a los perros, pero Fito me ha saltado tan rápidamente…**
Lucía:	**¿Fito? Es el perrito de doña Inés. Es pequeñito e inofensivo, siempre saluda alegremente a la gente.**

English conversation: An embarrassing situation

Karen in the park.

Karen:	**Go away! Don't do that!**
Dog owner:	**Fito… come here! For God's sake! I am really sorry.**
Karen:	**My white trousers! They're new.**
Dog owner:	**I don't know why that happened! Fito is normally a well-behaved dog. I am really sorry.**
Karen:	**Calm down, there's no reason to be upset.**
Dog owner:	**You naughty dog! What have you done? With that many people around he naturally gets a little nervous. Do you want to write down my phone number? You can call me if you have any trouble with washing the trousers.**
Karen:	**No, I don't think that's necessary.**
Dog owner:	**I have to apologize!**

At home.

Carmen:	**Lucía, where is Karen?**
Lucía:	**She went out for a walk in the park.**
Carmen:	**But she didn't say anything to me at all.**
Lucía:	**She wrote a note and left it on the table.**
Carmen:	**Well, I didn't see it…**
Lucía:	**Mum, … Karen is here; she's already back!**
Carmen:	**Karen, but… what have you done to those white trousers? What happened?**
Karen:	**A little dog barked at me in the park and jumped up on me with its wet paws.**
Carmen:	**Didn't it belong to anybody?**
Karen:	**Oh yes, the woman apologized a thousand times.**
Lucía:	**You were lucky it didn't bite you. But dogs that bark don't bite.**
Karen:	**Generally I am not afraid of dogs. But Fito jumped at me so quickly…**
Lucía:	**Fito? That's Doña Inés' little dog. He is small and harmless; he always greets people very enthusiastically.**

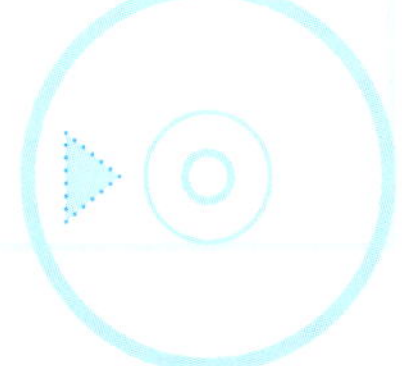

Grammar

Irregular past participles

The past participle form of some verbs is highly irregular:

hacer - ***hecho***	**poner** - ***puesto***
decir - ***dicho***	**volver** - ***vuelto***
ver - ***visto***	**escribir** - ***escrito***
abrir - ***abierto***	**romper** - ***roto***
ser - ***sido***	**ir** - ***ido***

Adverbs

Adverbs specify the **circumstances of an action**, e.g.:

Where?	**aquí** (here), **allí** (there), **enfrente** (on the other side), **arriba** (on top)
When?	**hoy** (today), **ahora** (now), **antes** (before), **pronto** (immediately), **temprano** (early), **tarde** (late), **mañana** (tomorrow)
How?	**bien** (good), **mal** (bad), **así** (so), **alto** (high)
How much?	**mucho** (much), **tanto** (so much), **bastante** (enough)

Some adverbs can be derived from adjectives:

feminine adjective + -mente = adverb

rápidamente	quickly
absolutamente	absolutely
normalmente	normally
generalmente	generally

The rule for **adverbs** is straightforward. They remain **unchanged** and are positioned **after a verb** or **in front of an adjective** or **another adverb**.

e.g. **El perro se pone naturalmente un poco nervioso.**

Diminutives

The diminutive applies to **nouns and adjectives** and is attached to the word stem. They agree with the gender and number of the noun to which they relate.
Diminutives are used not only to describe something smaller but also to give it a gentler, softer character.

perr*ito, -ita*	little dog
pequeñ*ito, -ita*	small

Exercises

Exercise 1

Fill in the correct past participle of these verbs.

ser .... ver ....

poner .... volver..

ir .... dar ....

hacer .... escribir ....

Exercise 2

Form adverbs with -mente.

1 Tienes que empezar a trabajar .... (inmediato).

2 La casa se encuentra .... (difícil) de noche.

3 (General) .... se levantan a las 8.00 de lamañana.

4 Lo hacemos todo .... (rápido).

5 Fito .... (normal) es un perro pacífico.

6 No saben .... (absoluto) nada.

Exercise 3

What belongs together? Form full sentences.

1 ¿Llegas a las once en punto?	a generalmente.
2 Voy a llamarla	b difícilmente.
3 Esto se puede hacer sólo	c cómodamente.
4 Los niños saludan	d directamente.
5 Se ha acostado	e Sí, exactamente.
6 No tengo miedo	f automáticamente.
7 La puerta se abre	g amablemente.
8 En el tren se viaja	h tranquilamente.

1........ 2........ 3........ 4........ 5........ 6........ 7........ 8........

Exercise 4

Translate the following into Spanish.

Fito is a little dog. Normally he is a well-behaved little animal. He has wet paws. Karen is generally not afraid of dogs. Fito greets people very enthusiastically.

....

....

....

....

....

Exercise 5

Infinitive or past participle?

1 Tengo que (trabajar) .... mucho esta semana.

2 Se ha (levantar) .... a las nueve.

3 Hay que (practicar) .... una lengua.

4 Voy a (comprar) .... billetes para el tren.

5 Karen ha (volver) .... ya.

Exercise 6

What's the opposite of the adjectives in italics?

1 ¿Por qué está tan *triste*? ....

2 Fito es un perro *grande*. ....

3 En España se desayuna *mucho*. ....

4 Este libro es *malo*. ....

5 Aprender el español es *fácil*. ....

6 La sopa está *fría*. ....

7 Los pantalones son *viejos*. ....

8 La puerta está *cerrada*. ....

Vocabulary

Below is a list of vocabulary encountered in this chapter.

absolutamente *absolutely*
acostarse *to go to bed, sleep*
alegre *joyful, happy; (here:) enthusiastic*
anotar *to write down*
antes *before*
arriba *on top, above*
cerrar *to close*
creer *to believe*
de verdad *really*
desagradable *embarrassing, unpleasant*
desvergonzado,-a *shameless; (here:) bad*
excusa *f* *apology*
excusarse *to excuse oneself*
fuera *go away*
generalmente *generally*
hacer falta *to be necessary*
húmedo, -a *damp, wet*
inmediato, -a *immediately*
inofensivo *harmless*
ladrar *to bark*
lavado *m* *laundry, wash*
miedo *m* *fear*
mil veces *a thousand times*
morder *to bite*
naturalmente *naturally*
nervioso, -a *nervous*
normalmente *normally*
nota *f* *note*
número *m* **de teléfono** *telephone number*
pacífico, -a *peaceful, friendly; (here:) well-behaved*
pantalones *m* **pl** *trousers Br/pants Am*
pata *f* *paw*
pedir excusas *to apologize*
perro *m* *dog*
pisar *to tread on*
practicar *to practise*
preocuparse *to be worried*
problema *m* *problem*
pronto *immediately*
rápidamente *quickly, fast*
romper *to break, damage*
saltar *to jump, leap*
situación *f* *situation*
sobre *on, over*
sopa *f* *soup*
suerte *f* *luck*
tener miedo a alguna cosa *to be afraid of something*
tranquilo, -a *calm, quiet*

Test 2

Work your way around the board. Each correct answer will take you to the next question until you have completed the exercise. Enjoy!

1
Choose one of the two answers, then go to the square with the number of your answer.

2
Tengo que ir… casa.
a ▶ 9
en ▶ 25

3
¡Falso!
Volver al n.º 9

8
¡Falso!
Volver al n.º 24

9
¡Muy bien!
¡Yo no… a María.
conosco ▶ 3
conozco ▶ 6

10
¡Falso!
Volver al n.º 21.

11
¡Muy bien!
Vienes al cine… ?
conmigo ▶ 15
consigo ▶ 16

16
¡Falso!
Volver al n.º 11

17
¡Fantástico!
No he comido…
nadie. ▶ 12
nada. ▶ 28

18
¡Falso!
Volver al n.º 28

19
¡Bien!
La secretaria ha… la carta.
escribido ▶ 7
escrito ▶ 24

24
¡Qué bien!
No he visto a…
nada. ▶ 8
nadie. ▶ 26

25
¡Falso!
Volver al n.º 2

26
¡Bravo!
El tren… salir.
va ▶ 30
va a ▶ 4

27
¡Fantástico!
Juan es un chico…
bien. ▶ 5
bueno. ▶ 19

4

¡Eso es!
… gustado la película.
Me he ▶ 13
Me ha ▶ 17

5

¡Falso!

Volver al n.º 27

6

¡Muy bien!
Este libro es… mí.
para ▶ 14
por ▶ 22

7

¡Falso!

Volver al n.º 19

12

¡Falso!

Volver al n.º 17

13

¡Falso!

Volver al n.º 4

14

¡Correcto!
Nosotros… a estudiar español.
empiezamos ▶ 29
empezamos ▶ 27

15

¡Fantástico!
! ¡Lo has hecho muy bien!

20

¡Falso!

Volver al n.º 23

21

¡Correcto!
¿Has visto a… ?
algún ▶ 10
alguien ▶ 23

22

¡Falso!

Volver al n.º 6

23

¡Qué bien!
Él es simpático… inteligente.
e ▶ 11
y ▶ 20

28

¡Muy bien!
El café… negro.
está ▶ 18
es ▶ 21

29

¡Falso!

Volver al n.º 14

30

¡Falso!

Volver al n.º 26

day: 15

Making calls

Day 15 discusses the gerund (i.e. how to say singing, dancing, eating, etc.). You will also learn how to formulate the verbs *decir (to say), oír (to hear), seguir (to continue)* and *volver a* (to talk about a repeated action). You will also learn how to make telephone calls in Spanish and discover the vocabulary you need to do this.

PHONE HOME…

To call abroad from Spain, dial 00 followed by: **61 (Australia); 1 (Canada** *and* **United States); 353 (Ireland); 64 (New Zealand); 44 (United Kingdom).** *You will usually have to omit the initial 0 of the area code of the city you're calling.*

Spanish conversation: Una llamada telefónica

Karen: **Carmen, ¿puedo utilizar su teléfono? Quisiera llamar a mis padres. Es una llamada a cobro revertido.**

Carmen: **Precisamente ahora estoy esperando una llamada urgente de México.**

Karen: **¿¿Dónde está la cabina telefónica más próxima?**

Carmen: **Está bastante lejos, pero hay una oficina telefónica que está más cerca.**

Karen en la oficina telefónica.

Karen: **Hola, buenos días. ¿Me puede dar una tarjeta telefónica?**

Empleada: **Ud. puede utilizar una de nuestras cabinas, no necesita tarjeta para ellas.**

Karen: **Muy bien, muchas gracias.**

Va a una cabina telefónica, descuelga el auricular y marca el numero. Pasa unos minutos esperando.

Karen: **¡Qué lástima! Está ocupado. Precisamente ahora mi madre está charlando con una de sus amigas. Seguramente va a seguir hablando por lo menos media hora más. Voy a llamar a Barcelona a mi amiga Manuela.**

Voz: **¡Dígame!**

Karen: **Oiga, ¿puedo hablar con Manuela?**

Voz: **Lo siento, está durmiendo. ¿De parte de quién?**

Karen: **Soy Karen.**

Voz: **¿Puede volver a llamarla? ¿O desea dejar algún recado?**

Karen: **¿Puede decirle, por favor, que la he llamado? Voy a volver a llamarla otra vez. Gracias.**

Voz: **De nada.**

English conversation: A telephone call

Karen: **Carmen, can I use your phone? I would like to call my parents. It's a collect call.**
Carmen: **Just this moment I am waiting for an urgent call from Mexico.**
Karen: **Where is the next phone booth then?**
Carmen: **It's pretty far, but there is a telephone office that is closer.**

Karen at the telephone office.

Karen: **Hello, good morning. Can you give me a telephone card?**
Employee: **You can use one of our booths. You don't need a card for them.**
Karen: **Very good. Thank you very much.**

Karen goes into the booth, picks up the receiver and dials the number. She waits a few minutes.

Karen: **What a shame! It's engaged (busy). Just now my mother has to chat with one of her friends. She'll no doubt be speaking for at least another half hour. I'll call my friend Manuela in Barcelona.**
Voice: **Hello.**
Karen: **Could I speak to Manuela, please?**
Voice: **I am sorry, she's sleeping right now. Who's calling?**
Karen: **I'm Karen.**
Voice: **Can she call you back? Or do you want to leave a message?**
Karen: **Could you please tell her that I called? I will call her another time. Thank you.**
Voice: **You're welcome.**

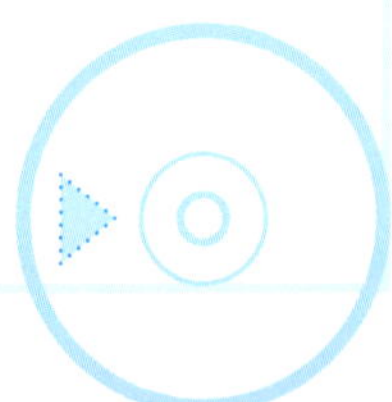

Grammar

The gerund

The gerund is used to describe actions that:

a) are just in the process of occurring:

estar + **gerund** = **presently** doing something

Karen se *está lavando*.	Karen is washing herself.

seguir + **gerund** = to continue to do something

***Sigue marcándolo* (el número).**	She continues dialling it (the number).

b) are occurring simultaneously:

Va de paseo *cantando*.	She goes for a walk singing.

The gerund of verbs ending in -ar is -ando, that of the verbs ending in -er and -ir is -iendo.

cantar to sing	beber to drink	escribir to write
cant*ando* singing	beb*iendo* drinking	escrib*iendo* writing

Note that **personal pronouns** must be positioned either **before** the conjugated **verb** or **attached to the gerund**.

***Le está dando* la mano.**

or

***Está dándole* la mano.**

Irregular gerund forms

pedir -p*idiendo*	**dormir - dur*miendo***
venir - v*iniendo*	**poder - pu*diendo***

With some verbs the unstressed -e- or -o- in the stem changes to -i- and/or -u-.
These include:

sentir - s*i*ntiendo	**morir - m*u*riendo**
reir - r*i*endo	**seguir - s*i*guiendo**
decir - d*i*ciendo	**repetir - rep*i*tiendo**

Irregular verbs ending in *-ir*

Decir (to say)		Oír (to hear)		Seguir (to continue)	
digo	I say	*oigo*	I hear	*sigo*	I continue
dices	*you say*	*oyes*	you hear	*sigues*	you continue
dice	he/she /it says	*oye*	he/she/it hears	*sigue*	he/she/it continues
decimos	we say	oímos	we hear	seguimos	we continue
decís	you (pl) say	oís	you (pl) hear	seguís	you (pl) continue
dicen	*they say*	*oyen*	they hear	*siguen*	they continue

Repeated actions

volver + **a** + **infinitive** = to repeat something/do it again

vuelvo a llamar	I call again
vuelves a cantar	you sing once more
vuelve a tener miedo	he is afraid again
volvemos a encontrarnos	we meet again
volvéis a hacer lo mismo	you (pl) do the same once more
vuelven a explicarlo	they explain it once more

Exercises

Exercise 1

Write out the gerund of the verbs in brackets.

1 El chico está (comer). ....

2 Carlos está (tomar) una cerveza de barril. ....

3 Están (cantar) una canción de su región. ....

4 Estoy (esperar) a mi hermano. ....

5 La estudiante está (hacer) un ejercicio. ....

Exercise 2

Answer the questions as in the example.

¿Trabajas todavía en Madrid? Sí, sigo trabajando en Madrid.

1 ¿Viven todavía en España? ....

2 ¿Esperas todavía en la calle? ....

3 ¿Venden todavía patatas? ....

4 ¿Duerme todavía? ....

5 ¿Os acostáis tarde todavía? ....

Exercise 3

Connect the actions that are happening simultaneously as in the example.

ir de paseo/charlar. Va de paseo charlando.

1 entrar en el bar/pedir cerveza ....

2 marcar los números/repetirlos ....

3 volver a buscar el bolso/no poder encontrarlo ....

4 salir de la escuela/correr ....

5 saludar/hacer una señal con la mano ....

Exercise 4

Form sentences using the gerund as in the example.

Trabajar mucho. Estoy trabajando mucho.

1 Esperar una llamada telefónica. ....

2 Bailar flamenco. ....

3 Preguntar por el camino. ....

4 Ir al teatro. ....

5 Llegar a casa. ....

Exercise 5

Infinitive, past participle or gerund?

1 Vamos a (charlar) .... un poco.

2 Ha (llegar) .... a Madrid hoy.

3 Estamos (esperar) .... a Luisa.

4 Sigue (repetir) .... los números.

5 Volvemos a (llamar) .... a Barcelona.

Vocabulary

Below is a list of vocabulary encoutered in this chapter.

abonado *m*	*(telephone) subscriber*
amiga *f*	*(female) friend*
auricular *m*	*(telephone) receiver*
cabina *f* **telefónica**	*phone booth*
caer	*to fall*
charlar	*to chat*
comunicar	*to connect*
correr	*to run, flow*
decir	*to say*
dejar	*to leave (behind)*
¿De parte de quién?	*Who's speaking?*
descolgar	*to pick up (the phone)*
ejercicio *m*	*exercise*
estudiante *m/f*	*pupil, student*
explicar	*to explain*
finalmente	*finally*
internacional	*international*
llamada *f*	*(phone) call*
llamada *f* **a cobro revertido**	*collect call*
llamar	*to phone, call*
marcar	*to dial*
más próximo, -a	*closest*
media hora más	*another half hour*
México *m*	*Mexico*
mientras	*during, while*
mismo, -a	*(the) same*
morir	*to die*
o	*or*
ocupado, -a	*engaged, busy*
oficina *f*	*office*
oír	*to hear*
por lo menos	*at least*
precisamente	*precisely*
recado *m*	*message*
repetir	*to repeat*
seguir	*to continue*
seguramente	*surely; (here:) no doubt*
señal *f*	*signal*
tarjeta *f* **telefónica**	*phone card*
teléfono	*telephone*
urgente	*urgent*
utilizar	*to use*
venir	*to come*

day: 16

Fashion

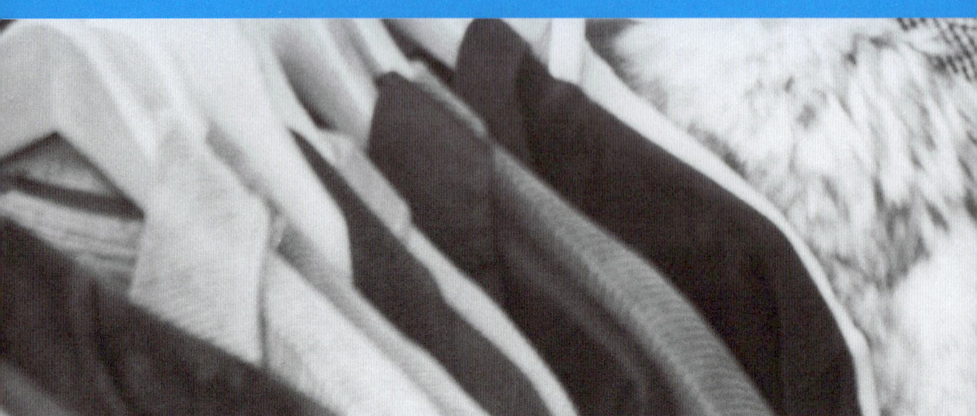

Day 16 is all about fashion (*la moda*). Learn the conditional tense (and its irregularities) to say what you would do, and learn how to use double pronouns. You will also learn the colors and the vocabulary for different types of clothing.

LA MODA…

Popular items of clothing include jeans ***(vaqueros)****, t-shirts* ***(camisetas)****, blouses* ***(blusas)*** *or shirts* ***(camisas)****. A one-stop shop is the large department store,* ***El Corte Inglés****. Traditional dress is not so common nowadays and it is more or less only the elder generation that wears the traditional black or the Basque beret* ***(boina)*** *or straw hat* ***(sombrero de paja)****.*

Spanish conversation: La Moda

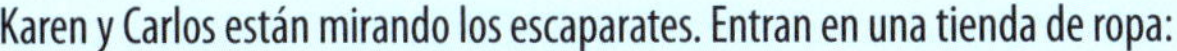

Karen y Carlos están mirando los escaparates. Entran en una tienda de ropa:

Dependiente: **Buenas tardes. ¿Qué desean?**

Karen: **Por favor, ¿me podría enseñar la falda del escaparate? Me gustaría probármela.**

Dependiente: **Sí, se la muestro con gusto, ¿cuál de ellas?**

Karen: **Aquella de la derecha, la roja.**

Dependiente: **¿Qué talla tiene Ud.?**

Karen: **La 38.**

Dependiente: **Lo siento, la falda del escaparate es la talla 36, pero tenemos también estos modelos nuevos de algodón, ¿le gusta alguno?**

Karen: **No sé… los negros me parecen un poco extravagantes…**

Carlos: **¿Podrías probarte la falda azul a rayas?**

Dependiente: **El probador está al fondo.**

Karen: **¿Carlos, te gusta? En la cintura me resulta un poco estrecha…**

Carlos: **Te queda perfectamente. Es muy sexy…**

Karen: **Entonces voy a adelgazar un poco.**

Carlos: **Me gustaría regalártela.**

Dependiente: **¿Desea regalársela? ¡Guau, […] qué regalo!**

Karen: **Vaya… ¡qué sorpresa!**

Carlos: **¿Cuánto cuesta?**

Dependiente: **Esta está a 33 euros, pero se la dejo en 30. Es una calidad muy buena, la puede meter en la lavadora y no necesita plancharla.**

Karen: **Gracias, ¿me la podría poner en una bolsa?**

Dependiente: **Sí, ahora mismo se la pongo en una bolsa de papel. ¿Necesitan Uds. algo más? ¿Un jersey o alguna blusa?**

Karen: **Gracias, por el momento no.**

English conversation: Fashion

Karen and Carlos are window-shopping. They are entering a clothing store.

Shop assistant:	**Good afternoon. What are you looking for?**
Karen:	**Could you please show me the skirt in the window? I'd like to try it on.**
Shop assistant:	**Yes, I'll be happy to show it to you. Which one of them?**
Karen:	**The one on the right, the red one.**
Shop assistant:	**What size do you take?**
Karen:	**Size 38.**
Shop assistant:	**I am sorry, the skirt in the window is a size 36, but we also have these new models in cotton. Is there one you like?**
Karen:	**I don't know, … the black ones seem too fancy to me…**
Carlos:	**Could you try on the blue striped skirt?**
Shop assistant:	**The changing room is at the back.**
Karen:	**Carlos, do you like it? It is a bit tight around the waist…**
Carlos:	**It fits you perfectly. It's very sexy…**
Karen:	**Well, then I will just have to lose a little weight.**
Carlos:	**I'd like to give it to you as a present.**
Shop assistant:	**You want to give it to her as a present? Wow, … what a present!**
Karen:	**Well! What a surprise!**
Carlos:	**How much is it?**
Shop assistant:	**This one costs 33 euros, but I'll give it to you for 30. It is very good quality; you can put it into the washing machine and it doesn't have to be ironed.**
Karen:	**Thank you, can you give me a bag for it?**
Shop assistant:	**Yes, I'll put it straight into a paper carrier bag. Do you need anything else? A sweater or a blouse?**
Karen:	**No thanks, nothing at the moment.**

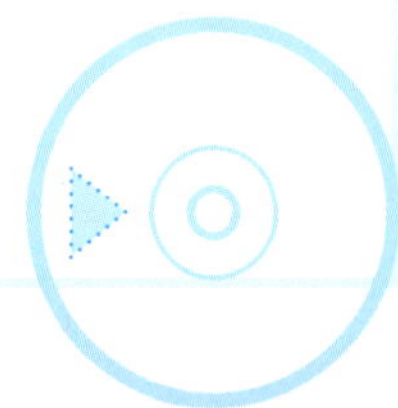

Grammar

Conditional tense

The conditional is used to **politely express a wish**, an **offer** or an **opinion**.

***Necesitaría* una blusa.**	I would need a blouse.
***Podría* ayudarte.**	I could help you.
No *hablaría* así.	I wouldn't talk like that.

To form the conditional tense (would…), take the infinitive of the verb and add:

-ía
-ías
-íamos
-íais
-ían

All regular verbs share the same endings:

bailar*ía*	I would dance	**beber*ía***	I would drink	**ir*ía***	I would go
bailar*ías*	you would dance	**beber*ías***	you would drink	**ir*ías***	you would go
bailar*ía*	he/she would dance	**beber*ía***	he/she would drink	**ir*ía***	he/she would go
bailar*íamos*	we would dance	**beber*íamos***	we would drink	**ir*íamos***	we would go
bailar*íais*	you would dance	**beber*íais***	you would drink	**ir*íais***	you would go
bailar*ían*	they would dance	**beber*ían***	they would drink	**ir*ían***	they would go

Irregular conditional forms

A number of verbs shorten their stem in the conditional, change it entirely or have a **-d-** inserted. You will need to learn these.

saber (to know)	**venir** (to come)	**querer** (to want)
sab*ría*	**vend*ría***	**quer*ría***
haber (to have)	**poner** (to put)	**decir** (to say)
hab*ría*	**pond*ría***	**di*ría***
poder (to be able to)	**salir** (to go out)	**valer** (to be worth)
pod*ría*	**sald*ría***	**vald*ría***
hacer (to do/make)	**tener** (to have)	
ha*ría*	**tend*ría***	

Note: Quisiera in the subjunctive tense is often used instead of **querría**

***Querría* saber dónde vives.**	I would like to know where you live.
***Quisiera* saber dónde vives.**	I would like to know where you live.

Double pronouns

te regalo la blusa	***te la* regalo**	I give it to you
te compro el traje	***te lo* compro**	I buy it for you
te enseño las casas	***te las* enseño**	I show them to you
te doy los bolsos	***te los* doy**	I give them to you

There are **two ways** these can be formed:
a) either both pronouns precede the conjugated verb form

***te lo* quiero comprar**	I want to buy it for you

b) both pronouns are attached to the infinitive or the gerund

quiero comprár*telo*	I want to buy it for you

(a ella/él/Ud.) *le* regalo *la* blusa	***se la* regalo**
(a ella/él/Ud.) *le* compro *el* traje	***se lo* compro**
(a ellas/ellos/Uds.) *les* enseño *las* casas	***se las* enseño**
(a ellos/ellas/Uds.) *les* doy *los* bolsos	***se los* doy**

In front of **la**, **las**, **lo**, **los** the pronouns **le**, **les** become **se** meaning him, her, you, them.

The indirect object (whom?) precedes the direct object (who/what?)

te	***la***	**regalo**
I give	it	(to) you

Colors

Note that some colors have both a masculine and a feminine ending.

amarillo, -a	yellow
blanco, -a	white
rojo, -a	red
negro, -a	black
azul	blue
verde	green
marrón	brown
gris	grey

Exercises

Exercise 1

Use the first person plural to say what you would like to do.

1 Ir de compras. ....

2 Acompañar a los abuelos. ....

3 Comer un helado. ....

4 Trabajar poco. ....

5 Salir al parque. ....

6 Subir al tercer piso. ....

7 Ducharse. ....

Exercise 2

Insert the the correct form for *you* as indicated in brackets.

1 ¿Me (poder) (Ud.) enseñar la falda?

2 ¿Le (decir) .... (tú) dónde está la estación?

3 ¿(Vosotros) (querer) .... acompañarme a Málaga?

4 ¿(Uds.) (jugar) .... con los niños?

5 ¿(Tú) (ir) .... de compras?

6 ¿(Ud.) (venir) .... más temprano del colegio?

7 ¿(Ella) (vivir) .... también en un piso alquilado?

Exercise 3

Fill in the personal pronouns.

1 Karen ha estudiado el español y .... sabe muy bien.

2 A tu hermana no .... conozco.

3 ¿Dónde está Almería? No .... sé.

4 Nos ofrecen su casa, pero no ....queremos.

5 (A mi amiga) .... he escrito pero (mi amiga) .... no me ha contestado.

6 Los pantalones .... (tú) quedan muy bien.

7 Si ellas no vienen hoy, ... voy a ver el lunes.

Exercise 4

Replace the words in italics with personal pronouns.

He dado mi coche a mi hermano. Se lo he dado.

1 Cuenta *sus problemas* a *Adela*. ....

2 Voy a comprar *el libro* a *Vicente*. ....

3 Pongo *el jersey* a *los niños*. ....

4 ¿Podrías comprar *unas cervezas* para *nuestros invitados*? ....

5 ¿Podrías dar *los libros* a *mi amiga*? ....

6 He regalado *las flores* a *la señora Ibáñez*. ....

Exercise 5

What belongs together?

1	¿Qué desea?	**a**	La 44.
2	¿Qué color desea?	**b**	Sí, me lo llevo.
3	¿De qué material?	**c**	Sí, me gusta mucho.
4	¿Para quién es?	**d**	No sé, de algodón o seda.
5	¿Qué talla tiene?	**e**	Me resulta un poco estrecho.
6	¿Le gusta?	**f**	Para mí.
7	¿Cómo le queda?	**g**	Un vestido.
8	¿Se lo lleva?	**h**	Algo en rojo.

1 .... **2** .... **3** .... **4** .... **5** .... **6** .... **7** .... **8** ....

Exercise 6

¿Esta or está? Insert the correct form where necessary.

.... chica no .... nunca en casa. Siempre .... de viaje. .... semana la he encontrado en Valencia y ahora ....de nuevo en Madrid. Vive en .... calle grande que .... al lado de .... iglesia famosa. No sé el nombre de .... iglesia, que .... en el centro.

Vocabulary

Below is a list of vocabulary encountered in this chapter.

acompañar	*to accompany*
adelgazar	*to lose weight*
ahora mismo	*right now*
al fondo	*at the back*
algodón *m*	*cotton*
blusa *f*	*blouse*
bolsa *f*	*carrier bag*
calidad *f*	*quality*
cintura *f*	*waist(line)*
contar	*to tell*
contestar	*to answer*
¿Cuál de ellas?	*Which one?*
dejar	*to leave*
derecha *f*	*right side, the right*
duchar	*to shower*
enseñar	*to show*
entonces	*then*
entrar en	*to enter (into)*
escaparate *m*	*shop window*
estrecho, -a	*tight*
extravagante	*fancy, extravagant*
falda *f*	*skirt*
fondo *m*	*back (of a room)*
invitado *m*	*guest*
jersey *m*	*sweater*
lavadora *f*	*washing machine*
meter	*to put into*
moda *f*	*fashion*
modelo *m*	*model*
momento *m*	*moment*
mostrar	*to show*
negro, -a	*black*
papel *m*	*paper*
perfectamente	*perfectly*
piso *m*	*floor, storey*
planchar	*to iron*
por el momento no	*not at the moment*
probador *m*	*changing room*
probarse alguna cosa	*to try something on,*
quedar	*(here:) to fit,suit*
a rayas	*striped*
regalar	*to give as a present*
regalo *m*	*gift, present*
resultar	*to turn out*
rojo, -a	*red*
seda *f*	*silk*
sexy	*sexy*
talla *f*	*(clothes) size*
tienda *f* **de ropa**	*clothing store*
valer	*to be worth*
¡Vaya!	*Well!*

day: 17

The police

Day 17 takes a more serious turn and talks about the Spanish police. You will also learn the *preterito indefinido* (past tense) of regular verbs and the multiple uses of the preposition *de* (from, of).

LA POLICÍA...

The main police forces in Spain are:

The ***Policía Municipal*** *(municipal police). They report to the local administration and are responsible for law and order in the city (writing parking tickets, recording complaints and charges, etc.). They wear blue uniforms.*

The ***Policía Nacional*** *(state police) is an armed rapid response unit that mainly deals with criminal offences. Their uniform is brown and white.*

The ***Guardia Civil*** *(civil guard) is a division of the army and reports to the Minister for the Interior. It is responsible for controling traffic and for policing public buildings and utilities. They wear a green uniform with a black beret.*

Spanish conversation: En la comisaría

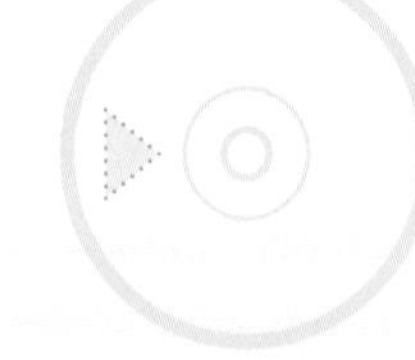

Policía:	**¿Qué le pasó?**
Karen:	**Me robaron el bolso con el pasaporte, las llaves de casa, un plano de Madrid, un monedero, … en plena calle.**
Policía:	**¿Cuándo ocurrió?**
Karen:	**Anoche a eso de las 10.00.**
Policía:	**¿Dónde pasó exactamente?**
Karen:	**Al salir de la estación del metro vi a un hombre que…**
Policía:	**Tiene que tener mucho ojo al salir y al entrar allí. ¿Podría describirme a ese hombre?**
Karen:	**Es difícil, se lo llevó tan rápidamente y sin tener compasión. Solamente lo vi por detrás. Al verlo… empecé a dar gritos: »¡Mi bolso, … mi bolso!« El ladrón entró en la estación, le perseguí, pero le perdí de vista en la muchedumbre dentro de la estación.**
Policía:	**¿Y nadie le ayudó?**
Karen:	**No, nadie… Todo ocurrió en un abrir y cerrar de ojos.**
Policía:	**Bueno, ahora vamos a hacer una declaración y rellenar este formulario.**
Karen:	**¿Cree Ud. que se puede encontrar…?**
Policía:	**No sé. De todos modos va a ser un poco difícil. Tiene que andar Ud. con mucho ojo en la ciudad. Nosotros nos vamos a ocupar del caso. Por favor, su nombre y dirección.**
Karen:	**Mi nombre es Karen Muller, vivo en el Paseo de la Castellana n.º 6.**
Policía:	**Sin la copia de la denuncia no puede solicitar un pasaporte nuevo. Tiene que solicitar uno en el consulado.**

English conversation: At the police station

Policeman: **What happened to you?**
Karen: **Someone stole my bag with my passport, my house keys, a map of Madrid, my wallet, … right in the middle of the street.**
Policeman: **When did it happen?**
Karen: **Last night at about 10 p.m.**
Policeman: **Where exactly did it happen?**
Karen: **When I left the subway station I saw a man, who…**
Policeman: **You have to keep your eyes open when entering or leaving there. Could you describe this man for me?**
Karen: **That's difficult, he grabbed it so quickly and ruthlessly. I only saw him from behind. When I saw him… I started screaming: "My bag, … my bag!" The thief went into the station, I followed him but lost sight of him in the crowd at the station.**
Policeman: **And no one helped you?**
Karen: **No, nobody… It all happened in the blink of an eye.**
Policeman: **OK, we will take down your statement and fill out this form.**
Karen: **Do you think you'll be able to find it… ?**
Policeman: **I don't know. It will be difficult in any case. You have to keep you eyes open when walking around in the city. We will look into your case. Your name and address, please.**
Karen: **My name is Karen Muller, I live at Paseo de la Castellana No. 6.**
Policeman: **Without a copy of this report you cannot apply for a new passport. You will have to apply for one at your consulate.**

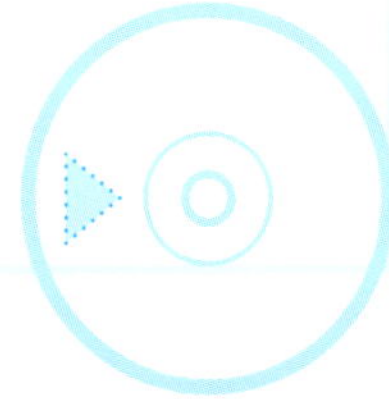

Grammar

The preterite

The preterite tense is used to signify an **action that has been completed in the past** and that is **not related to the present**.

The preterite is used in connection with expressions of time such as **ayer** (yesterday), **anteayer** (the day before yesterday), **anoche** (last night), **la semana pasada** (last week), **el año pasado** (last year) and years, e.g. 2005.

***Viví* en Madrid en 1986.**

I lived in Madrid in 1986.

La semana pasada *encontramos* a Pedro.

Last week we met Pedro.

hablar		perder		abrir	
habl*é*	I spoke	**perd*í***	I lost	**abr*í***	I opened
habl*aste*	*you spoke*	**perd*iste***	*you lost*	**abr*iste***	*you opened*
habl*ó*	he/she spoke	**perd*ió***	he/she lost	**abr*ió***	he/she opened
habl*amos*	*we spoke*	**perd*imos***	*we lost*	**abr*imos***	*we opened*
habl*asteis*	you (pl) spoke	**perd*isteis***	you (pl) lost	**abr*isteis***	you (pl) opened
habl*aron*	*they spoke*	**perd*ieron***	*they lost*	**abr*ieron***	*they opened*

Verbs ending in **-er** and **-ir** have the same endings in the **preterite**.

Note that some verbs change their spelling!

pagar (to pay) becomes **pa*gué***

sacar (to take out) becomes **sa*qué***

For verbs that have a ***z*** in the middle, before **-e-** and **-i-**, **-z-** changes to **-c-**:

empezar - **empe*c*é**

Where **-i-** exists between two vowels, it becomes **-y-** :

ca*ió* to **ca*yó***

caer to **ca*yó*** (see **oír** in Day 15)

Note

al + **infinitive** can be used to describe the moment at which an event occurs: *when; while; during*

Saluda *al entrar*. = He greets when entering.

sin + **infinitive** can be used in the same way to mean *without*

Se va *sin mirarlo*. = He leaves without looking at him.

De

The preposition **de** can be used to mean many things:

origin and designation of location

soy *de* Barcelona	= I am from Barcelona
vengo *de* la ciudad	= I come from the city
la falda *del* escaparate	= the skirt in the shop window

ownership, relation to

el libro *de* Antonio	= Antonio's book
la señora *de* García	= Mr. García's wife

compound phrases

la bolsa *de* papel	= the paper carrier bag
la estación *del* metro	= the subway station
cordones *de* zapatos	= the shoelaces

attribute

la falda *de* rayas	= the striped skirt
el señor *de* las gafas	= the man with the glasses

reference

ocuparse *del* caso	= to look into the case
grita *de* miedo	= she screams in fear.

quantities after nouns

un poco *de* sal	= a little bit of salt
un litro *de* leche	= a litre of milk

times, dates

a las tres *de* la tarde	= at three in the afternoon
el 10 *de* marzo	= the 10th of March
***de* día**	= during the day

used with certain verbs

estar *de* pie	= to stand
estar *de* acuerdo	= to agree

Exercises

Exercise 1

Fill in the verb forms according to the example given for hablar.

hablar hablé hablaste hablarías hablaríais

1 comprar ....

2 leer ....

3 cantar ....

4 abrir ....

5 vivir ....

6 perder ....

Exercise 2

Put the verbs into the indefinido.

1 Ayer (yo, visitar) .... a unos amigos.

2 (yo, llamar) .... a la puerta.

3 Me (abrir) .... una chica.

4 Me (dejar) .... pasar y me (ofrecer) .... un vaso de vino.

5 Después del vino (nosotros, tomar) .... unas gambas.

6 A mí no me (gustar) .... nada.

7 (yo, salir) .... a dar un paseo.

8 (yo, ver) .... muchas flores bonitas.

9 Luego (yo, tomar) .... el autobús y (volver) .... a casa.

Exercise 3

Fill in de, del or de la.

1 La puerta .... casa está abierta.

2 ¿Cuál es la dirección .... consulado?

3 Vivimos muy cerca .... Plaza de la Cibeles.

4 La señora .... Sánchez da clases .... español.

5 Nos vamos a ocupar .... caso.

Exercise 4

Rewrite the sentences according to the example given.

Cuando salió perdió el bolso. Al salir perdió el bolso.

1 Cuando salí de casa me quedé sin llaves.

....

2 Cuando vimos esta película, nos reímos a carcajadas.

....

3 Cuando leí el periódico me puse triste.

....

Exercise 5

Rewrite the sentences according to the example given.

e.g. No soy tu amigo pero te voy a ayudar. Sin ser tu amigo te voy a ayudar.

1 No las conozco, no las voy a acompañar.

....

2 Juan no es muy listo pero sabe mucho.

....

3 No tengo mucho dinero pero viajo mucho.

....

4 No veo a la chica, no abro la puerta.

....

Vocabulary

Below is a list of vocabulary encountered in this chapter.

andar	*to walk (around)*
anoche	*last night*
anteayer	*day before yesterday*
caso *m*	*case*
comisaría *f*	*police station*
compasión *f*	*compassion*
consulado *m*	*consulate*
copia *f*	*copy*
creer	*to believe*
dar gritos	*to scream*
de atrás	*from behind*
de día	*during the day*
de todos modos	*in any case*
declaración *f*	*(here:) statement*
denuncia *f*	*report*
denunciar	*to report*
describir	*to describe*
en plena calle	*right in the middle of the street*
¿En qué puedo servirle?	*What can I do for you?*
en un abrir y cerrar de ojos	*in the blink of an eye*
encontrar (-ue-)	*to find*
estar de acuerdo	*to agree with*
estar de pie	*to stand, to be standing*
formulario *m*	*form*
gafas *f pl*	*spectacles/glasses*
grito *m*	*scream*
ladrón *m*	*thief*
listo, -a	*clever, smart*
llevarse alguna cosa	*to take something along*
monedero *m*	*purse*
muchedumbre *f*	*crowd*
ocuparse de alguna cosa	*to look into something*
ocurrir	*to happen*
perder de vista	*to lose sight of*
perseguir (-i-)	*to follow, pursue*
reirse a carcajadas	*to laugh loudly*
rellenar	*to fill in (e.g. form)*
robar	*to steal*
robo *m*	*theft*
servir	*to serve*
solamente	*only*
solicitar	*to order, apply for*
tener mucho ojo	*to keep one's eyes open*

day: 18

Camping in Spain

Day 18 talks about camping in Spain and you will learn the vocabulary associated with it. You will also learn all about negation (how to say *no*!) and irregular verbs in the preterite (past) tense.

CAMPGROUNDS...

There are over one thousand campgrounds in Spain, ranging from the basic to the luxurious. Most campgrounds located along the coastline; in the interior of the country they are few and far between. The best time to camp in Spain is in late spring, as it avoids the heat that hits in June, July and August, as well as the crowds that converge during these months. While some campgrounds are open most of the year, it is advisable to check details in advance.

Spanish conversation: Vamos de cámping

Carlos:	**Karen, podríamos ir de cámping toda la semana, ¿qué te parece?**
Karen:	**Es una idea fantástica. Los García estuvieron el mes pasado en Valencia e hicieron un viaje en autocaravana.**
Carlos:	**Y a ti, ¿adónde te gustaría ir?**
Karen:	**A mí me gustaría ir a la costa a bañarme, poder tomar el sol y descansar a pierna suelta y por las noches ir a bailar.**
Carlos:	**Podríamos ir a la Costa Brava, allí conozco un cámping con todo lo que necesitamos, incluso una discoteca.**

El día de la salida.

Carlos:	**Karen, ¿qué dijeron los García de este viaje a la Costa Brava?**
Karen:	**Pues, tuvieron que aceptar. Se quedaron con la boca abierta. ¿Pusiste anoche la tienda y los sacos de dormir en el coche?**
Carlos:	**Sí, los puse. Y tú, ¿has traído un anorak? De día hace calor, pero de noche hace un poco de frío.**
Karen:	**No, pero tengo un jersey en la mochila. Bueno, ahora podemos partir.**
Carlos:	**Quise traer algo para comer y beber, pero no tuve tiempo ni para ir de compras ni para despedirme de mi madre.**
Karen:	**He traído algunas galletas, pan integral, queso, zumo de naranja y siete u ocho mandarinas. ¿Quieres este pan u otro?**
Carlos:	**¡Eres un ángel! Este. Ñam, ñam… Hace dos años pasé por aquí con unos amigos…**
Karen:	**¿Cuánto se paga por acampar?**
Carlos:	**No sé exactamente, vamos a ver.**
Karen:	**¿Tienes un carnet de cámping?**
Carlos:	**No, no tengo.**
Karen:	**¿Hay servicios, duchas y lavabos allí?**
Carlos:	**Sí … hay electricidad y agua potable.**
Karen:	**¿No es peligroso por las noches?**
Carlos:	**No, el cámping está vigilado.**

English conversation: We're going camping

Carlos: **Karen, we could go camping for the whole week. What do you think about that?**

Karen: **That's a fantastic idea. The Garcías were in Valencia last month and they travelled around in a mobile home.**

Carlos: **And what about you? Where would you like to go?**

Karen: **I'd like to go swimming at the seaside, to sunbathe and laze around and go dancing in the evening.**

Carlos: **We could go to the Costa Brava; I know a campsite there that has everything we need, including a disco.**

On the day of departure.

Carlos: **Karen, what did the Garcías say about this trip to the Costa Brava?**

Karen: **Well, they must have agreed to it. They were speechless. Did you put the tent and the sleeping bags into the car last night?**

Carlos: **Yes, I did. And what about you, did you bring an anorak? It is hot during the day, but at night it gets a little cold.**

Karen: **No, but I have a pullover in my backpack. OK, we can leave now.**

Carlos: **I wanted to bring something to eat and to drink, but I neither had time to go shopping nor to say goodbye to my mother.**

Karen: **I brought a few biscuits, wholemeal bread, cheese, orange juice and seven or eight tangerines. Do you like this bread or another kind?**

Carlos: **You're an angel! This one here. Mhmm, ... two years ago I passed by here with a few friends...**

Karen: **How much do we pay for the campsite?**

Carlos: **I don't know exactly, we'll see.**

Karen: **Do you have a camping permit?**

Carlos: **No I don't have one.**

Karen: **Are there toilets, showers, washrooms?**

Carlos: **Yes, ... there's a power outlet and drinking water.**

Karen: **Isn't it dangerous at night?**

Carlos: **No, the campsite is guarded.**

Karen: **Well then, we couldn't ask for anything more!**

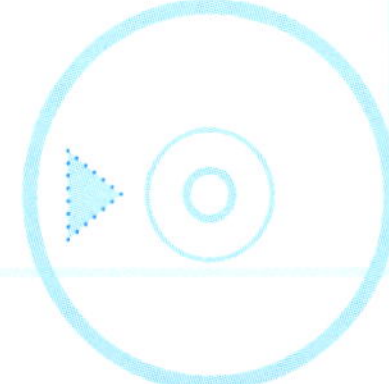

Grammar

Irregular preterite forms

Some verbs have irregular preterite forms:

estar (to be)		tener (to have)		hacer (to have)	
estuve	I was	*tuve*	I had	*hice*	I did
estu*viste*	*you were*	*tuviste*	*you had*	*hiciste*	*you did*
estuvo	*he/she/it was*	*tuvo*	*he/she/it had*	*hizo*	*he/she/it did*
estu*vimos*	*we were*	*tuvimos*	*we had*	*hicimos*	*we did*
estu*visteis*	*you (pl) were*	*tuvisteis*	*you (pl) had*	*hicisteis*	*you (pl) did*
estu*vieron*	*they were*	*tuvieron*	*they had*	*hicieron*	*they did*

Be careful with the spelling of hizo: the c becomes z in front of the o!

poner (to put)		querer (to want)		decir (to say)	
puse	I placed	quise	I wanted	dije	I said
pusiste	*you placed*	quisiste	*you wanted*	dijiste	*you said*
puso	*he/she/it placed*	quiso	*he/she/it wanted*	dijo	*he/she/it said*
pusimos	*we placed*	quisimos	*we wanted*	dijimos	*we said*
pusisteis	*you (pl) placed*	quisisteis	*you (pl) wanted*	dijisteis	*you (pl) said*
pusieron	*they placed*	quisieron	*they wanted*	dijeron	*they said*

The i in the ending -ieron is dropped after j: di*jeron*.

Negation: *no… ni… ni…*

No… ni…ni… corresponds to the English **neither… nor**

***No* tuve tiempo *ni* para ir de compras ni para despedirme.**

I had neither time to go shopping, nor to say goodbye.

No… ni on the other hand means **not even**

***No* tuve tiempo *ni* para ir de compras.**

I did not even have the time to go shopping.

Or

o (meaning **or**) becomes **u in front of o/ho:**

ocho *o* nueve mandarinas but siete *u* ocho mandarinas

eight or nine mandarins

¿quieres éste *o* el otro? but ¿quieres éste *u* otro?

Do you want this one or the other one?

Exercises

Exercise 1

Tell the story below using the preterite tense. Start with Ayer. . . .

Hoy he hecho un viaje en tren. Me he levantado muy temprano, me he duchado y me he vestido. Luego he tomado una tostada con café. Después he cogido mi bocadillo para el almuerzo y lo he metido en la mochila. Entonces he salido de casa. Mi madre me ha llevado a la estación de autobuses y allí he esperado media hora en vano. Entonces he hecho autostop. He tenido que esperar otros diez minutos y he llegado a la estación justamente un minuto antes de la salida del tren. Lo he cogido y ¡todo ha salido a pedir de boca!

Ayer..

Exercise 2

Write sentences using the example below as a guide.

tener dinero/comprar pan: No tengo dinero ni para comprar pan.

1 querer/salir

....

2 tener tiempo/dar un paseo

....

3 poder/hablar

....

Exercise 3

Insert o or u as necessary.

Nos encontramos ayer entre las siete .... ocho de la tarde en un café. Tomamos un helado, uno o dos zumos y unas tapas. Nos sirvió un chico .... hombre andaluz de dieciocho .... veinte años. A eso de las diez .... once regresamos a casa.

Exercise 4

Insert the correct tense of the verb in brackets. Should it be the present, perfect or preterite?

1 Hoy (nosotros, trabajar) .... mucho. (Estar) .... cansados.

2 Esta noche (yo, ir) .... a bailar.

3 El domingo pasado (nosotros, estar) .... en un restaurante.

4 ¿Qué (vosotros, hacer) .... ayer por la noche?

5 ¿(tú, comprar) .... leche esta mañana?

6 (Nosotros, querer) .... ir este verano a la playa.

Exercise 5

Write sentences using the example below as a guide.

e.g. **encontrar/Pedro/Marta:** **No he encontrado ni a Pedro ni a Marta.**

1 entrar/iglesia/catedral

....

2 visitar/abuelos/tíos

....

3 comer/huevos/patatas

....

4 comprar/zumo/galletas

....

5 leer/libro/periódico

....

6 ir/de viaje/de paseo

....

7 ver/como anda/como baila

....

8 oír/perros/ladrones

....

Vocabulary

Below is a list of vocabulary encountered in this chapter.

a pedir de boca	*exactly as one wants it (literally: as the mouth desires)*
a pierna suelta	*carefree (literally:with a dangling leg)*
a tiempo	*on time*
acampar	*to camp*
accidente *m*	*accident*
aceptar	*to agree*
(el) agua *f* **potable**	*drinking water*
andar	*to go*
ángel *m*	*angel*
anorak *m*	*anorak (waterproof jacket)*
autocaravana *f*	*RV, mobile home*
bañarse	*to bathe, swim*
boca *f*	*mouth*
calor *m*	*heat*
cámping *m/* **campamento**	*campsite*
carnet *m* **de cámping/campamento**	*camping permit*
coger	*to take*
costa *f*	*coast*
de día	*during the day*
de noche	*at night*
descansar	*to rest*
despedirse	*to say goodbye*
día *m* **de la salida**	*departure day*
discoteca *f*	*disco/nightclub*
ducha *f*	*shower*
electricidad *f*	*electricity*
en vano	*in vain*
fantástico, -a	*fantastic*
frío *m*	*cold*
galleta *f*	*biscuit/cookie*
hace calor	*it's hot (weather)*
hace frío	*it's cold (weather)*
incluso	*inclusive*
ir de cámping/ campamento	*to go camping*
lavabo *m*	*washroom*
mandarina *f*	*tangerine*
mochila *f*	*rucksack, backpack*
pan *m* **integral**	*wholemeal/ whole-wheat bread*
peligroso, -a	*dangerous*
pierna *f*	*leg*
regresar	*to come back, return*
saco *m* **de dormir**	*sleeping bag*
se quedaron con la boca abierta	*they were left speechless*
servicios *m pl*	*toilets, bathrooms*
tienda *f*	*tent*
tomar el sol	*to sunbathe*
traer	*to bring*
vestirse	*to get dressed*
vigilado, -a	*guarded*
zumo *m* **de naranja**	*orange juice*

day: 19

Traveling by car

Day 19 discusses traveling by car in Spain. You will learn more irregular verb forms in the preterite (past) tense. You will also learn how to use adjectives and further build your vocabulary.

RULES OF THE ROAD...

The wearing of safety belts is mandatory in Spain, as is making sure that the car is equipped with a warning triangle and reflective vests in case of a breakdown. Spaniards love to toot their horns, especially when overtaking. The speed limit on **autopistas** *is 120 km/h, on* **autovías** *it is 100 km/h, on secondary roads* **(carreteras)** *90 km/h and inside built-up areas 60 km/h. Most highways in Spain are subject to tolls. Note that it is illegal for private vehicles to take other cars in tow.*

Spanish conversation: Un viaje en coche

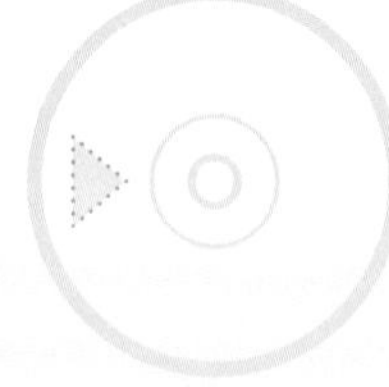

Camino a la Costa Brava.

Carlos:	**Necesitamos gasolina, debe de haber por aquí una estación de servicio.**
Karen:	**¿Cuánto gasta tu coche?**
Carlos:	**Casi 8 litros por cada 100 kilómetros. Lo supe hace unos meses al no quedarme ni una gota en el depósito.**
Karen:	**¿Qué tipo de gasolina?**
Carlos:	**Sin plomo.**
Karen:	**¿Cuándo lo compraste y cuánto pagaste por él?**
Carlos:	**Lo compré hace dos años y pagué unos 12 000 euros.**
Karen:	**Carlos, ¡allí hay una gasolinera!**
Carlos:	**También hay un taller. Podemos almorzar mientras ellos hacen un chequeo. ¿Qué te parece?**
Karen:	**Buena idea.**
Carlos:	**(al mozo) Sin plomo, lleno, por favor. ¿Puede hacerme una inspección al coche? Oí un ruido muy raro.**
Mozo:	**¡Cómo no! Ahora mismo miro el motor.**
Carlos:	**¿Quiere comprobar la presión de los neumáticos, el agua y el líquido de frenos? Creo que también falta aceite.**
Mozo:	**¿Algo más?**
Carlos:	**Sí, ¿cuánto tiempo va a tardar?**
Mozo:	**Una hora más o menos. Mientras tanto pueden tomar algo en el restaurante.**

Mientras ellos esperan.

Carlos:	**El año pasado fui al sur e hice un viaje por Andalucía. Un buen amigo me siguió hasta Cádiz. Estuvimos en Cádiz en un buen hotel… Nos sentimos de maravilla.**
Karen:	**Mis padres y yo fuimos a Italia. Estuvimos en Brenzone en una pensión grande. Nos divertimos mucho… fueron unas vacaciones fantásticas. Carlos, tienes muy mala cara hoy.**
Carlos:	**Anoche dormí muy mal y como no pude dormir estoy hecho polvo.**
Karen:	**¡Oh pobrecito! ¡Yo dormí como un tronco! Vamos, el coche ya debe estar listo.**

English conversation: Traveling by car

On the way to the Costa Brava.

Carlos:	**We need petrol (gas), there should be a petrol station somewhere around here.**
Karen:	**How much does your car use?**
Carlos:	**Nearly 8 litres per 100 kilometres. I found that out a few months ago when I had not a drop left in the tank.**
Karen:	**What kind of petrol?**
Carlos:	**Unleaded.**
Karen:	**When did you buy the car and how much did you pay for it?**
Carlos:	**I bought it two years ago and paid about 12,000 euros.**
Karen:	**Carlos, there's a petrol station!**
Carlos:	**There's also a garage. We could have lunch while they check the car. What do you think?**
Karen:	**Good idea.**
Carlos:	**(to the attendant) Unleaded, please fill it up. Could you take a look at the car? I heard a very strange noise.**
Attendant:	**Why not! I'll look at the engine right away.**
Carlos:	**Would you mind checking the tyre pressure, the water and the brake fluid? Also, I think it needs oil.**
Attendant:	**Anything else?**
Carlos:	**Yes, how long will it take?**
Attendant:	**About an hour. In the meantime you can have something to eat at the restaurant.**

While they wait.

Carlos:	**Last year I went south and travelled through Andalusia. A good friend of mine followed me all the way to Cádiz. We stayed in a nice hotel in Cádiz… We felt great.**
Karen:	**My parents and I went to Italy. We stayed in a large guesthouse in Brenzone. We really enjoyed ourselves… it was a fantastic holiday. Carlos, you look really bad today!**
Carlos:	**I slept very badly last night… and because I couldn't sleep I am totally worn out.**
Karen:	**Oh, you poor thing! I slept like a log! Come on, the car should be ready now.**

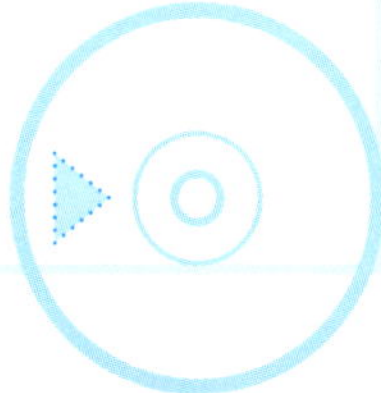

Grammar

The preterite: irregular forms

saber (to know)		poder (to be able to/can)		ir/ser (to go/to be)	
supe	I found out	pude	I could/was able	fui	I went/was
supiste	you found out	pudiste	you could/were able	fuiste	you went/were
supo	he/she/it found out	pudo	he/she/it could/was able	fue	he/she/it went/was
supimos	we found out	pudimos	we could/were able	fuimos	we went/were
supisteis	you (pl) found out	pudisteis	you (pl) could/were able	fuisteis	you (pl) went/were
supieron	they found out	pudieron	they could/were able	fueront	they went/were

Note that the verbs ir (to go) and ser (to be) share the **same forms** in the preterite.

The preterite emphasises the **beginning of an action in the past**. Therefore some verbs will **change their meaning**: e.g. **sabe** (he knows) becomes **supo** (he found out)

sentir (to feel)		seguir (to follow)		dormir (to sleep)	
sentí	I felt	seguí	I followed	dormí	I fell asleep
sentiste	you felt	seguiste	you followed	dormiste	you fell asleep
sintió	he/she/it felt	*siguió*	he/she/it followed	*durmió*	he/she/it fell asleep
sentimos	we felt	seguimos	we followed	dormimos	we fell asleep
sentisteis	you (pl) felt	seguisteis	you (pl) followed	dormisteis	you (pl) fell asleep
sintieron	they felt	*siguieron*	they followed	*durmieron*	they fell asleep

Sentir, seguir, servir as well as dormir and morir have regular endings but change the **stem** -e to -i- and the -o- to -u- in the **3rd person** singular and plural.

Assumptions

deber + (de) + **infinitive** = should, ought to
Debe + de + **infinitive** is used to express an **assumption based on known facts**:

Debe de haber un restaurante por aquí.	There should be a restaurant around here.

de is often dropped in constructions like this one below:

El coche debe estar listo.	The car should be ready.

Adjectives

bueno, malo, grande	
bueno + singular masculine noun	**buen**
malo + singular masculine noun	**mal**
grande + singular noun	**gran**

Before **masculine nouns in the singular** **bueno** and **malo** drop the ending **-o**:

un buen amigo

grande drops the ending **-de** before **masculine and feminine nouns in the singular**:

una gran persona

When positioned after the noun and if the noun is **plural** their endings remain:

una persona gran*de*	**unos amigos buen*os***

Be aware of the difference in meaning that the position of **grande** implies:

una ciudad *grande*	a big city
una *gran* ciudad	a great city

Note also how the verb that precedes an adjective can change its meaning:

ser + **listo** = to be smart

estar + **listo** = to be ready

Exercises

Exercise 1

Form the preterite of the verbs in brackets.

El año pasado mis padres y yo (hacer) un viaje a Madrid. Ellos no (saber) por qué no nos (ir) a Barcelona. (Ser) porque yo (estar) el año pasado en Madrid y esta ciudad me (gustar) mucho. Allí (conocer) la amabilidad de mucha gente. También mis padres se (sentir) de maravilla cuando (llegar) allí y me lo (decir) muchas veces.

Exercise 2

Fill in the preterite of the verbs.

1 Anoche Carlos (dormir) .... muy mal.

2 Nunca (ellos, saber) .... cómo pasó.

3 Los alumnos (hacer) .... una excursión.

4 Todos (sentir) .... mucho su desgracia.

5 (Nosotros, querer) .... acompañarlas pero no nos (poder) .... ir.

6 Ayer (yo, ir) .... a visitar a Karen.

7 Le (él, seguir) .... la huella.

Exercise 3

Complete the table with the preterite forms.

tú nosotros ustedes

1 ir ....

2 sentir ....

3 ducharse ....

4 afeitarse ....

5 poner ....

6 decir ....

Exercise 4

Translate the following text into Spanish.

There should be a restaurant around here. Last year I was here with some friends. The restaurant should be open.

....

....

....

....

Exercise 5

Make the adjectives agree with the nouns.

1 (bueno) .... tiempo

2 (grande) .... alegría

3 (malo) .... amigo

4 (ciento) .... kilómetros

5 (primero) .... mes

6 (ninguno) .... hombre

7 (alguno) .... hotel

8 (malo) .... noticia

Exercise 6

Create a dialogue by joining the sentences.

1 sentirse	con la boca abierta	....
2 dormir	polvo	....
3 hay que tener	a carcajadas	....
4 reirse	de maravilla	....
5 quedarse	de boca	....
6 descansar	como un tronco	....
7 salir a pedir	mucho ojo	....
8 estar hecho	a pierna suelta	....

Vocabulary

Below is a list of vocabulary encountered in this chapter.

ahora mismo	*right now*
alegría *f*	*joy*
amabilidad *f*	*friendliness*
Andalucía *f*	*Andalusia*
camino a	*on the way to*
camino *m*	*way, path*
cara *f*	*face*
casi	*nearly, almost*
chequeo *m*	*check*
¡Cómo no!	*Why not!*
comprobar	*to check, examine*
de maravilla	*wonderful, great*
deber de	*should, ought to be*
deber	*to have to, must*
depósito *m*	*(petrol/gas) tank*
desgracia *f*	*misfortune*
divertirse	*to enjoy oneself*
dormir como un tronco	*to sleep like a log*
enamorado, -a	*in love*
estación *f* **de servicio**	*petrol/gas station*
estar hecho polvo	*to be broken, (literally: to be ground to dust)*
faltar	*to miss*
gasolina *f*	*petrol/gas*
gasolinera *f*	*petrol/gas station (small)*
gastar	*to consume, use (up)*
gota *f*	*drop*
hace unos meses	*a few months ago*
huella *f*	*track*
inspección *f*	*inspection*
kilómetro *m*	*kilometer*
líquido *m*	*liquid, fluid*
líquido *m* **de frenos**	*brake fluid*
lleno, -a	*full*
mientras tanto	*during, while*
motor *m*	*engine, motor*
mozo *m*	*attendant*
neumático *m*	*tyre*
noticia *f*	*message*
pensión *f*	*B & B, guesthouse*
plomo *m*	*lead*
pobrecito *m*	*poor thing*
polvo *m*	*dust*
presión *f*	*pressure*
raro, -a	*rare, strange*
ruido *m*	*noise*
seguir	*to follow*
sentirse de maravilla *f*	*to feel wonderful*
sin plomo	*unleaded*
sur *m*	*south*
taller *m*	*garage, repair shop*
tardar	*to be late; to take (one's time)*
tener mala cara	*to look bad*
tipo *m*	*type, kind*

day: 20

An accident

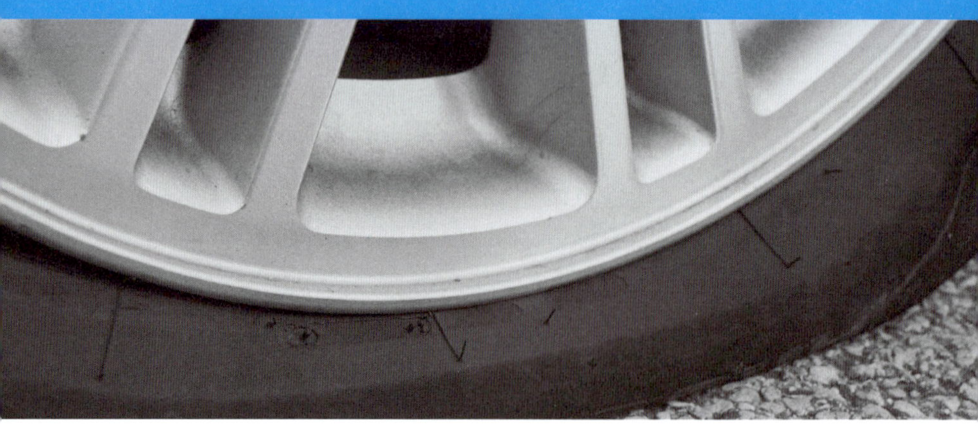

Day 20 talks about accidents and you will learn more about driving in Spain. You will learn the imperfect tense, when to use it and its irregular forms. You will also further build your vocabulary. Don't forget to continue to practice what you have learned in the exercise sections - you can check your answers in the back of the book!

DANGEROUS DRIVING...

Perhaps the greatest danger you will face on Spanish roads is the impatient driving style of the Spaniards, as most accidents happen due to dangerous overtaking manoeuvres. If you are involved in an accident with personal injuries you can bail yourself out by paying a fine, which will normally have to be paid on the spot. It is also mandatory in Spain to carry spare bulbs for your headlights in the car.

Spanish conversation: Un accidente

Vuelta a Madrid.

Karen: **¡Qué tráfico! ¡Cuántos coches! ¡Cuidadoooo!**

Carlos: **¡Oh, gracias a Dios! ¡Qué cara de ese conductor! Karen, ¿estás bien?**

Karen: **Sí, ¡qué susto!, casi chocamos. Me pregunto si ese conductor tiene el permiso de conducir.**

Carlos: **Hace unos años me pasó lo mismo en esta autopista.**

Karen: **¿De verdad? ¿Qué te pasó?**

Carlos: **Llovía, yo conducía en la calzada, vino un camión de la derecha y se me adelantó sin respetar la preferencia. Tuve la impresión que no me veía. Di un frenazo de emergencia, pero no pude evitar el choque contra la parte trasera del camión.**

Karen: **Y ¿qué pasó después?**

Carlos: **El conductor del camión y yo tuvimos que esperar a la policía. No teníamos testigos. Mientras esperábamos hubo otro accidente casi a nuestro lado.**

Karen: **¡Qué horror!**

Carlos: **Ambos estábamos pálidos y no sabíamos qué hacer. Yo siempre en estos casos estaba tranquilo pero aquel día no. Y cuando llegaron los policías estábamos muy nerviosos.**

Karen: **¿Reconoció el otro conductor que él tenía la culpa?**

Carlos: **Sí, él dijo que yo iba demasiado deprisa, pero estaba claro que él era el culpable.**

Karen: **¿Llevabas puesto el cinturón de seguridad?**

Carlos: **Sí, lo llevaba puesto.**

Karen: **Cuando llueve, nieva o hace niebla es muy peligroso conducir. ¿Qué fue de tu coche?**

Carlos: **El coche estaba hecho polvo.**

Karen: **¡Qué pena!**

Carlos: **Lo remolcaron y para la declaración de los hechos tuvimos que darles nuestros nombres, apellidos, direcciones y la póliza del seguro. Era un desastre.**

English conversation: An accident

On the way back to Madrid.

Karen: **The traffic! So many cars! Watch out!**

Carlos: **Oh, thank God! What nerve that driver had! Karen, are you OK?**

Karen: **Yes, I got a fright! We nearly crashed. I wonder whether that driver has a licence.**

Carlos: **A few years ago the same thing happened to me on this motorway.**

Karen: **Really? What happened to you?**

Carlos: **It was raining and I was driving in this lane. Suddenly a truck came from the right and cut right in front of me without acknowledging my right of way. I think he didn't see me. I had to make an emergency stop but could not avoid crashing into the rear of the truck.**

Karen: **And, what happened then?**

Carlos: **The truck driver and I had to wait for the police. We had no witnesses. While we were waiting another accident happened almost right next to us.**

Karen: **How terrible!**

Carlos: **Both of us went pale and did not know what to do. I am normally calm in such situations but not this time. And when the police came both of us were very anxious.**

Karen: **Did the other driver admit that it was his fault?**

Carlos: **Yes, he said that I had been going too fast, but it was obvious that he was the one at fault.**

Karen: **Were you wearing your safety belt?**

Carlos: **Yes, I was wearing it.**

Karen: **When it rains, snows or is foggy, it is very dangerous to drive. What happened to your car?**

Carlos: **The car was destroyed.**

Karen: **What a shame!**

Carlos: **They towed it away and for the accident report we had to give our first names, last names, addresses and the insurance policy. It was a disaster.**

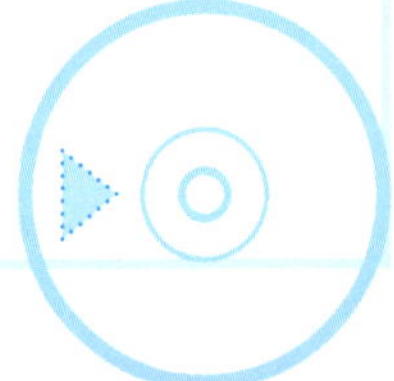

Grammar

Imperfect tense

bailar (to dance)		comer (to eat)		decir (to say)	
bail*aba*	I danced	com*ía*	I ate	dec*ía*	I said
bail*abas*	you danced	com*ías*	you ate	dec*ías*	you said
bail*aba*	he/she/it danced	com*ía*	he/she/it ate	dec*ía*	he/she/it said
bail*ábamos*	we danced	com*íamos*	we ate	dec*íamos*	we said
bail*abais*	you (pl) danced	com*íais*	you ate	dec*íais*	you (pl) said
bail*aban*	they danced	com*ían*	they ate	dec*ían*	they said

The **first** and **third person singular** are **identical**, while verbs ending in -er and -ir always share the same endings.

Irregular forms

ver (to see)		ser (to be)		ir (to go)	
veía	I saw	era	I was	iba	I went/drove
veías	you saw	eras	you were	ibas	you went
veía	we saw	era	he/she/it was	iba	he/she/it went
veíamos	we saw	éramos	we were	íbamos	we went
veíais	you (pl) saw	erais	you (pl) were	ibais	you (pl) went
veían	they saw	eran	they were	iban	they went

When to use the imperfect	
a) Describing actions that were happening in the past:	
***Hacía* sol.**	The sun was shining.
Los niños *jugaban*.	The children were playing.
b) A recurring action in the past:	
De joven *jugaba* al tenis.	When I was young I played tennis.
Siempre *esperaba* a Carlos delante del café.	She always waited for Carlos in front of the café.
c) An action that was already ongoing, when another action started; the newly beginning action takes the **preterite**:	
Mientras *esperábamos*, *hubo* otro accidente.	While we waited another accident happened.
Cuando *iba* al teatro encontré a María.	When I went to the theatre I met Mary.
d) parallel actions in the past:	
***Estábamos* pálidos y *no sabíamos* qué hacer.**	We turned pale and did not know what to do.
***Estaba tocando* la guitarra mientras *cantaba*.**	He played the guitar while he was singing.

The imperfect tense is often used in connection with time indicators such as **siempre** (always), **todas las noches** (every night), **todos los años** (every year), **de joven** (when young), **antes** (previously), **mientras** (while).

Two more irregular forms

venir (to come)		dar (to give)	
vine	I came	**di**	I gave
viniste	you came	**diste**	you gave
vino	he/she/it came	**dio**	he/she/it gave
vinimos	we came	**dimos**	we gave
vinisteis	you (pl) came	**disteis**	you (pl) gave
vinieron	they came	**dieron**	they gave

The context of the sentences will reveal whether **vino** means "wine" or "he came".
You will have noticed earlier that the Spaniards don't slam on their brakes but "give" an emergency stop – **di un frenazo**.

Exercises

Exercise 1

Write the imperfect forms as in the following example.

leer leías leíais leíamos

1 poner ....

2 saludar ....

3 adelantarse ....

4 ver ....

5 saber ....

6 ir ....

7 estar ....

8 ser ....

Exercise 2

Complete the sentences in the imperfect tense.

1 De joven (yo, ir) .... todos los días a la escuela.

2 Todas las mañanas (ella, dar) .... un paseo.

3 (Nosotros, mirar) .... las flores.

4 Cuando (tú, ser) .... pequeño, (tú, tocar) .... la guitarra.

5 (Vosotros, no soler) .... cenar antes de dormir.

Exercise 3

What's your reaction?

1	No puedo acompañarte hoy.	**a**	¡Qué cara!
2	Se sentó en nuestra mesa sin preguntar.	**b**	¡Qué horror!
3	No nos pasó nada en el accidente.	**c**	¿De verdad?
4	Los tomates están en oferta.	**d**	¡Gracias a Dios!
5	He olvidado el bolso en el metro.	**e**	¡Qué pena!
6	Ha habido un fuerte huracán en Florida.	**f**	Lo siento.

1......... **2**......... **3**......... **4**......... **5**......... **6**.........

Exercise 4

The expression ¿Qué es de…? is used to inquire about various things. Rewrite the phrases accordingly.

¿Cómo está tu hermano? ¿Qué es de tu hermano?

1 ¿Has terminado tu tesis? ....

2 ¿Qué tal están tus padres? ....

3 ¿Qué pasó con tu coche? ....

4 ¿Cómo está tu madre? ....

Vocabulary

Below is a list of vocabulary encountered in this chapter.

a nuestro lado *next to us*
accidente *m* *accident*
adelantarse *overtake; (here:) to cut in (front)*
ambos, -as *both*
apellido *m* *surname*
autopista *f* *motorway/expressway*
camión *m* *lorry/truck*
cara *f* *face*
carril *m* *lane*
chocar *to crash*
choque *m* *crash*
cinturón *m* **de seguridad** *safety belt/seat belt*
conducir *to drive*
conductor *m* *driver*
culpa *f* *guilt*
culpable *guilty, at fault*
dar un frenazo *to brake*
deprisa *fast*
declaración *f* *report; explanation*
declaración *f* **de los hechos** *(here:) accident report*
desastre *m* *disaster*
¿De verdad? *Really?*
evitar *to avoid*
frenazo *m* *braking*
frenazo *m* **de emergencia** *emergency stop*
¡Gracias a Dios! *Thank God!*
hubo *there was (from haber)*
huracán *m* *hurricane*
impresión *f* *impression*
llover *to rain*
nervioso, -a *nervous, anxious*
nevar *to snow*
niebla *f* *fog, mist*
olvidar *to forget*
pálido, -a *pale*
parte *f* **trasera** *rear (part)*
peligroso, -a *dangerous*
permiso *m* **de conducir** *driving licence*
póliza *f* **del seguro** *insurance policy/card*
preferencia *f* *right of way*
prisa *f* *hurry*
¡Qué cara! *Such nerve! (literally: What a face!)*
¡Qué horror! *How awful!*
¡Qué pena! *What a pity!*
reconocer *to admit*
remolcar *to tow away*
respetar *to pay attention to*
susto *m* *scare, fright*
tener lugar *to happen, occur*
tesis *f* *thesis*
testigo *m* *witness*
tráfico *m* *traffic*
vuelta *f* *return journey*

day: 21

Sport

Day 21 is all about sport. You will learn how to say what you like doing and the vocabulary you need to describe different activities. You will also be reminded of the difference between the imperfect tense and preterite and when to use each one.

BULL FIGHTING...

*Bullfighting **(la corrida)** remains a popular spectator sport in Spain. There are four different categories: **corridas** with fully mature bulls **(toros)** and experienced **toreros**, who are licensed to fight in a big arena. The **novilladas** is with three-year-old bulls **(novillos)** and **toreros** who are not yet allowed to fight in a big arena. The **becerradas** is with young bulls of up to two years of age and **toreros** who are just starting their career. The **rejoneo** is fought with the **torero** sitting on a horse and is often staged before the actual bullfight itself. The season runs from March to October.*

Spanish conversation: ¡Viva el deporte!

Karen:	**Carlos, ¿qué deporte practicabas cuando estabas en Argentina?**
Carlos:	**En Argentina a mí me gustó el tenis. Se puede decir que siempre me ha gustado.**
Karen:	**¿Qué deporte le gusta a la gente en Argentina?**
Carlos:	**La gente en Argentina es fanática del fútbol. También yo soy muy aficionado al fútbol. De chico iba todos los domingos con mis amigos al campo de fútbol. Cuando el partido era bueno volvíamos a casa contentísimos y muy cansados.**
Karen:	**El sábado pasado Pedro y David fueron al estadio, jugaba el Real Madrid. Cuando llegaron a casa estaban muy sudados y sedientos... Quise ir con ellos pero ya no había entradas. Cuando cerraron las taquillas me fui a hacer footing. Quisiera ver un partido de fútbol alguna vez: Real Madrid contra un equipo latinoamericano, por ejemplo de Brasil o Argentina...**
Carlos:	**Le voy a preguntar a José, él trabaja como vendedor en las taquillas del estadio Santiago Bernabéu.**
Karen:	**¡Caramba! No está mal. ¿Sabes cuánto cuesta la entrada?**
Carlos:	**Depende de si es un partido nacional o internacional.**
Karen:	**Le preguntas a José, ¿vale?**
Carlos:	**Sí, de acuerdo. ¿Y tú juegas al tenis?**
Karen:	**No, fui a clase hace años, pero... Realmente a mí no me interesaba ni me gustaba mucho, pero ahora me gustaría hacer un curso.**
Carlos:	**Bravo, ¡viva el deporte! Si quieres podemos jugar mañana.**

English conversation: Long live sport!

Karen:	**Carlos, what kind of sport did you do when you were in Argentina?**
Carlos:	**I liked playing tennis in Argentina. You could say that I have always enjoyed playing tennis.**
Karen:	**What kind of sport do the people in Argentina enjoy?**
Carlos:	**People in Argentina are football (soccer) fanatics. I am a great fan of football, too. As a little boy I went with my friends to the football pitch (soccer field) every Sunday. If the game was good, we would come home really happy and very tired.**
Karen:	**Last Saturday Pedro and David went to the stadium; Real Madrid played. When they returned home they were all sweaty and thirsty… I had wanted to go with them but there were no tickets left. When they closed the ticket counter I went jogging. I would like to watch a football match once: Real Madrid against a team from Latin America, for example from Brazil or Argentina…**
Carlos:	**I'll go and ask José. He works as a ticket seller at the Santiago Bernabéu stadium.**
Karen:	**Wow! That's not bad. Do you know how much it costs to get in?**
Carlos:	**It depends whether it is a national or an international game.**
Karen:	**You'll ask José, won't you?**
Carlos:	**Yes, OK. And you play tennis?**
Karen:	**No, I had lessons a few years ago, but… I wasn't really interested and didn't enjoy it very much, but I'd like to take lessons now.**
Carlos:	**Great, long live sport! If you want we can play tomorrow.**

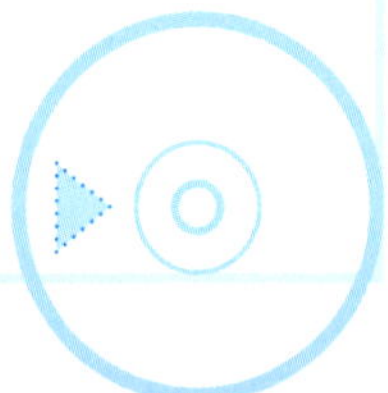

Grammar

Comparison between the imperfect and the preterite

Preterite

a) **completed action in the past (What happened?)**

Llovió mucho aquel año.	That year it rained a lot.

Imperfect

a) **past tense without reference to the beginning or end of an action (How was something?)**

Entonces llovía mucho.	Back then it rained a lot.

Comparison between the imperfect and the preterite tense

Preterite

b) **actions or events that started in the past (What happened then?)**

***Supe* de su suerte.**	I found out about his luck.

c) **one-off, single action**

El domingo *se fueron* a la iglesia.	On Sunday they went to church.

d) **actions in sequence**

***Cantaron* y *salieron*.**	They sang and (then) left.

Imperfect

b) **actions or events that are already in the process of occurring (What was going on?)**

***Sabía* de su suerte.**	I knew about his luck.

c) **habitual actions**

Los domingos *iban* a la iglesia.	On Sundays they went to church.

d) **parallel actions**

Mientras *cantaban salían*.	They left (while) singing.

Remember that some verbs change their meaning in the imperfect/preterite tense:

sabía	I knew (how to)	**supe**	I found out
tenía	I had	**tuve**	I got
conocía	I knew	**conocí**	I got to know
iba	I went	**fui**	I drove (away)

Repeating object pronouns

Day 10 has already pointed out that Spaniards play it safe by repeating pronouns.
This rule also holds true when stressing a **preceding noun** that is then repeated using a **pronoun**:

***A los* chicos *les* gusta el deporte.**	The boys like sport.
***El* café Triana *lo* conozco.**	I know the café Triana.

In **spoken language** the object is often repeated using a pronoun **independent of its position** in front or after the verb:

¿Le conoces *a mi padre*?	Do you know my father?
Le preguntamos *a José*.	We ask José.

me gusta – me gustan

With constructions like:

Me gusta el deporte.	I enjoy sport.
Les encantan las flores.	They like the flowers.

The **object pronoun precedes** and the **subject follows** the verb. The verb always agrees with the subject.

muy/mucho

Mucho **precedes nouns** and **follows verbs**. It agrees in gender and number with the noun it relates to:

Me gusta mucho *el deporte*.	I enjoy sport very much.
Hay much*as* flores por aquí.	There are lots of flowers here.

Muy **precedes adjectives or adverbs:**

Está *muy bien*.	He is doing very well.
Llegaron *muy sedientos*.	They arrived very thirsty.

jugar (to play)

Note the following construction that is specific to Spanish:

jugar + a + **article** + **noun**

jugar al tenis to play tennis	**jugar a los naipes** to play cards

but for **musical instruments** you use tocar

tocar la guitarra to play the guitar	**tocar el acordeón** to play the accordion

Days of the week

lunes *m*	Monday
martes *m*	Tuesday
miércoles *m*	Wednesday
jueves *m*	Thursday
viernes *m*	Friday
sábado *m*	Saturday
domingo *m*	Sunday

Exercises

Exercise 1

Imperfect or preterite?

1 Normalmente (nosotros, comer) .... paella los domingos, pero aquel domingo (nosotros, tomar) .... un cocido madrileño.

2 Mientras (ellos, cenar) .... (ver) .... la tele.

3 Mientras (yo, cocinar) .... (ella, arreglar) .... las camas.

4 Antes (él, fumar) .... más que ahora.

5 Cuando (yo, llegar) .... a casa, la puerta (estar) .... cerrada.

6 (ella, llegar) .... tarde, cuando la (esperar) .... Juan.

7 Todos los domingos (ellos, irse) .... al teatro, pero aquel domingo (ellos, irse) .... al cine.

8 Todas las Navidades mi madre (hacer) .... churros, la pasada Navidad (hacer) .... un pastel.

Exercise 2

Repeat the nouns in italics with the corresponding pronouns.

1 La *puerta* .... he abierto yo.

2 Anoche .... encontramos a *Paco y Juana* en un bar.

3 *Estos libros* .... quería regalar a mi marido.

4 .... he encontrado a *Carlos* muy contento.

5 *Este abrigo* me .... compré hace dos semanas.

Exercise 3

Write out the sentences and add a pronoun, where necessary.

1 Este coche compró hace dos años.

....

2 ¡Qué hambre tenemos!

....

3 Preguntaremos a María si nos hace una paella.

....

4 Este libro debes comprar de todos modos.

....

Exercise 4

Me gusta or me gustan?

A mí me .... jugar al fútbol, pero a Juanita le .... el alpinismo. A mí me .... los churros, pero a mi madre le .... más los pasteles. A mí me .... la música clásica, pero a mi hermano le .... el folklore.

Exercise 5

Muy, mucho, muchos, mucha or muchas?

No me gusta .... trabajar en esa oficina, porque pasan .... coches y .... gente por allí, el aire está .... sucio. Además tengo que escribir .... Antes me gustaba ...., había .... árboles y el aire estaba .... limpio, todos estábamos .... contentos, nos quedábamos más tiempo en la oficina.

Vocabulary

Below is a list of vocabulary encountered in this chapter.

abrigo *m*	*coat*
acordeón *m*	*accordion*
aire *m*	*air*
alpinismo *m*	*mountain climbing*
árbol *m*	*tree*
¡Bravo!	*Great!*
campo *m* **de fútbol**	*football pitch/ soccer field*
¡Caramba!	*Damn!; (here:) Wow!*
churro *m*	*fritter*
¿De acuerdo?	*OK?*
deporte *m*	*(type of) sport*
encantar a alguien	*to appeal to someone*
entrada *f*	*ticket*
equipo *m*	*team*
esquí *m*	*skiing*
estadio *m*	*stadium*
fanático, -a de footing *m*	*mad about jogging*
fumar	*to smoke*
fútbol *m*	*football/soccer*
iglesia *f*	*church*
internacional	*international*
latino	*Latin*
limpio, -a	*clean*
nacional	*national*
naipe *m*	*playing card*
natación *f*	*swimming*
Navidad *f*	*Christmas*
palabra *f*	*word*
partido *m* **de fútbol**	*football/soccer game*
por ejemplo	*for example*
practicar	*to practice*
realmente	*really, in fact*
sediento	*thirsty*
ser aficionado, -a a alguna cosa	*to be enthusiastic about something*
sucio, -a	*dirty*
sudoroso, -a	*sweaty*
taquilla *f*	*ticket counter*
técnica *f*	*technology*
tenis *m*	*tennis*
vendedor *m*	*vendor*
viva	*(long) live*

Test 3

Work your way around the board. Each correct answer will take you to the next question until you have completed the exercise. Enjoy!

1
Choose one of the two answers, then go to the square with the number of your answer.

2
Ellos… frío.
tienen ▶ 4
han ▶ 29

3
¡Falso!

Volver al n.º 11

8
¡Falso!

Volver al n.º 5

9
¡Bien hecho!
Muchas gracias. De…
nadie ▶ 26
nada ▶ 11

10
¡Falso!

Volver al n.º 28

11
¡Qué bien!
En Irlanda el paisaje es siempre…
gris ▶ 3
verde ▶ 30

16
¡Fantástico!
¡Colorín, colorado, este test se ha acabado!

17
¡Bien!
Gracias… tu ayuda.
para ▶ 19
por ▶ 5

18
¡Falso!

Volver al n.º 22

19
¡Falso!

Volver al n.º 17

24
¡Falso!

Volver al n.º 4

25
¡Bien!
¿Has… la mesa?
ponido ▶ 15
puesto ▶ 22

26
¡Falso!

Volver al n.º 9

27
¡Falso!

Volver al n.º 7

4

¡Correcto!
Ayer Carlos… al cine.
fui ▶ 24
fue ▶ 9

5

¡Muy bien!
Me… los deportes.
gusta ▶ 8
gustan ▶ 28

6

¡Falso!

Volver al n.º 30

7

¡Muy bien!
Tengo… sed.
muy ▶ 27
mucha ▶ 23

12

¡Falso!

Volver al n.º 23

13

¡Muy bien!
Eres un… amigo.
bueno ▶ 21
buen ▶ 17

14

¡Fantástico!
¿… los platos en la mesa?
pono ▶ 20
pongo ▶ 16

15

¡Falso!

Volver al n.º 25

20

¡Falso!

Volver al n.º 14

21

¡Falso!

Volver al n.º 13

22

¡Correcto!
Hoy… a Jaime.
encontré ▶ 18
he encontrado ▶ 7

23

¡Correcto!
Madrid es una ciudad…
grande ▶ 14
gran ▶ 12

28

¡Fantástico!
¡… un día muy bonito!
es ▶ 25
está ▶ 10

29

¡Falso!

Volver al n.º 2

30

¡Correcto!
¿Dónde… las llaves?
son ▶ 6
están ▶ 13

day: 22

Finding work

Day 22 discusses finding work in Spain and how to discuss future plans. You will learn the future tense and its irregular forms and how to use the subject pronouns *uno/una* to mean "one". Finally, you will continue to further boost your vocabulary.

CONTACTS...

There are different ways of finding work in Spain. You can take a look at the job offers in the national and regional newspapers, check some online job sites (such as **Infojobs.com***), send a spontaneous application to a particular company you are interested in, etc. Unfortunately, Spain is known for not being much of a meritocracy so it is quite common to hear that someone has gotten a job thanks to their contacts, not their skills or achievements.*

Spanish conversation: Busco un nuevo trabajo

Karen: **Mañana compraré El País y miraré los anuncios de trabajo.**
Carlos: **¿No te gusta el trabajo que tienes ahora?**
Karen: **Una se aburre, hago siempre lo mismo. El trabajo en la casa de los García no me llena.**
Carlos: **Iremos entonces a comprar el periódico y leeremos juntos las ofertas de trabajo.**
Karen: **Trabajaré en un hospital o en una clínica como enfermera.**
Carlos: **¡Es duro el trabajo en un hospital!**
Karen: **Una se acostumbra a todo, además me gusta atender a los enfermos. Si mañana no encontramos anuncios interesantes, escribiré cartas a hospitales y clínicas solicitando un puesto de trabajo.**
Carlos: **¿Qué es de Paula? Ella buscaba un trabajo como enfermera…**
Karen: **La próxima semana empezará a trabajar en la consulta del Dr. Jiménez, le pagará muy bien y como siempre tirará el dinero.**

Después de leer el periódico.

Karen: **Llamaré por teléfono y concertaré una entrevista para mañana.**
Carlos: **¿Qué les dirás a los García?**
Karen: **Les diré que saldré de casa una hora antes, así podré llegar a tiempo a la entrevista. Mañana tendré que levantarme temprano para preparar la comida. Me pondré la chaqueta roja, ¿no?**
Carlos: **Sí, esa te queda estupendamente… y además lloverá mañana. A ver si tienes suerte.**

Karen al teléfono.

Karen: **Buenos días, he leído su anuncio en el periódico de hoy…**
Secretaria: **¿Cuál es su profesión? ¿Tiene experiencia laboral?**
Karen: **Sí, soy enfermera y antes trabajaba en un hospital.**
Secretaria: **¿Lleva Ud. mucho tiempo en Madrid?**
Karen: **Llevo tres meses aquí.**
Secretaria: **¿Podría venir mañana a las 3.00 de la tarde para presentarse?**
Karen: **Sí, de acuerdo. Hasta mañana.**

English conversation: I am looking for a new job

Karen:	**Tomorrow I'll buy El País and look at the job advertisements.**
Carlos:	**Don't you like the job you have at the moment?**
Karen:	**It is boring, I always do the same thing. The job at the García's house isn't enough for me.**
Carlos:	**Then we'll go and buy a newspaper and look through the job advertisements together.**
Karen:	**I'll work as a nurse in a hospital or a clinic.**
Carlos:	**Working in a hospital is hard work!**
Karen:	**One can get used to anything, besides, I enjoy caring for the sick. If we can't find an interesting advertisement tomorrow I'll write letters to the hospitals and clinics to enquire about a job.**
Carlos:	**What about Paula? She was looking for work as a nurse…**
Karen:	**She's starting work next week in the practise of Dr. Jiménez. He'll pay her really well and, as usual, she'll squander it all.**

After reading the newspaper.

Karen:	**I'll call and set up a job interview for tomorrow.**
Carlos:	**What will you tell the Garcías?**
Karen:	**I'll tell them that I am going to leave the house an hour earlier so that I'll be able to get to the interview on time. Tomorrow I'll have to get up early to prepare the meal. I'll put on the red jacket, or what do you think?**
Carlos:	**Yes, it fits you very well… and by the way, it's going to rain tomorrow. Let's see if you are going to be lucky.**

Karen on the phone.

Karen:	**Good morning, I saw your ad in today's newspaper…**
Secretary:	**What is your profession? Do you have any work experience?**
Karen:	**Yes, I am a nurse and I've worked in a hospital before.**
Secretary:	**Have you been in Madrid long?**
Karen:	**I've been here for three months.**
Secretary:	**Could you come tomorrow at three in the afternoon for an interview?**
Karen:	**Yes, I could. Until tomorrow then.**

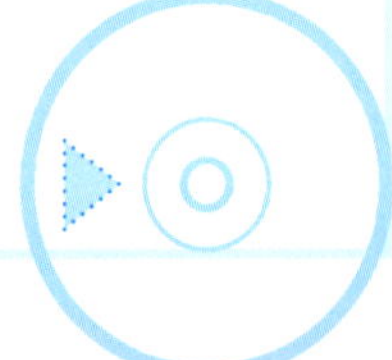

Grammar

Future tense

To form the future tense, you take the infinitive of the verb and add the endings:
-é, -ás, -a, -emos, -éis, -an

Note that all verbs take the same endings in the future, irrespective of whether they end in -ar, -er or -ir.

tomar (to take)		beber (to drink)		vivir (to live)	
tomar*é*	I will take	beber*é*	I will drink	vivir*é*	I will live
tomar*ás*	you will take	beber*ás*	you will drink	vivir*ás*	you will live
tomar*á*	he/she/it will take	beber*á*	he/she/it will drink	vivir*á*	he/she/it will live
tomar*emos*	we will take	beber*emos*	we will drink	vivir*emos*	we will live
tomar*éis*	you (pl) will take	beber*éis*	you (pl) will drink	vivir*éis*	you (pl) will live
tomar*án*	they will take	beber*án*	they will drink	vivir*án*	they will live

The future tense is used to describe an action, process or state **in the future**.

***Solicitaré* trabajo.**	I will look for work.
***Lloverá* mañana.**	It will rain tomorrow.
***Viviré* bien.**	I will live well.

Irregular future forms

Note that verbs that change their stem in the conditional also do so in the future tense:

saber	sab*ré*	venir	ven*dré*	querer	quer*ré*
haber	hab*ré*	poner	pon*dré*	decir	di*ré*
poder	pod*ré*	salir	sal*dré*	valer	val*drá*
hacer	ha*ré*	tener	ten*dré*		

Subject pronoun *uno/una*

The **subject pronoun** uno/una can only be used with **reflexive verbs** because these verbs cannot form the impersonal se.

***uno/una* se aburre**	= one gets bored
***uno/una* se afeita**	= one shaves (oneself)
***uno/una* se va de paseo**	= one goes for a walk

Exercises

Exercise 1

Fill in the verb forms following the example.

comprar compraran compraréis compraré

1 poder ....

2 comer ....

3 vivir ....

4 hacer ....

5 vender ....

Exercise 2

Rewrite the sentences using the example.

No voy al teatro. No iré al teatro.

1 No ponen música. ....

2 No sabe la lección. ....

3 Estoy feliz. ....

4 Hace frío. ....

5 Volvemos pronto. ....

6 José estudia español. ....

7 No quiero ir al café. ....

Exercise 3

Fill in the future tense of the verbs in brackets.

El próximo domingo (yo, organizar) .... una fiesta. Me (poner) .... mi traje más bonito e (invitar) .... a mucha gente. (Yo, tocar) .... la guitarra. (Nosotros, bailar y cantar) .... hasta las cinco de la madrugada. (Ser) .... muy divertido. Todos (estar) .... felices y (decir) .... que es la mejor fiesta de todo el año.

Exercise 4

Rewrite the sentences using the subject pronoun as in the example.

Por la mañana me levanto temprano. Por la mañana uno se levanta temprano.

1 En España me suelo acostar tarde.

....

2 Nos divertimos mucho jugando al fútbol.

....

3 Los sábados no me aburro nunca.

....

4 Nos alegramos mucho de su suerte.

....

5 Cuando hace frío me pongo el abrigo.

....

6 Nosotros nos presentamos al profesor.

....

7 No me quedo nunca en casa.

....

Exercise 5

The following list contains a number of professions you have learned. Insert them into the appropriate sentences: profesor, enfermera, pintor, secretaria, camarero, azafata

1 Trabajo en un restaurante, soy ....

2 Doy clases de español, soy ....

3 Hago cuadros, soy ....

4 Tengo que escribir muchas cartas en inglés, soy...........................

5 Trabajo en un avión, soy ....

6 Me gusta atender a los enfermos, soy ....

Exercise 6

Read the following advertisement and decide whether the statements are correct or incorrect by ticking Sí or No.

Escuela de lenguas necesita profesor. Personas de 25 a 28 años. Se requiere experiencia mínima de 2 años. Se valorará positivamente tener unos buenos conocimientos generales. Trabajo en Madrid centro. Sueldo inicial aproximadamente de 20.000 euros anuales. Los interesados llamen al teléfono 275 46 70 para concertar una entrevista.

	Sí	No
1 Una clínica necesita a un profesor.	....	....
2 Se necesita experiencia.	....	....
3 Necesitan personas de 25 a 28 años.	....	....
4 El trabajo está en Madrid centro.	....	....
5 Se pagan exactamente 20.000 euros al mes.	....	....
6 Se exigen pocos conocimientos generales.	....	....
7 Los interesados tienen que escribir una carta.	....	....
8 Hay que concertar una entrevista por teléfono.	....	....

Exercise 7

You are looking for a job. What do you do first? Arrange the sentences in the correct order.

1 Presentarse y tener una entrevista. ....

2 Comprar el periódico todos los días. ....

3 Empezar a trabajar. ....

4 Escribir cartas y solicitar un puesto de trabajo. ....

5 Buscar un nuevo trabajo. ....

6 Leer los anuncios de trabajo. ....

Vocabulary

Below is a list of vocabulary encountered in this chapter.

acostumbrarse a alguna cosa	*to get used to something*
alegrarse	*to be happy*
anual	*annually*
anuncio *m* **de trabajo**	*job advertisement*
aproximadamente (aprox.)	*approximately*
atender a alguien	*to care for someone*
buscar	*to search, look for*
cabeza *f*	*head*
carta *f*	*letter*
chaqueta *f*	*jacket*
clínica *f*	*clinic*
concertar (-ie-)	*to arrange*
conocimientos *m pl* **generales**	*general education*
consulta *f*	*GP's practice/doctor's office*
despedir a alguien	*to lay someone off*
dinero *m*	*money*
dolor *m*	*pain*
duro, -a	*hard*
El País	*Spanish newspaper*
emplear	*to employ*
enfermo *m*	*sick person*
entrevista *f*	*(job) interview*
escuela *f* **de lenguas**	*language school*
espalda *f*	*back*
estómago *m*	*stomach*
estupendo, -a	*excellent*
exigir	*to request*
experiencia *f*	*experience*
experiencia *f* **laboral**	*work experience*
feliz	*happy*
hombro *m*	*shoulder*
hospital *m*	*hospital*
imaginarse	*to imagine*
inicial	*initially*
interesado *m*	*applicant*
laboral	*work-related*
lección *f*	*lesson*
llenar	*to fill in*
lluvia *f*	*rain*
madrugada *f*	*early morning*
médico *m*	*physician, doctor*
mínimo, -a	*minimum*
oferta *f* **de trabajo**	*job offer*
pelo *m*	*hair*
pierna *f*	*leg*
presentarse	*to present/introduce oneself*
profesión *f*	*profession*
puesto *m* **de trabajo**	*job, position*
requerir	*to request*
secretaria *f*	*secretary*
solicitar a.c.	*to ask for something*
sueldo *m*	*salary*
tirar	*to throw away*
valer	*to be of use, value*
valorar	*to value*

day: 23

The flea market

Day 23 takes you to a flea market. You will learn how to use the future tense to make an assumption and how to use the definite article (el, la, los, las) as a demonstrative pronoun. You will also learn how to make comparisons with *más/menos que* (more/less than).

AT THE MARKET...

Madrid's ***Rastro*** *is said to be the biggest of its kind in the world. Sunday mornings the streets in the southern part of the San Isidro district are awash with people wanting to buy, sell or barter. Everything from clothing, pots and pans, old wares and antiques – whether genuine or not – change hands. Also to be found are traveling people practicing acrobatic skills or showing off trained animals.*

Spanish conversation: En el Rastro

Carmen: **Karen, ¿por qué no nos tuteamos? Somos amigas, ¿no?**

Karen: **De acuerdo, gracias. A propósito, en la clínica buscaban a alguien para tres años por lo menos, así que me voy a quedar con vosotros.**

Carmen: **¡Estupendo! ¿Me quieres acompañar mañana al rastro?**

Karen: **Sí, con gusto. Esto me gusta más que cuidar a los niños.**

Carmen: **Todos los domingos por la mañana en las calles en el sur del barrio de San Isidro hay más gente de la que uno se puede imaginar. Allí se compra, se vende y – lo más importante, se regatea.**

En el Rastro.

Karen: **¡Por Dios! ¡Qué marea de gente!**

Carmen: **Sí… ¿Has visto ya esas lámparas? Son bonitas.**

Karen: **Sí, son más bonitas que las que están en la mesa.**

Carmen: **Seguramente serán caras y costarán más de lo que queremos pagar.**

Karen: **Vamos a preguntar por el precio, por si las moscas…** (Al vendedor) **Señor, ¿por cuánto me daría esas lámparas?**

Vendedor: **¿Las de la mesa? Se las dejo por 38 euros, ¿las quiere?**

Karen: **¡Qué barbaridad! No, gracias.** (A Carmen) **Son más caras de lo que pensábamos.**

Carmen: **¿Qué te parece este reloj?**

Karen: **¿El del baúl? Será antiguo, ¿no?**

Carmen: **Antiquísimo. También esas tazas me chiflan. Serán de porcelana…**

Karen: **¿A cuánto estarán? ¿Las compramos?** (Al vendedor) **¿Cuánto valen estas tazas?**

Vendedor: **Esas 6 tazas valen 20 euros.**

Karen: **Son muy caras…**

Vendedor: **¿Cuánto me da?**

Carmen: **Por todo le doy 15 euros.**

Vendedor: **¡Vale! Voy a empaquetárselas.**

Carmen: **Pues es una verdadera ganga, ¿no?**

English conversation: At the flea market

Carmen:	Karen, why don't we address each other with 'you' (the informal Spanish 'tú')? We are friends, aren't we?
Karen:	I agree, thank you. By the way: the clinic was looking for someone to stay a minimum of three years, so I'll stay with you.
Carmen:	Excellent! Do you want to come with me to the flea market tomorrow?
Karen:	Yes, I'd love to. I'd like that more than looking after the kids.
Carmen:	More people than you can imagine gather every Sunday morning on the streets in the southern part of the San Isidro district. There you buy, sell and – most importantly – you barter things.

At the flea market.

Karen:	Oh my God! What a crowd of people!
Carmen:	Yes, … Have you seen those lamps? They are nice.
Karen:	Yes they're nicer than those on the table.
Carmen:	They're probably expensive and cost more than what we want to spend.
Karen:	Let's ask the price just to make sure… (To the vendor) How much are you asking for these lamps?
Vendor:	Those on the table? I'll give them to you for 38 euros. Do you want them?
Karen:	That's exorbitant! No, thanks. (To Carmen) They're more expensive than we thought.
Carmen:	What do you think of this clock?
Karen:	The one on the trunk? It's probably old, right?
Carmen:	Ancient. I am also crazy about these cups. They are probably porcelain…
Karen:	How much could they be? Shall we buy them? (To the vendor) How much are these cups?
Vendor:	Those six cups are 20 euros.
Karen:	They are very expensive…
Vendor:	How much will you give me for them?
Carmen:	I'll give you 15 euros for the lot.
Vendor:	OK! I'll wrap them up for you.
Carmen:	That's a real bargain, isn't it?

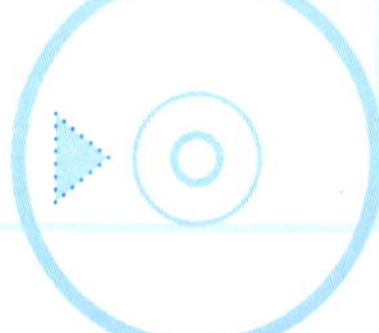

Using the future tense to make an assumption

Será **caro.**	That is probably expensive.
¿A cuánto ***estarán*****?**	How much could they be?

Besides **deber (de)** + **infinitive**, the **future tense** is also often used to make an assumption.

The definite article used as a demonstrative pronoun

In combination with de, the definite article can be used like a demonstrative pronoun:

No me gustan estas tazas. ***Las de*** **la mesa me gustan más.**

I don't like these cups. I like **the ones** on the table better.

Este reloj es antiguo, pero ***el del*** **baúl es antiquísimo.**

This clock is old, but **the one** on the trunk is ancient.

Comparisons with *más/menos que*

Esto me gusta ***más/menos*** **que cuidar a los niños.**

I like that more/less than looking after the children.

Where the comparison is concluded with a **noun** or a **verb in the infinitive** use **más/menos que**.

Hay más gente ***de la que*** **uno se puede imaginar.**

There are more people than you can imagine.

Compramos más tazas ***de las que*** **necesitamos.**

We buy more cups than we need.

Hacen más pan ***del que*** **pueden comer.**

They bake more bread than they can eat.

Tenemos más amigos ***de los que*** **queremos invitar.**

We have more friends than (those) we want to invite.

Comparisons that end (**más/menos** + **noun**) with a **conjugated verb** have **de** + **article of the noun** referred to **(la, las, el, los)** in front of que and the verb.

Costarán más ***de lo que*** **queremos pagar.**

They will probably cost more than we want to pay.

Esto es más complicado ***de lo que*** **cree.**

That is more complicated than you think.

If the first sentence has **más/menos** **by itself** or **with an adjective** it is followed by **de** + **lo** **before** **que** **and the verb**.

Exercises

Exercise 1

Make assumptions by replacing the words in italics with the future tense.

Hoy no *ha venido* .... al colegio. No *está* .... en Madrid. Se *ha ido* .... a la playa a tomar el sol. *Ha ido* .... en tren.

Se *queda* .... una semana. Me *llama* .... seguramente por teléfono para decirme cuando vuelve. Me *compra* .... un regalo.

Exercise 2

Convert the following questions into assumptions using the following example.

¿Se han ido ya? Se habrán ido ya.

1 ¿Le dan el coche? ....

2 ¿Han terminado ya? ....

3 ¿Van a tu fiesta? ....

4 ¿Sabe inglés? ....

5 ¿Hace buen tiempo? ....

6 ¿Está de acuerdo? ....

7 ¿Ha escrito la carta? ....

8 ¿Llega mañana? ....

Exercise 3

Select the correct form.

1 Estas flores son más bonitas ..... parecían.

a de lo que **b** de las que **c** que

2 Aprender el español es más fácil ..... aprender el alemán.

a de lo que **b** que **c** del que

3 En marzo ya hace menos frío ..... en enero.

a que **b** del que **c** de lo que

4 Escribe más cartas ...... recibe.

a de lo que **b** que **c** de las que

5 Ahora tiene más hambre ..... tenía hace una hora.

a que **b** de la que **c** de lo que

6 Había más gente en la calle ..... uno se puede imaginar.

a de la que **b** de lo que **c** que

1 .... **2** .... **3** .... **4** .... **5** .... **6** ....

Exercise 4

Fill in the blanks.

1 Necesita más dinero en un día .... le pagan en una semana.

2 Compra más libros .... puede leer.

3 Ahora tiene más años .... tenía cuando era joven.

4 Tienes más trajes .... puedes llevar.

5 Habla mucho más .... pensábamos.

6 Las lámparas valen más .... queríamos pagar.

7 Le dan menos dinero .... merece.

8 He comprado mucho más pan .... necesitamos.

9 Tiene más amigos .... yo.

10 Le gusta más bailar .... trabajar.

Exercise 5

What is it?

		a	**b**	**c**
1	rastro	a razor	a flea market	a bowl of rice
2	regatear	to barter	to cheat	to row
3	ganga	a gang	a hallway	a bargain
4	reloj	a clock	a tea cup	a chandelier
5	apañarse	to bake bread	to get by	to make pancakes

1 .... **2** .... **3** .... **4** .... **5** ....

Exercise 6

Which sentence is correct?

1 **a** Muchísimos gracias.
b Muchísimas gracias.

2 **a** Esto es más fácil de la que se cree.
b Esto es más fácil de lo que se cree.

3 **a** Con mucho gusto.
b Con mucho gusta.

4 **a** Le gusta más de cuidar a los niños.
b Le gusta más que cuidar a los niños.

5 **a** El reloj parece antiquísimo.
b El reloj parece antiquísima.

6 **a** ¿A cuánto estáran?
b ¿A qué estarán?

1 .... **2** .... **3** .... **4** .... **5** .... **6** ....

Vocabulary

Below is a list of vocabulary encountered in this chapter.

a propósito	*by the way*
antiguo, -a	*old*
barrio *m*	*neighborhood/district*
baúl *m*	*trunk*
chiflar	*to go crazy*
complicado, -a	*complicated*
costar	*to cost*
cuidar a alguien	*to look after someone*
empaquetar	*to wrap up*
¡Estupendo!	*Excellent!*
ganga *f*	*bargain*
lámpara *f*	*lamp*
merecer	*to be worth*
pagar	*to pay*
por lo menos	*at least*
por si las moscas…	*just in case*
porcelana *f*	*porcelain, china*
¡Qué barbaridad!	*That's exorbitant!*
¡Qué marea de…!	*What a lot… !*
recibir	*to receive*
regatear	*to barter*
reloj *m*	*watch, clock*
seguramente	*surely*
taza *f*	*cup*
tutearse	*to address one another with the informal "tú"*
vender	*to sell*
verdadero, -a	*really, truly*

day: 24

Running errands

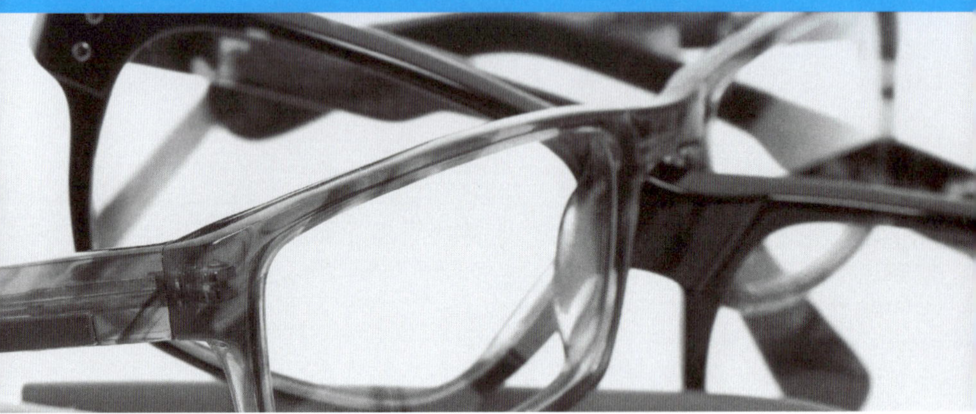

Day 24 introduces the passive voice whereby you can talk about actions that have taken place. You will also learn how to say that you must do something using *deber* + infinitive and discover the difference between *quería* and *querría*. Finally, you will continue to build your vocabulary and put into practice all that you have learnt.

EL ESTANCO…

If you need stamps in Spain you can buy them in the post offices as well as the ***estancos****. The latter are state-run tobacco kiosks that are easily recognized by their shop windows, which are dressed in the Spanish national colors, red-yellow-red. Buy your stamps in these stores and you get a free and friendly chat included.*

Spanish conversation: Hacer unos recados

Carmen:	**No sé dónde he puesto las llaves del coche, no las encuentro.**
Karen:	**Están colgadas en el llavero de la cocina.**
Carmen:	**Sí, aquí están, gracias.**
Karen:	**Carmen, la lavadora todavía no ha sido reparada. No podemos lavar este fin de semana.**
Carmen:	**¿Desde cuándo está estropeada?**
Karen:	**Desde hace cuatro días.**
Carmen:	**Pero, ¿por qué no me lo dijiste antes?**
Karen:	**Se lo dije a Pedro hace dos días.**
Carmen:	**Pedro está muy ocupado, su exposición ha sido prevista para la semana que viene.**
Karen:	**Desde el martes trato de llamar al servicio de reparaciones, ese teléfono debe estar averiado, siempre está ocupado.**
Carmen:	**La lavadora ha sido instalada por un vecino. En la guía de teléfono debe estar escrito su número de teléfono, se llama Víctor Sánchez.**
Karen:	**Han llamado de la óptica. Dicen que tus gafas han sido arregladas.**
Carmen:	**Ah… mis gafas. ¿Tienes tiempo para hacerme un par de recados?**
Karen:	**Sí, hoy es viernes y esta tarde no tengo clase.**
Carmen:	**Necesito recoger las gafas de la Óptica Paredes y comprar unos sellos, luego tengo que pasar por la panadería y la carnicería. No debo olvidarme, mis zapatos negros necesitan media suela y los marrones un arreglo de tacones.**
Karen:	**La zapatería está cerrada ahora. Allí iré más tarde.**
Carmen:	**Quería llevar también el vestido negro a la tintorería porque lo necesito para acompañar a Pedro a la exposición. ¿Te importaría llevarlo? Debe ser lavado en seco.**
Karen:	**Ah, qué bien, de paso iré a la relojería y así mato dos pájaros de un tiro.**

English conversation: Running some errands

Carmen:	**I don't know where I put the car keys; I can't find them.**
Karen:	**They are on the key rack in the kitchen.**
Carmen:	**Yes, there they are, thank you.**
Karen:	**Carmen, the washing machine has not been repaired. We can't do the laundry this weekend.**
Carmen:	**How long has it been broken?**
Karen:	**For four days.**
Carmen:	**But why didn't you tell me earlier?**
Karen:	**I told Pedro two days ago.**
Carmen:	**Pedro is very busy, his exhibition is scheduled for next week.**
Karen:	**I've been trying to reach customer service since Tuesday. That telephone must be broken; it's always been engaged (busy).**
Carmen:	**The washing machine was installed by a neighbour. His number must be in the telephone directory; his name is Victor Sánchez.**
Karen:	**The optician called and said your glasses have been repaired.**
Carmen:	**Ah, my glasses. Do you have time to run a few errands for me?**
Karen:	**Yes, today is Friday and I don't have any lessons in the afternoon.**
Carmen:	**I must get my glasses from Paredes Optics and buy a few stamps, then I have to go to the bakery and the butcher's. I must not forget that my black shoes need new soles and the brown ones have to be reheeled.**
Karen:	**The shoemaker's shop is closed now. I'll go there later.**
Carmen:	**I also wanted to take my black dress to the cleaners because I need it to accompany Pedro to the exhibition. Would you mind taking it there for me? It has to be dry-cleaned.**
Karen:	**Ah, that's good, on the way there I'll stop at the watchmaker's and I'll kill two birds with one stone.**

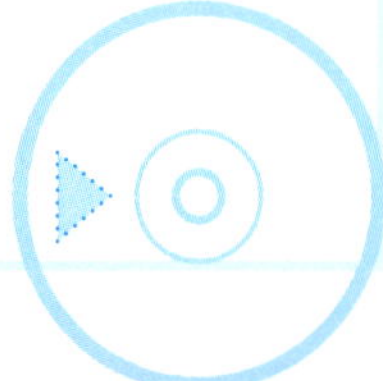

Grammar

Passive voice

Note that the passive voice is not used as often in Spanish as it is in English and Spanish people will often use another tense to get around using it! To form the passive voice, you use **ser** + **past participle**.

La lavadora *ha sido reparada*.	The washing machine has been repaired.
El libro *es escrito* por él.	The book is written by him.
Las gafas van a *ser arregladas*.	The glasses will be repaired.
El partido *fue ganado* por nuestro equipo.	The game was won by our team.

The past participle changes in the passive voice.

Descriptive passive

estar + **past participle** = descriptive passive (Result of an action)

passive voice	*descriptive passive*
La lavadora ha sido arreglada.	**La lavadora está arreglada.**
The washing machine is repaired.	The washing machine has been repaired.

Passive forms with *se*

In spoken Spanish the passive is often replaced by the combination of **se** + **verb** (the impersonal form) or by the **third person plural**.

Se ha reparado la lavadora.	***Han reparado* la lavadora.**
One has repaired the washing machine.	They have repaired the washing machine.

Obligations expressed with *deber* + infinitive

deber + **infinitive** = **must, to have to**

Lesson 19 already introduced **debe (de)** + infinitive as an expression of assumption.

Deber + **infinitive (without de)** is a milder version of saying **tener que**, meaning **must**:

Debo ir a la panadería.	I have to go to the bakery.
No debes olvidar.	You must not forget.

quería – querría

Watch out for the differences in spelling and pronunciation:

Quería comprar este vestido.	I wanted to buy this dress.

Quería comprar este vestido.	I'd like to buy this dress.

desde, hace, desde hace

desde **(since) – start of a time span** that extends into the present:

***Desde* el martes trato de llamar.**	I've been trying to call him **since** Tuesday.

desde hace **(since/for) – time span** that lasts into the **present**:

Está estropeada *desde hace* tres días.	It's been broken **for** three days.

hace **(ago) – a specific time in the past**:

Se lo dije *hace* dos días.	I told him two days **ago**.

Exercises

Exercise 1

Rewrite the sentences in the passive voice using the following example.

Un ladrón robó el bolso. El bolso fue robado por un ladrón.

1 La escuela de lenguas buscó a un profesor.

....

2 El huracán ha destruido toda la región.

....

3 El Real Madrid va a ganar el partido.

....

4 La chica ha denunciado el robo.

....

Exercise 2

Change the passive form of the sentences back into the active using the following example. e.g. El libro fue leído por los alumnos. Los alumnos leyeron el libro.

1 El premio fue ganado por mi hermano.

....

2 Las cartas han sido escritas por mí.

....

3 El coche fue robado por un ladrón.

....

Exercise 3

Rewrite the sentences in the passive voice with se and the third person plural.

1 Pasado mañana (terminar) el trabajo.

....

2 Nunca (saber) la verdad.

....

3 Algún día (encontrar) el bolso.

....

Exercise 4

Select the correct expression.

1 Para ser profesor ..... estudiar mucho.

a se debden b deben de c hay que

2 El teléfono ..... estar averiado.

a hay que b debe de c se debe de

3 ..... tener mucho ojo en una ciudad como ésta.

a Debes de b Hay que c Deben

4 ..... practicar mucho el español para aprenderlo bien.

a Tienes que b Debes que c Se deben que

1 .... 2 .... 3 .... 4 ....

Exercise 5

Hace, desde hace or desde? Insert the correct form below.

1 Nos visitaron .... unos días.

2 ¿............................ cuánto tiempo estudias español?

3 ¿............................ cuándo no has salido de casa?

4 Estudio español .... un año.

5 La lavadora está estropeada .... quince días.

Exercise 6

Translate the following text into Spanish.

Good morning. I'd like to speak to Carlos. I wanted to ask him whether he has bought any tickets. I'd like to watch a football match one day.

....

....

....

....

....

....

Vocabulary

Below is a list of vocabulary encountered in this chapter.

arreglado, -a	*repaired*
arreglo *m*	*repair*
averiado, -a	*broken, defective*
carnicería *f*	*butcher's*
colgar (-ue-)	*to hang (up)*
de paso	*on the way*
desde hace	*since, for*
desde	*since*
estropeado, -a	*broken*
exposición *f*	*exhibition*
fin *m* **de semana**	*weekend*
guía *f* **de teléfono**	*telephone directory*
instalar	*to install*
lavadora *f*	*washing machine*
lavar en seco	*to dry-clean*
marrón	*brown*
matar dos pájaros de un tiro	*to kill two birds with one stone*
matar	*to kill*
ocupado, -a	*busy, engaged*
óptica *f*	*optician*
pájaro *m*	*bird*
panadería *f*	*bakery*
portallaves *m*	*key rack*
prever	*to plan ahead*
recados *m pl*	*errands*
recoger	*to pick up, collect*
relojería *f*	*watch/clock shop*
reparar	*to repair*
sello *m*	*stamp*
semana *f* **que viene**	*next week*
servicio de atención al cliente	*customer service*
suela (de zapatos)	*(shoe) sole*
tacón *m*	*heel*
te importaría	*would you mind*
tintorería *f*	*dry-cleaner's*
tiro *m*	*shot*
tratar de *(+ inf.)*	*to try to*
vecino *m*	*neighbor*
zapatería *f*	*shoemaker's/shoe repair shop*
zapato *m*	*shoe*

day: 25

A night out

Day 25 takes you on a night out. It introduces the present subjunctive tense which is used to express a mood or a feeling. You will also learn about flamenco. Finally, you will further build your vocabulary and be able to put everything you have learned into practice in the exercise section.

FLAMENCO...

*Although deeply rooted in Andalusia, **flamenco** is now a complex intertwined art form. The melancholy song, music and dance accompanied by guitars, castanets, rythmic clapping and movements work together to capture the pain, passion and sensuality at the heart of **flamenco**. It remains at its best in intimate spaces in late-night sessions but performances also take place in theaters, jazz clubs and concert halls.*

Spanish conversation: Madrid de noche

Karen:	Carlos, me gustaría que salgamos juntos toda una noche por Madrid.
Carlos:	¿Quieres conocer la vida nocturna madrileña?
Karen:	Sí, tú llevas más tiempo aquí. Quiero que me hagas una sugerencia.
Carlos:	Bueno, yo propongo que salgamos el viernes. La famosa noche madrileña empieza el viernes por la tarde y termina el lunes.
Karen:	¿En serio? No lo creo.
Carlos:	¡Si ya te lo he dicho! Los madrileños son unos locos. Son insaciables y tienen reglas fijas para divertirse.
Karen:	Quiero que me lo expliques de forma más detallada.
Carlos:	Vamos a conocer una serie de locales. Me parece bien que el viernes a las 2.00 de la tarde tomemos algo en una taberna. Pediremos que nos sirvan unas tapas y una copa de Rioja. Después quiero que nos pasemos al café Gijón en el Paseo de Recoletos.
Karen:	Bueno, la noche es muy larga ¿no?
Carlos:	¿Quieres que saque entradas para el Teatro Monumental?
Karen:	A decir verdad, me gustaría más que veamos un buen flamenco.
Carlos:	Hay también clubs nocturnos donde bailan flamenco… En "La Casa Patas" la entrada incluye una bebida.
Karen:	¿De allí vamos a una discoteca?
Carlos:	Todavía no. Según las reglas no se va a la discoteca antes de las 2.00 de la madrugada.
Karen:	Toda la gente pasea por la Gran Vía a medianoche, ¿no?
Carlos:	Claro. Yo propongo que conozcas la discoteca "Oh Madrid" que está en la carretera de La Coruña. Tienen una piscina.
Karen:	Carlos, ¡quiero que pasemos allí la noche!
Carlos:	Luego vamos a la discoteca "Voltereta", está en el sótano de un gran almacén. Abren a las 7.00 de la mañana.
Karen:	¿A las 7.00 de la mañana?
Carlos:	Si te lo he dicho: los madrileños son insaciables.

English conversation: Madrid at night

Karen: **Carlos, I would like to make a night of it together with you in Madrid.**

Carlos: **Do you want to get a taste of the Madrid nightlife?**

Karen: **Yes, you've been here much longer. I want you to make a suggestion.**

Carlos: **Well, I suggest that we go out on Friday. The famous Madrid night starts Friday afternoon and ends on Monday.**

Karen: **Are you serious? I don't believe that.**

Carlos: **Yes, I've already told you that! The locals of Madrid are slightly crazy. They're insatiable and keep to a few hard rules on how to entertain themselves.**

Karen: **I'd like you to explain that to me in more detail.**

Carlos: **We will get to know a number of restaurants and pubs. I think it would be good if we had something to eat in a tavern at 2 in the afternoon on Friday. We'll ask them to serve us a few "tapas" and a glass of red wine from Rioja. After that I want us to go to the café Gijón at Paseo de Recoletos.**

Karen: **OK, the night is going to be long, right?**

Carlos: **Do you want me to buy tickets for the Teatro Monumental?**

Karen: **To be honest, I'd prefer to watch a good Flamenco show.**

Carlos: **There are also nightclubs where they dance the Flamenco… At the "Casa Patas" the admission includes one drink.**

Karen: **Are we going to the disco from there?**

Carlos: **Not yet. According to the rules you don't go to the disco before 2 in the morning.**

Karen: **Everybody goes for a walk along the Gran Vía at midnight, right?**

Carlos: **That's right. I suggest getting to know the disco "Oh Madrid", which is along the road to La Coruña. They have a swimming pool.**

Karen: **Carlos, I want us to spend the night there!**

Carlos: **Afterwards we'll go to the disco "Voltereta", it's in the basement of a large department store. It opens at 7 in the morning.**

Karen: **At 7 in the morning?**

Carlos: **Like I told you: the locals of Madrid are insatiable.**

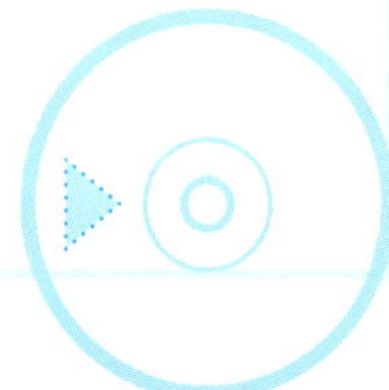

Grammar

Subjunctive mood

The subjunctive is used first and foremost to express a **personal attitude or mood** (doubt, uncertainty, negativity, etc.) and to set something into perspective or to qualify something that has been said.
It is mostly introduced with **que** in **subordinate clauses**, but it can occur in main clauses as well as in certain forms of the imperative.

Present subjunctive

The present tense forms of the subjunctive derive from the 1st person singular of the present indicative:

cant*ar*	**cant*o***	**cante**			
to sing	**cant*es***				
	cante				
	cant*emos*				
	cant*éis*				
	cant*en*				
pon*er*	**pong*o***	**pon*ga***	**serv*ir***	***sirvo***	***sirva***
to put	**pong*as***		*to serve*	***sirvas***	
	pong*a*			***sirva***	
	pong*amos*			***sirvamos***	
	pong*áis*			***sirváis***	
	pong*an*			***sirvan***	

Verbs ending in **-ar** end in the subjunctive in **-e**, verbs ending in **-er** and **-ir** end in **-a**. Some verbs, however, change their spelling: **pagar** – **pag*ue*** / **sacar** – **sa*que***
The 1**st and 3rd person singular** are formed **in the same way**.
Verbs ending in **-er** and **-ir** share **the same endings**.

The subjunctive mood after expressions of wishes and feelings

The subjunctive follows **verbs** that express a **wish**.

***Quiero que* me acompañes.**	I want you to accompany me.
***Deseo que* le visitemos a él.**	I want us to visit him.
***Propone que* conozcas el barrio.**	He suggests that you get to know the neighborhood.
***Espero que* venga.**	I hope that he comes.
***¿Me permites que* fume?**	May I smoke? (Is it okay with you if I smoke?)
***Me gustaría que* tomemos algo.**	I would like us to eat something.

The subjunctive follows **verbs** that express **satisfaction**, **pleasure**, **joy**, **regret** etc.

***Me parece bien que* salgamos.**	I think it is good that we are going out.
***Me alegro de que* me escribas.**	I am delighted that you are writing to me.
***Lamento que* estén cerrado.**	I regret that they are closed.

si

You have probably already noticed that **si** is generally used for **if** or **whether**:

Si quieres, vamos al teatro.	If you want, we can go to the theatre.
No sé si viene.	I don't know whether he is coming.

Si can also be used for **affirmation** or **emphasis**:

¡Si te lo había dicho!	Like I told you!

Exercises

Exercise 1

Complete each row with the 3rd person singular in the present indicative and the subjunctive mood as in the following example.

traducir traduce traduzca

1 conducir ....

2 tener ....

3 leer ....

4 escribir ....

5 subir ....

6 aprender ....

7 venir ....

Exercise 2

Say what you are wishing for.

1 (nosotros, salir) toda una noche. ....

2 (nosotros, visitar) un bar. ....

3 (tú, sacar) una entrada para el teatro. ....

4 (tú, ver) una película. ....

Exercise 3

Which form is correct.

1 Karen desea que (salen, salgan) .... toda una noche.

2 Karen y Carlos (salen, salgan) .... toda una noche.

3 Me parece bien que nos (visitáis, visitéis) .... este fin de semana.

4 Vosotros nos (visitáis, visitéis) .... este fin de semana.

5 Propone que (toman, tomen) .... algo en una taberna.

6 (Toman, tomen) .... algo en una taberna.

7 Lamento que no la (ayudas, ayudes) .... con los ejercicios.

Exercise 4

Ask for permission. Put the verbs below in the correct form.

¿Me permite que…?

1 (abrir) .... la puerta?

2 (fumar) .... un cigarrillo?

3 (salir) .... con su hija?

4 (hacer) .... una pregunta?

5 (visitar) .... a su familia?

6 (entrar) .... en su casa?

Vocabulary

Below is a list of vocabulary encountered in this chapter.

a decir verdad	*to be honest, to tell the truth*
abanico *m*	*fan*
atraer	*to put on*
castañuelas *f pl*	*castanets*
cigarrillo *m*	*cigarette*
club *m* **nocturno**	*nightclub*
contagiar	*to infect*
detallado, -a	*detailed*
discoteca *f*	*disco*
electrizar	*to electrify*
¿En serio?	*Seriously?*
entrada *f*	*admission (ticket)*
espectáculo *m*	*show*
fiebre *f*	*fever*
fijo, -a	*firm, hard*
flamenco *m*	*flamenco*
gran almacén *m*	*department store*
incluir	*to include*
insaciable	*insatiable*
lamentar	*to regret, lament*
largo, -a	*long*
local *m*	*restaurant, pub*
loco *m*	*crazy person*
madrugada *f*	*early morning*
mantón *m*	*shawl*
melancólico, -a	*melancholic*
nórdico, -a	*nordic, from the north*
orgullo *m*	*pride*
palmoteo *m*	*rhythmic clapping*
pasarse	*to go to*
pasearse	*to go for a walk*
pasión *f*	*passion*
permitir	*to permit*
piscina *f*	*swimming pool*
proponer	*to suggest*
puro, -a	*pure*
regla *f*	*rule*
ritmo *m* **gitano**	*gypsy rhythm*
según	*according to*
sentimiento *m*	*sentiment, feeling*
sótano *m*	*basement, cellar*
sugerencia *f*	*suggestion*
tablao *m* **de flamenco**	*Flamenco stage*
taconeo *m*	*tap dancing*
tener a disposición	*to have at one's disposal*
terminar	*to end*
toda una noche	*all through the night*
traducir (-zc-)	*to translate*
tristeza *f*	*sadness*
un montón de	*a lot of*
una serie de	*a series of*
vida *f* **nocturna**	*nightlife*

day: 26

Happy Birthday!

Day 26 focuses on the subjunctive mood in more detail and introduces irregular subjunctive forms and expressions that must take the subjunctive. You will also learn more about Spanish culture.

CELEBRATIONS...

La Pascua *refers generally to the major Christian feasts:* ***La Pascua de Navidad,*** Christmas; ***La Pascua Florida*** *or* ***de Resurrección****, Easter; and* ***La Pascua de Pentecostés****, Pentecost.*

Las Pascuas *means the time following on one of the major Christian feasts, i.e. the time from Christmas Eve to Epiphany and, at Easter, the Holy Week from Palm Sunday through Easter Monday. Some major feast days include:* ***Año Nuevo*** *(New Year),* ***Los Reyes Magos*** *(Epiphany),* ***Nochebuena*** *(Christmas Eve, December 24th),* ***Nochevieja*** *(New Year's Eve).*

Spanish conversation: ¡Feliz cumpleaños!

Carmen: **¡Muchas felicidades por tu cumpleaños, Karen!**

El resto de la familia: **¡Feliz cumpleaños!**

Karen: **Gracias. ¡Qué bonita está la mesa!**

Carmen: **La hemos puesto los niños y yo. Puede ser que esté un poco festiva. Queremos que sepas que te queremos mucho.**

Karen: **Muchas gracias, sois tan amables todos. ¿Qué es esto?**

Lucía: **Son tus regalos. Este es mi regalo para ti.**

Karen: **¡Qué bien envueltos están! Estoy muy curiosa.**

Lucía: **Quiero que empieces con mi regalo. Ojalá no sea difícil abrirlo.**

Karen: **A ver, a ver que es... ¡Una bufanda! Qué bonita!**

Lucía: **¿Te gusta? Es para cuando haga frío.**

Karen: **Me encanta, Lucía. Muchas gracias.**

David: **Este es mi regalo para ti.**

Karen: **A ver, ¡oh! Un retrato. No creo que lo hayas hecho tú.**

David: **Sí, para tí. Quizá no te reconozcas. Estás muy joven.**

Karen: **Muchas gracias, David. No dudo que un día serás un gran pintor, como tu padre.**

Pedro: **Ese es el regalo de Carmen y mío. Esperamos que te guste.**

Karen: **Una blusa de seda. En rojo, mi color predilecto.**

Carmen: **Sabemos que este color te va bien. Ahora nos sentamos todos a la mesa. La tarta la hemos preparado Lucía y yo. Es posible que no esté tan rica como se ve.**

Pedro: **Vamos a probarla. No creo que esté mal.**

Karen: **¡Qué rica está! Dejemos también un trozo para mi madre.**

Pedro: **¿Viene tu madre?**

Karen: **Sí, ¿no os lo he dicho? Llega el lunes en avión.**

Pedro: **Entonces, iremos por ella al aeropuerto.**

Carmen: **Y si quieres puedes invitar a Carlos y a otros amigos a festejar esta noche en casa.**

Karen: **Con mucho gusto. Hoy estoy realmente feliz. Gracias.**

English conversation: Happy birthday

Carmen:	**Happy birthday, Karen!**
The rest of the family:	**Happy birthday!**
Karen:	**Thank you. The table is set so beautifully!**
Carmen:	**The children and I set it. Perhaps it does look a little festive. We wanted you to know that we like you very much.**
Karen:	**Many thanks. You are all so nice. What's that?**
Lucía:	**These are your presents. This is my present for you.**
Karen:	**They're wrapped so nicely! I am very curious.**
Lucía:	**I want you to start with my present. Hopefully it won't be too difficult to open.**
Karen:	**Let's see, let's see what it is… A scarf! How nice!**
Lucía:	**Do you like it? It's for when it gets cold.**
Karen:	**I like it a lot, Lucía. Thank you very much.**
David:	**This is my present for you.**
Karen:	**Let's see. Oh! A portrait. I don't believe you did it.**
David:	**Yes I did, for you. Maybe you don't recognize yourself. You look very young.**
Karen:	**Thank you very much, David. I have no doubt that one day you will be a great painter, like your father.**
Pedro:	**This is a present from Carmen and myself. We hope you like it.**
Karen:	**A silk blouse. In red, my favourite color.**
Carmen:	**We know that this colour suits you well. Now let's all sit by the table. Lucía and I have prepared a tart. It may not taste as good as it looks.**
Pedro:	**We will try it. I don't think it'll taste bad.**
Karen:	**How delicious it is! Let's also leave a piece for my mother.**
Pedro:	**Is your mother coming?**
Karen:	**Yes, didn't I tell you? She's arriving by plane on Monday.**
Pedro:	**Then we'll pick her up at the airport.**
Carmen:	**And, if you want, you can invite Carlos and your other friends to have a party at our home tonight.**
Karen:	**I'd very much like to do that. I am really happy today. Thank you.**

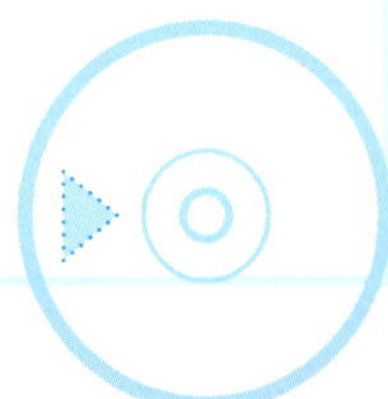

Grammar

Irregular subjunctive forms

ser (to be)	estar (to be)	saber (to know)	ir (to go)	haber (to have)
sea	esté	sepa	vaya	haya
seas	estés	sepas	vayas	hayas
sea	esté	sepa	vaya	haya
seamos	estemos	sepamos	vayamos	hayamos
seáis	estéis	sepáis	vayáis	hayáis
sean	estén	sepan	vayan	hayan

In Day 1 and Day 2 we looked at the different uses for ser and estar.
Note the different meanings here with the same adjectives:

ser joven	*estar* joven	*ser* bonito	*estar* bonito
to be young	to look young	to be pretty	to look pretty
ser rico	*estar rico*	*ser listo*	*estar listo*
to be rich	to taste good	to be smart	to be ready

Dipthong changes in the subjunctive

empezar (to start)	querer (to want)	poder (to be able)	dormir (to sleep)
emp*ie*ce	qu*ie*ra	p*ue*da	d*ue*rma
emp*ie*ces	qu*ie*ras	p*ue*das	d*ue*rmas
emp*ie*ce	qu*ie*ra	p*ue*da	d*ue*rma
empecemos	queramos	podamos	durmamos
empecéis	queráis	podáis	durmáis
emp*ie*cen	qu*ie*ran	p*ue*dan	d*ue*rman

Verbs where the -e- or -o- in their stem changes to -ie- or -ue- in the indicative mood retain this irregular pattern in the subjunctive.

The subjunctive is used with expressions of **doubt** and **hope:**

esperar que	to hope (that)
no creer que	to believe (that)
dudar que	to doubt (that)

The subjunctive is used to express **uncertainty**.

Espero que no sea difícil.	I hope it is not difficult.
No creo que te guste.	I don't think you will like it.
Dudo que te quede bien.	I doubt that it will suit you well.

The subjunctive is also used after **ojalá** and **quizá**/**quizás**:

Ojalá te guste.	Hopefully you will like it.
Quizá no te reconozcas.	Maybe you don't recognize yourself.

The subjunctive is used after **impersonal expressions**

es probable que	it is likely (that)
puede ser que	it is could be (that)
es posible que	it is possible (that)
es mejor que	it is better if
es preciso que	it is necessary (that)

Examples:

Es probable que venga.	It is possible that he'll come.
Puede ser que haya llegado.	It could be that he has arrived.
Es posible que esté aquí.	It is possible that he is here.
Es mejor que se quede en casa.	It is better if he stays home.

The subjunctive is used to express an **action or event in the future**

Cuando haga frío, te pones el abrigo.	If (as soon as) it gets cold you'll put your coat on.
Cuando te vayas a Inglaterra, será invierno.	When you go to England it will be winter.

Note:

Depending on the degree of probability, **quizás** and **cuando** can also be followed by the indicative mood.

Cuando + **indicative** expresses a **habitual action**

Cuando hace frío te pones el abrigo.	Whenever it gets cold, you'll put your coat on.

Exercises

Exercise 1

Rewrite the sentences following the example below.

e.g. **Creo que vienen. No creo que vengan.**

1 No hay duda que estáis contentos. Dudo que ....

2 Javier cree que tendrá suerte. Javier no cree que ....

3 Creo que sabes cantar. No creo que ....

4 Creo que van a Granada este año. No creo que ....

Exercise 2

Rewrite the sentences following the example below.

e.g. **¿Es interesante? ¡Ojalá sea interesante!**

1 ¿Tenéis tiempo? ....

2 ¿Llevan abrigos? ....

3 ¿Hace sol? ....

4 ¿Hablas español? ....

Exercise 3

Rewrite the sentences.

1 Nos es imposible acompañaros. Es imposible que ....

2 Sería mejor para él quedarse en la cama. Es mejor que ....

3 Necesitamos salir. Es preciso que ....

4 Probablemente llega hoy. Es probable que ....

Exercise 4

Complete the verb forms following the example below.

e.g. ¿Cuándo vas a pagar tus deudas? Cuando tenga dinero.

1 ¿Cuándo (tu, venir) a visitarnos? Cuando (yo, tener tiempo).

....

2 ¿Cuándo (Karen, invitar) a sus amigos? Cuando (ser) su cumpleaños.

....

3 ¿Cuándo (ir) tus padres de vacaciones? Cuando (querer).

....

4 ¿Cuándo (terminar) Pedro el cuadro? Cuando lo (necesitar).

....

Exercise 5

Ser or estar? Insert the correct form below.

1 Juan .... un chico muy listo, pero .... muy cansado hoy.

2 Mi abuela tiene ya 73 años, pero .... muy joven.

3 ¿Te gusta el pastel? Sí, ... muy rico.

4 Esa falda .... de algodón y te .... mejor.

5 .... un día bonito hoy.

6 ¡Qué bonita .... esta niña!

Exercise 6

Indicative or subjunctive? Insert the correct form below.

1 Me alegro tanto de que mi madre (haber) .... venido.

2 ¿Sabes cuándo (él, volver) ....?

3 Sé que (tú, tener) .... razón.

4 ¿Es verdad que (ellos, hablar) .... muy bien el español?

5 Ojalá (vosotros, descansar) .... esta noche.

6 Espero que no (tú, enfadarse) .... conmigo.

Vocabulary

Below is a list of vocabulary encountered in this chapter.

bufanda *f*	*scarf*
¡Buen fin de semana!	*Have a nice weekend*
¡Buen viaje!	*Have a good trip!*
cumpleaños *m*	*birthday*
curioso, -a	*curious*
dejar	*to leave*
deuda *f*	*debt (money)*
dinero *m*	*money*
dudar	*to doubt*
¡Enhorabuena!	*Congratulations*
enfadarse	*to be angry*
envuelto, -a	*wrapped up*
examen	*exams*
favorito	*favorite*
fin de semana	*weekend*
felicitar	*to congratulate*
¡Felices vacaciones!	*Enjoy your holidays!*
¡Feliz cumpleaños!	*Happy birthday!*
¡Feliz Navidad!	*Merry Christmas!*
¡Felices Pascuas!	*Enjoy the holidays!*
¡Feliz Año Nuevo!	*Happy New Year!*
festejar	*to party, celebrate a feast*
festivo, -a	*festive*
imposible	*impossible*
¡Mucha suerte!	*Good luck!*
¡Mucho éxito!	*All the best!*
¡Muchos felicidades!	*Congratulations!*
ojalá	*hopefully*
Pascuas/ Navidades	*religious holidays*
pastel *m*	*cake*
predilecto	*favorite*
quizá(s)	*maybe, perhaps*
regalo *m*	*present, gift*
resto *m*	*rest*
retrato *m*	*portrait*
rico, -a	*rich, (here:) delicious*
sentarse (-ie-)	*to sit down*
ser preciso	*to be necessary*
ser probable	*to be likely*
tarta *f*	*tart*
tener razón	*to be right*
trozo *m*	*piece*
un día	*one day*
usar	*to use*
vacaciones	*holidays/vacations*

day: 27

At the hotel

Day 27 talks about trips away and places to stay. You will learn the subjunctive of the verb *dar* (to give) and when to use it (after certain conjunctions). You will also learn how to say you have just done something using *acabar de*.

PLACES TO STAY...

Spain offers visitors a full range of accommodations, from the humble youth hostel ***(albergue juvenil)*** *to the five-star* ***hotel****. Alternatively, try the* ***refugios*** *(small inns found in remote and mountainous regions),* ***hostales*** *(modest hotels that are often family run) or* ***pensión*** *(boarding house). An* ***apartamento amueblado*** *is a furnished apartment, mainly found in resorts. For a special treat, try one of the* ***Paradores Nacionales****. These are old castles, monasteries or palaces that have been converted into hotels. For complete listings, check out a* ***Guía de hoteles y pensiones*** *online or at the local tourist office.*

Spanish conversation: 50 euros por noche

Recepcionista: **Hotel Europa, buenas noches.**
Karen: **Buenas noches, ¿tienen Uds. habitaciones libres?**
Recepcionista: **Sí, ¿desea una doble o una individual?**
Karen: **Una individual con baño que sea tranquila y que dé al patio.**
Recepcionista: **¿Para cuándo la necesita?**
Karen: **A partir del lunes.**
Recepcionista: **¿Para cuántas noches la desea?**
Karen: **Para tres noches. ¿Cuánto cuesta la habitación?**
Recepcionista: **50 euros por noche. El desayuno está incluido en el precio. ¿A nombre de quién?**
Karen: **De Helga Muller.**
Recepcionista: **Ya he tomado nota, gracias.**

Karen habla con Carmen.

Karen: **Acabo de reservar una habitación para que se aloje mi madre. ¡Ojalá le guste!**
Carmen: **¿En qué hotel?**
Karen: **En el Hotel Europa. Es un hotel como para ella, es confortable y realmente barato.**
Carmen: **¿Tu madre viene sólo para visitarte?**
Karen: **No, no sólo para eso. Ahora tiene la oportunidad de conocer este país y después pasará unos días de vacaciones viajando por España. Bueno, a no ser que Madrid le guste más. Pero no creo que se quede mucho tiempo. A ella no le gustan las ciudades grandes.**
Carmen: **¿Qué le gustaría ver a ella?**
Karen: **Le gustaría visitar un par de provincias, luego irse a una isla para bañarse y disfrutar del sol, del agua… Quizá regrese luego a Madrid. No es mala idea, ¿no?**
Carmen: **En caso que ella necesite algunas direcciones, tenemos amigos por todas partes. Por mucho que ella viaje o lea no llegará a conocer España tan bien como con españoles. ¡Eso ya lo sabes tú!**
Karen: **Sí, es verdad. Hasta que ella llegue podré conseguir más informaciones sobre España para que ella pueda planear: un guía, un mapa, un plano de la ciudad. ¡Estoy tan contenta de que ella venga!**

English conversation: 50 euros per night

Receptionist:	**Hotel Europa, Good evening.**
Karen:	**Good evening. Do you have any vacancies?**
Receptionist:	**Yes, do you want a double or a single room?**
Karen:	**A quiet, single room with a bathroom, facing the courtyard.**
Receptionist:	**When do you need it?**
Karen:	**As of Monday.**
Receptionist:	**For how many nights do you want it?**
Karen:	**For three nights. How much does the room cost?**
Receptionist:	**50 euros per night. Breakfast is included in the price. In whose name?**
Karen:	**Helga Muller.**
Receptionist:	**I've written it down, thank you.**

Karen speaks to Carmen.

Karen:	**I have just booked a room for my mother to stay in. I hope she likes it.**
Carmen:	**At which hotel?**
Karen:	**At the Hotel Europa, that's just right for her. It is comfortable and inexpensive.**
Carmen:	**Is your mother coming just to visit you?**
Karen:	**No, not just for that. She's using the opportunity to get to know the country, and then she's taking a few days' holiday travelling through Spain. Well, unless she prefers to stay in Madrid. But I don't think she'll stay long. She doesn't like big cities.**
Carmen:	**What would she like to see?**
Karen:	**She would like to visit a few provinces, then go to an island to go swimming and enjoy the sun and the water… She might return to Madrid afterwards. Not a bad idea, is it?**
Carmen:	**Just in case she needs a few addresses, we have friends all over the place. No matter how much she travels or reads, she will never get to know Spain as well as she would being with Spaniards. But you know that already!**
Karen:	**Yes, that's right. By the time she arrives, I will have gathered more information about Spain so that she can plan ahead: a travel guide, a map and a city guide. I am so looking forward to her coming!**

Grammar

Subjunctive of *dar*

dar (to give)	
dé I give	**demos** we give
des you give	**deis** you (pl) give
dé he/she/it gives	**den** they give

Subjunctive after specific conjunctions

Conjunctions that express an **intention**, **doubt**, **probability** or a **hypothetical situation** or those that refer to a **future action** are followed by the **subjunctive mood**.

***para que* pueda viajar**	**so that** she can travel
***a no ser que* Madrid le guste más**	**unless** she likes Madrid better
***en caso de que* ella necesite algunas direcciones**	**in case** she needs a few addresses
El perro no ladra *sin que* se lo permita.	The dog does not bark **without** my permission.
Tengo que estar en casa *antes de que* venga mi madre.	I have to be home **before my** mother comes.
***Por mucho que* ella viaje y lea...**	**As much as** she travels and reads...
Hasta que ella no llegue, no podré conseguir más información.	**Until** she arrives, I won't be able to gather any more information.

Subjunctive in relative clauses

The **subjunctive** is used in relative clauses to express **wishes** or **conditions**:

Una habitación individual con baño *que sea* tranquila y *que dé* al patio.

A quiet, single room with a bathroom, facing the courtyard.

Immediate past

acabar + **de** + **infintive** = just having done something

***Acabo de llamar* a mi madre.**	I just called my mother.
***Acaban de llegar* a casa.**	They just got home.

¿cuánto?

¿Cuánto? is used to enquire after a quantity. It changes like an adjective in relation to the noun.

¿Cuánto cuesta la habitación?	How much does the room cost?
¿Para cuántas noches la necesita?	For how many nights do you need it?

Exercises

Exercise 1

Put the verbs into the 3rd person singular of the present subjunctive using the following example: tener – tenga

oír	ir	haber ....
venir....................................	estar	empezar..............................
decir	sentir	ser ....
dar	dormir.................................	bailar ....
querer	salir	vivir ....

Exercise 2

Insert the correct verb form.

1 En caso de que (tú, querer) .... salir por las noches tienes que comportarte bien.

2 Por mucho que (ir) .... al estadio no aprenderemos nunca a jugar al fútbol.

3 Cuando (llegar) .... tu abuelo me avisas.

4 Transcurre el año sin que (nosotros, ir) .... a España.

5 Cuando (yo estar) .... en Madrid, iba todos los días al Retiro.

6 Hasta que tú no me (decir) .... la verdad, no te miraré.

7 Le llamo antes de que me (ver) ....

Exercise 3

You just did what you are being asked to do. Answer as in the example below.

e.g. ¿Has preparado la comida? Acabo de prepararla.

1 ¿Has puesto la mesa? ....

2 ¿Has encontrado a Adela? ....

3 ¿Has comprado pan para mañana? ....

4 ¿Has visto esta película? ....

5 ¿Has solicitado un pasaporte nuevo? ....

6 ¿Has reservado una habitación para tu amiga? ....

Exercise 4

Select the correct verb form.

1 Tenemos una secretaria que ..... perfectamente inglés.

a habla b hable 1.........

2 Buscamos a un profesor que ..... tocar la guitarra.

a sabe b sepa 2.........

3 ¿Cuándo me ..... el dinero?

a prestas b prestes 3.........

4 Espero que os ..... el pastel que he hecho.

a gusta b guste 4.........

5 Creo que ..... aún de viaje.

a estén b están 5.........

6 Es posible que no nos ..... .

a visitan b visiten 6.........

Exercise 5

Replace the word in italics with its opposite.

1 La habitación es muy *barata*/ ....

2 Hoy es el *último*/ .... día de trabajo.

3 La panadería está *abierta*/ ....

4 En la calle hay *poca*/ .... gente.

5 Este libro es muy *interesante*/ ....

6 Nos levantamos siempre *tarde*/ ....

7 Esta ciudad es *antigua*/ ....

8 El jardín de mis amigos es *grande*/ ....

Exercise 6

Select the correct form.

1 *¿Cuánto/cuántos* cuestan los tomates? ....

2 ¿Para *cuántos/cuántas* días las necesita? ....

3 *¿Cuánta/cuántas* gente viene a tu fiesta? ....

4 ¿Para *cuántos/cuánto* tenemos que cocinar? ....

5 *¿Cuántas/cuántos* canciones sabes tocar con la guitarra? ....

6 *¿Cuánto/cuántos* tiempo llevas en Madrid? ....

Vocabulary

Below is a list of vocabulary encountered in this chapter.

a no ser que	*unless, except*
a partir de	*from, as of*
acabar	*to end, be finished*
alojarse	*to stay (at s.o.'s place)*
avisar a alguien	*to inform someone*
bañarse	*to bathe*
como para	*as for*
comportarse	*to behave*
confortable	*comfortable*
conseguir (-i-)	*to obtain*
contento, -a	*content, satisfied*
en casa de	*at home with*
en caso de que	*in case*
habitación *f* **doble**	*double room*
habitación *f* **individual**	*single room*
hotel *m*	*hotel*
isla *f*	*island*
jardín *m*	*garden*
oportunidad *f*	*opportunity*
planear	*to plan*
por mucho que	*even if*
prestar	*to borrow*
provincia *f*	*province*
recepcionista *m/f*	*receptionist*
tomar nota	*to note, write down*
transcurrir	*to go by, pass*
un par de	*a few*

day: 28

Meeting friends

Day 28 talks about meeting friends. You will learn how to use the imperative (to give commands), as well as possessive pronouns. You will further build your vocabulary and be able to put into practice what you have learnt so far.

ETIQUETTE...

Spaniards are fairly flexible when it comes to time. This holds true for dates and appointments as well as for invitations.

Salud *does not only mean "health" but also "cheers". However, it is not customary in Spain to wait for everyone to get their drinks before raising glasses. Everyone starts as soon as he or she is served his/her glass.*

Before starting to eat one says ***¡Qué aproveche!*** *or* ***¡Buen provecho!*** *Enjoy your meal!*

Spanish conversation: Una noche con los amigos

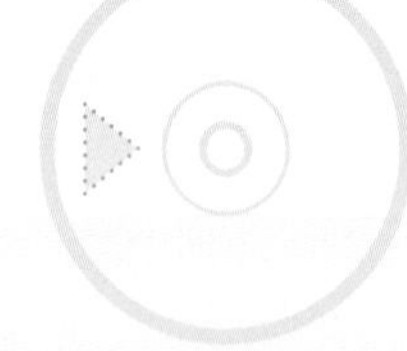

Carlos:	**Karen, acaba de llamar un amigo mío. Nos ha invitado a cenar esta noche en su casa.**
Karen:	**¿Un amigo tuyo?**
Carlos:	**Sí, Mario Ibáñez, es madrileño de pura cepa. Lleva casi un año trabajando en Barcelona. Su madre desea celebrar su visita.**

En casa de los Ibáñez.

Mario:	**Carlos, ¡cuánto tiempo sin verte, hombre! Entrad.**
Carlos:	**¡Caramba, Mario! ¡Qué sorpresa! Mira, te presento a Karen.**
Mario:	**Encantado. Sentaos, ahí viene mi madre.**
Carlos:	**Doña Eva, ¿cómo está?… Los años no han pasado para Ud.**
Eva:	**Gracias. Carlos, tú no has cambiado nada, como siempre tan galante. Karen, bienvenida a casa.**
Karen:	**Muchas gracias, Sra. Ibáñez.**
Eva:	**Hace tanto calor aquí por el horno. Mario, abre la ventana, por favor.**
Mario:	**Mi madre ha preparado las famosas empanadas para que las pruebe Karen.**
Eva:	**Sírvase, Karen. Las tiene que probar calientes. Mario, Carlos, servíos.**
Karen:	**¿Son todas iguales?**
Eva:	**No. Estas son de pollo, estas de carne picada y esas de verdura.**
Karen:	**¡Qué sabrosas!… Carlos, pruébalas. Están buenísimas.**
Mario:	**Carlos, tomemos primero un vino tinto.**
Eva:	**Mario, he olvidado la botella en la cocina. Llévate estos vasos porque no los vamos a necesitar si bebemos vino, por favor.**
Mario:	**¿Y dónde está el vino?**
Eva:	**Abre el armario de la izquierda, allí están las botellas. Karen, la casa suya está cerca, así que visíteme. Generalmente estoy en casa. Pero llámeme por teléfono para mayor seguridad.**
Karen:	**Sí, lo haré con gusto.**
Eva:	**Mario, quedan algunas empanadas en el horno. Apágalo, por favor.**

English conversation: An evening with friends

Carlos:	**Karen, a friend of mine just called. He invited us for dinner at his house tonight.**
Karen:	**A friend of yours?**
Carlos:	**Yes, Mario Ibáñez, he is a true "local of Madrid". He's been working in Barcelona for almost a year now. His mother wants to celebrate his visit.**

At home with the Ibáñez family

Mario:	**Carlos, long time no see, man! Come in.**
Carlos:	**My goodness, Mario! What a surprise! Here, let me introduce you to Karen.**
Mario:	**Nice to meet you. Let's sit down. Here comes my mother.**
Carlos:	**Mrs. Eva, how are you?… The years have not changed you at all.**
Eva:	**Thank you. Carlos, you haven't changed one bit, either, charming as always. Karen, welcome to our home.**
Karen:	**Thank you very much, Mrs. Ibáñez.**
Eva:	**It's the oven that's making it so hot in here. Mario, please open the window.**
Mario:	**My mother made the famous empanadas for Karen to try.**
Eva:	**Help yourself, Karen. You must try them while they are hot. Mario, Carlos, help yourselves.**
Karen:	**Are they all the same?**
Eva:	**No, these are with chicken, those with ground meat and these here with vegetables.**
Karen:	**How tasty!… Carlos, try these. They're excellent.**
Mario:	**Carlos, let's first have a glass of red wine.**
Eva:	**Mario, I forgot the bottle in the kitchen. Take back these glasses, please, we won't need them if we are drinking wine.**
Mario:	**And where is the wine?**
Eva:	**Open the left side of the cupboard, that's where the bottles are. Karen, your house is nearby, do come and visit me. I am normally in. But call me to make sure.**
Karen:	**Yes, I would like to do that.**
Eva:	**Mario, there are a few empanadas left in the oven. Turn it off, please.**

Grammar

Imperative

	tú	Ud.	vosotros	Uds.
comprar	compr*a*	compr*e*	compr*ad*	compr*en*
beber	beb*e*	beb*a*	beb*ed*	beb*an*
escribir	escrib*e*	escrib*a*	escrib*id*	escrib*an*

The **imperative** (command) is used to express a **request** or a **demand**.
The 2nd person singular (tú) hereby corresponds with the 3rd person singular of the present indicative:

¡*Pasa* por mi casa!	Stop by my house!
¡*Lee* el libro!	Read the book!
¡Recibe a mis amigos!	Welcome my friends!

The polite formal forms (Ud., Uds.) are formed with the endings of the present subjunctive.

¡Pas*en* Uds. por mi casa!	Stop by my house!
¡Le*a* el libro!	Read the book!
¡Recib*an* a mis amigos!	Meet my friends!

In the **2nd person plural** (vosotros) the endings -ad (for verbs ending in -ar) and/or -ed and -id (for verbs ending in -er and -ir) are attached to the **stem**.

¡Pas*ad* por mi casa!	Stop by my house!
¡Le*ed* el libro!	Read the book!
¡Recib*id* a mis amigos!	Meet my friends!

Reflexive verbs drop the -d-: sentados ' sent*aos*

Pronouns and the affirmative imperative

The personal pronoun is attached to the imperative form, the indirect object taking precedence before the direct object:

¡Pruébe*selas!*	Try them on!	¡Sírv*ete*!	Help yourself!

Possessive pronouns

singular masc./fem.		
mío/mía	**míos/mías**	mine
tuyo/tuya	**tuyos/tuyas**	yours (informal)
suyo/suya	**suyos/suyas**	his/hers/yours (formal)
plural masc./fem.		
nuestro/nuestra	**nuestros/nuestras**	ours
vuestro/vuestra	**vuestros/vuestras**	yours (informal)
suyo/suya	**suyos/suyas**	theirs/yours (formal)

While the possessive determiners **mi**, **tu**, **su** etc. always precede the noun, the stressed possessive pronouns are used in the following constructions:
un + **noun** + **mío**: **un amigo mío** (**a** friend of **mine**)
ser + **mío**: **la blusa *es mía*** (this blouse **belongs to me**)
el + **mío**: **este abrigo *es el mío*** (this coat is **mine**) ¡noun + **mío**!: **¡Dios mío!** (My God!)

The stressed **possessive pronoun** behaves like an adjective; it agrees with the **noun** in **gender** and **number**.

tan and *tanto*

Tanto, **-a**, **-os**, **-as** **(so much, so many)** precedes the noun and agrees with it in gender and number:

***tanto* calor**	***tantos* hombres**	***tanta* gente**	***tantas* amigas**

Tanto, like **mucho**, can also be used as an adverb in which case it remains **unchanged**:

bebe *tanto*	he drinks so much	**se lamenta *tanto***	he complains so much

Tan **(so, so much)**, like **muy**, precedes adjectives and adverbs:

sois *tan amables*	you are so nice	**toca *tan bien* la guitarra**	he plays the guitar so well

Exercises

Exercise 1

Fill in the verb forms in the affirmative imperative.

	tú	vosotros
1 conducir	....	....
2 recibir	....	....
3 volver	....	....
4 jugar	....	....
5 vender	....	....

Exercise 2

Answer in the imperative using the following example.

¿Puedo ir a casa? Sí, vaya a casa (usted).

1 ¿Puedo fumar? .... (tú)

2 ¿Puedo abrir la ventana? .... (Ud.)

3 ¿Podemos cantar y bailar? .... (vosotros)

4 ¿Cierro la puerta? .... (tú)

5 ¿Hablamos español? .... (Uds.)

6 ¿Compro pan? .... (tú)

7 ¿Puedo conducir yo? .... (Ud.)

8 ¿Podemos acompañar a Pilar? .... (vosotros)

Exercise 3

Rewrite the sentences in the imperative and add the pronouns using the following example: Comprar el vestido. (tú) Cómpralo.

1 Mirar la televisión. (Ud.) ....

2 Preparar la comida. (vosotras) ....

3 Escribir la carta. (tú) ....

4 Arreglar la cama. (tú) ....

5 Comprar el periódico. (Ud.) ....

6 Sacar entradas. (Uds.) ....

Exercise 4

Fill in the appropriate possessive pronoun.

1 Estas gafas son .... (yo)

2 El libro es .... (usted)

3 El coche es .... (vosotros)

4 ¿Es .... (nosotros) esta maleta?

5 Los zapatos marrones son .... (tú).

6 Una hermana .... (él) me va a visitar esta tarde.

7 ¡Hija .... ! ¿Qué has hecho?

Exercise 5

Tan, tanto or tanta?

1 Estoy cansada de .... trabajo.

2 Gracias, sois .... amables.

3 Hay .... gente en la calle que no se puede caminar.

4 Tiene .... dinero que no sabe como gastarlo.

5 Este año ha llovido ..... poco como nunca.

Exercise 6

Which answer is correct?

1 ¿Dónde trabaja?

a En una oficina. **b** Soy médico.

2 ¡Visítame! Podemos salir juntas.

a Sí, me gusta muchísimo. **b** Gracias, con gusto.

3 ¡Qué joven estás!

a Sí. **b** Gracias.

4 Mira, te presento a mi marido.

a Encantado. **b** ¿En qué trabaja?

1 .... **2** .... **3** .... **4** ....

Vocabulary

Below is a list of vocabulary encountered in this chapter.

apagar	*to switch/turn off*
armario *m*	*cupboard*
cambiar	*to change*
carne *f* **picada**	*ground [minced] meat*
celebrar	*to celebrate*
como siempre	*as always*
de pura cepa	*genuine, true, pure*
empanadas *f pl*	*pies with different fillings*
galante	*charming*
horno *m*	*oven*
igual	*the same*
izquierda *f*	*left*
lamentarse	*to complain, lament*
mío	*mine*
para mayor seguridad	*for safety's sake*
recibir	*to meet, greet*
sabroso, -a	*tasty*
seguridad *f*	*safety*
sentarse (-ie-)	*to sit down*
servirse (-i-)	*to help oneself*
suyo, -a	*yours (usted)*
tuyo, -a	*yours*
visita *f*	*visit*

day:29

At the doctor's

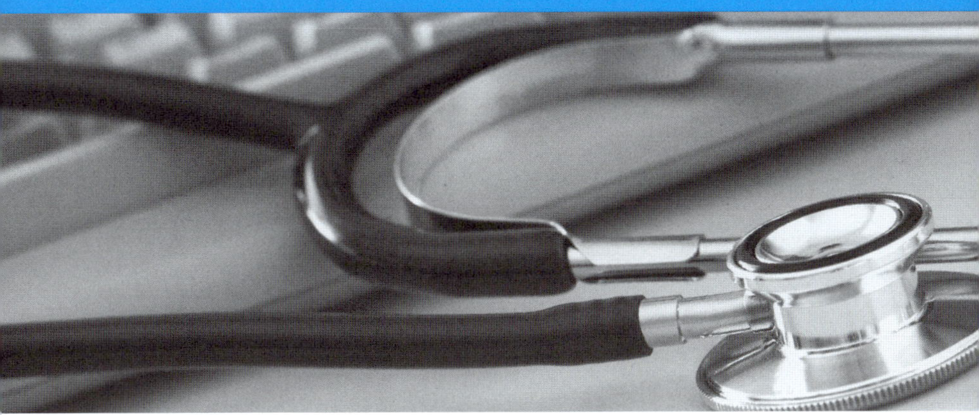

As you near the end of this course, Day 29 takes you to the doctor's and introduces irregular imperative forms. You will learn all the vocabulary you will need for these situations. Don't forget to look at the section on Spanish accents!

MEDICAL ASSISTANCE...

For minor consultations or should you require medical help in Spain, contact the ***médico de medicina general*** *(doctor) or the nearest* ***puesto de socorro*** *(A&E/ER). Should you or someone in your group fall seriously ill, contact your country's Consulate-General or Embassy.*

Spanish pharmacies are open during normal business hours. The address of the nearest emergency pharmacy ***(farmacia de guardia)*** *in the area has to be displayed on the door of all the other pharmacies at all times.*

Spanish conversation: En la consulta

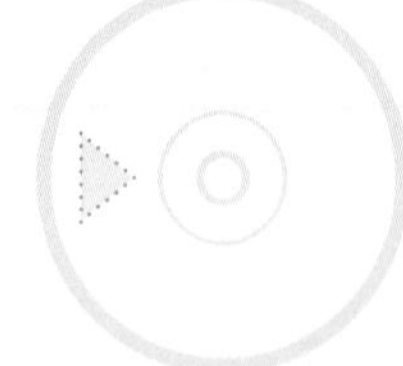

Karen hace una cita por teléfono. Su amiga Paula trabaja en la consulta del Dr. Jiménez.

Karen:	**¿Paula? Soy Karen.**
Paula:	**Hola, bonita. Dime.**
Karen:	**No me siento bien. Desearía pedir hora con el Dr. Jiménez. ¿A qué hora tiene consulta?**
Paula:	**Los jueves todo el día, los viernes sólo por la mañana.**
Karen:	**¿Podría ir hoy?**
Paula:	**Oye, ven ahora mismo.**
Karen:	**Gracias, hasta pronto.**

Karen en la consulta del médico.

Paula:	**Hola, tienes mala cara. Es la primera vez que vienes, ¿verdad?**
Karen:	**Así es. Ten mi volante del seguro.**
Paula:	**Ponlo allí. Espero que ya estés bien para tu despedida. Rellena esta ficha y vete a la sala de espera.**
Doctor:	**Buenos días… entre, por favor. Dígame, ¿qué le pasa?**
Karen:	**No me siento bien. Tengo tos y un poco de fiebre. Me duele la garganta, creo que está hinchada.**
Doctor:	**Siéntese, vamos a ver. ¿Desde cuándo se siente Ud. mal?**
Karen:	**Desde hace dos días.**
Doctor:	**Abra la boca, … saque la lengua, por favor. Diga "Aaaa".**
Karen:	**Aaaa…**
Doctor:	**Respire profundamente y contenga la respiración. Tosa, por favor.**
Karen:	**¿Es algo grave?**
Doctor:	**No, una gripe. Coma cosas ligeras y beba mucho. Debe quedarse unos días en la cama.**
Karen:	**¿Unos días en la cama? Todo va a estar patas arriba en casa.**
Doctor:	**No creo que esté enferma muchos días. Voy a recetarle algunos medicamentos. Tome una pastilla por la mañana y otra por la tarde antes de las comidas. Haga también una inhalación antes de acostarse. Vaya a la farmacia con esta receta. Tenga.**
Paula:	**Bonita, pronto te sentirás mejor y para tu despedida ya estarás sana. Hazme el favor de alegrar esa cara. ¡Qué te mejores!**

English conversation: At the doctor's

Karen makes an appointment over the phone. Her friend Paula works at Dr. Jiménez' practise (office).

Karen: **Paula? This is Karen.**
Paula: **Hello, sweetie. What's up?**
Karen: **I'm not feeling well. I'd like to make an appointment with Dr. Jiménez. When are his consulting hours?**
Paula: **Thursdays all day and Fridays only in the morning.**
Karen: **Could I come today?**
Paula: **OK, come right away.**
Karen: **Thank you, see you soon.**

Karen at the doctor's practise.

Paula: **Hello, you do look bad. This is the first time you have been here, isn't it?**
Karen: **Yes, it is. Here's my insurance card.**
Paula: **Put it there. I hope you will be fine by the time you leave. Fill out this form and go into the waiting room.**
Doctor: **Good morning, … please come in. Tell me what's the matter.**
Karen: **I don't feel well. I have a cough and I've got a slight temperature. My throat hurts, and I think it is swollen.**
Doctor: **Have a seat, let's see. Since when have you been feeling sick?**
Karen: **For two days now.**
Doctor: **Open your mouth, … stick out your tongue, please. Say "Aaah".**
Karen: **Aaah…**
Doctor: **Take a deep breath and hold it in. Cough, please.**
Karen: **Is it something serious?**
Doctor: **No, the flu. Eat only light meals and drink a lot. Stay in bed for a few days.**
Karen: **A few days in bed? The whole house will be turned upside down.**
Doctor: **I don't think that you will be ill for long. I'll write you a prescription for some medication. Take one tablet in the morning and one at night before your meals. Inhale before you go to bed. Take this prescription and go to the pharmacy. Here you are.**
Paula: **Well, sweetie, you'll be better soon and all fit again by the time you leave. Come on, cheer up and smile. Get well soon!**

Grammar

Irregular imperative forms

	tú	Ud.	vosotros	Uds.
decir	di	diga	decid	digan
hacer	haz	haga	haced	hagan
ir	ve	vaya	id	vayan
poner	pon	ponga	poned	pongan
salir	sal	salga	salid	salgan
ser	sé	sea	sed	sean
tener	ten	tenga	tened	tengan
venir	ven	venga	venid	vengan

In the affirmative imperative, these verbs have their own **you-form** *(inform.)*.

Alternatives to the imperative	
¿puede…?	
¿Puedes abrir la ventana?	Can you open the window?
¿por qué no…?	
¿Por qué no abres la ventana?	Why don't you open the window?

vamos + a + **infinitive**:

Vamos a cenar.	Let's go eat.

This alternative uses the 1st person plural.
a + **infinitive**:

¡A comer!	Come and eat!

Verbs

ir - venir

Ir does not only mean **to go/to drive**, but also to come, from the perspective away from the speaker.
Venir means **to come** in the direction of the speaker:

¿Vienes?	Are you coming? (towards the speaker)
Sí, voy.	Yes, I am coming. (away from the speaker)

Accents are important!

Accents in Spanish distinguish a word's meaning when the spelling is similar.

Pagu*é* en euros	I **paid** in euros.
Quiere que pagu*e* en euros	He wants me to **pay** in euros.
¿Quieres que te *dé* un consejo?	Do you want me to **give** you advice?
Madrid es la capital *de* España	Madrid is the capital **of** Spain.
¿Eres *tú*?	Is that **you**?
Es *tu* bolso.	It is **your** bag.

Exercises

Exercise 1

Fill in the affirmative imperative forms.

	Tú	Ud.	Vosotros	Uds.
1 hablar	....	....	....	....
2 repetir	....	....	....	....
3 empezar	....	....	....	....
4 hacer	....	....	....	....
5 pasar	....	....	....	....
6 decir	....	....	....	....

Exercise 2

Put the verbs into the imperative in the form requested in brackets.

1 (Tener) .... mucho ojo al salir de la estación. (vosotros)

2 (Ser) .... bueno y (hacer) .... lo que te digan. (tú)

3 (Ir) .... con nosotros. (Uds.)

4 (Decir) .... lo que saben. (Uds.)

5 (Pasar) .... por la carnicería y (comprar) .... carne picada. (tú)

6 (Comprobar) .... la presión de los neumáticos. (Ud.)

Exercise 3

Give the infinitive of each verb below.

1 escriba ....

2 tenga ....

3 diga ....

4 rellene ....

5 trabaje ....

6 pregunte ....

7 mira ....

Exercise 4

Ir, venir or llegar? Insert the correct verb form in the sentences below.

1. ¿Cuándo .... el tren?

2. El mes que .... vamos de vacaciones.

3. Hoy no puedo .... de compras.

4. Mañana .... a visitar a unos amigos.

5. ¿... (vosotros) a nuestra fiesta el **próximo sábado? Sí,** .... **(nosotros).**

6. La Sra. García .... todos los días a la **oficina.**

7. ¿Ha .... (él) tarde hoy?

8. Mi madre ha .... de Alemania.

9. Mi hermano ha .... a México.

10. ¿Puedo .... ahora mismo?

Exercise 5

Translate the following sentences into Spanish.

1 I have a headache. ....

2 My throat hurts. ....

3 I think I have a temperature. ....

4 I don't feel well. ....

5 I have a cough. ....

6 Get better soon! ....

Vocabulary

Below is a list of vocabulary encountered in this chapter.

alegrar	*to cheer up*
bonita *f*	*(here:) sweetie*
cabeza *f*	*head*
consulta *f*	*consulting hours*
contener (-g-)	*to hold*
despedida *f*	*farewell*
doler (-ue-)	*to hurt*
enfermo, -a	*sick, ill*
farmacia *f*	*pharmacy*
ficha *f*	*form*
fiebre *f*	*fever*
garganta *f*	*throat*
grave	*serious*
gripe *f*	*flu, cold*
hinchado, -a	*swollen*
inhalación *f*	*inhalation*
lengua *f*	*tongue*
ligero, -a	*light*
medicamento *m*	*medication*
médico *m*	*GP/ doctor*
mejorarse	*to get well*
operación *f*	*operation*
pastilla *f*	*tablet, pill*
pedir hora	*to make an appointment*
preferir (-ie-)	*to prefer*
profundamente	*deep, profound*
¡Qué te mejores!	*Get well soon!*
receta *f*	*prescription*
recetar	*to prescribe*
recomendar (-ie-)	*to recommend*
rellenar	*to fill out*
respiración *f*	*breathing*
respirar	*to breathe*
sacar	*(here:) to stick out*
sala *f* **de espera**	*waiting room*
sano, -a	*healthy*
tener tos	*to have a cough*
todo está patas arriba	*everything is upside down*
tos *f*	*cough*
toser	*to cough*
volante *m* **del seguro**	*insurance card*

day:30

Goodbye

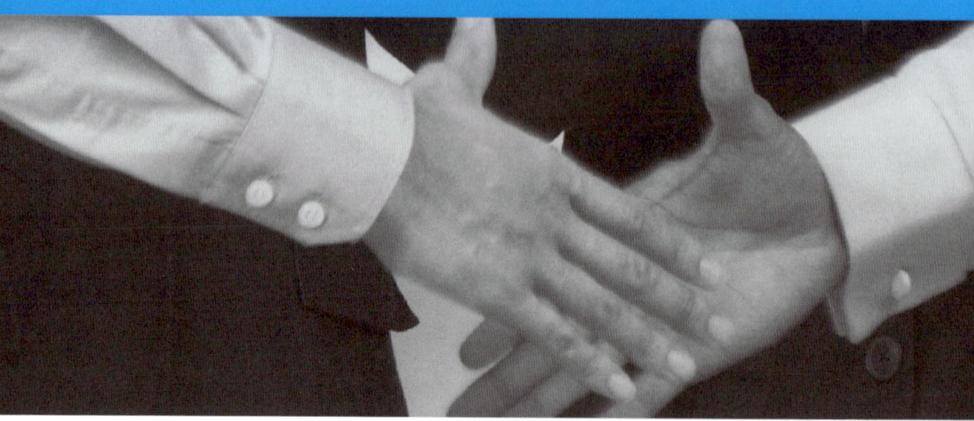

Congratulations, you've reached the final chapter of this course. Day 30 marks the end of your trip to Spain. By now, you should be quite confident understanding, speaking, and writing Spanish in a variety of situations. You should have acquired a comprehensive vocabulary, and be comfortable with Spanish grammar. Well done!

UN BESO...

*A kiss (**un beso**) on either cheek is customary between men and women and between women. A simple handshake will do for more distant relations. The standard term for saying farewell is **adiós** or **chao**.*

Spanish conversation: La despedida

Toda la familia García y Carlos acompañan a Karen al aeropuerto que está en las afueras de Madrid.

Carlos:	**Karen, no olvides facturar el equipaje.**
Karen:	**No te preocupes, estamos ya delante de los mostradores de Iberia.**
Empleada:	**¿Cuál es su maleta?**
Karen:	**La que está entre la maleta negra y la gris.**
Empleada:	**¿Es esto todo su equipaje?**
Karen:	**Sí, excepto este bolso que llevaré como equipaje de mano.**
Empleada:	**No lo ponga en la báscula, por favor.**
Karen:	**¿Tengo que pagar exceso de peso?**
Empleada:	**Pasa los 20 kilos, pero no se preocupe. Puerta n.º 9A. Al lado del control de pasaportes.**
Karen:	**¡Este año con vosotros ha sido fantástico!**
Carmen:	**El tiempo ha pasado rapidísimo.**
Pedro:	**Vamos a echarte de menos.**
Karen:	**No os pongáis tristes. Sois los mejores amigos que tengo, os agradezco lo que habéis hecho por mí.**
Carlos:	**Las despedidas siempre son tristes…**
Karen:	(A Lucía) **No olvides escribirme.**
Lucía:	**Descuida, te escribiré y te mandaré una foto de Nicolás que puedes colocar encima de tu escritorio.**
Karen:	**Ahora tengo que marcharme, están llamando para mi vuelo… No me mires tan triste, Carmen.**
Carmen:	**Ven para que te abrace. ¡Muchos saludos a tu madre!**
Karen:	**Adiós, Pedro… Adiós, Lucía… Chao, David… Adiós, Carlos.**
Carlos:	**Adiós, Karen. ¡Buen viaje!**
Carmen:	**¡No te olvides de nosotros! !Qué te vaya bien!**

English conversation: Farewell

The whole García family and Carlos accompany Karen to the airport, which is located outside of Madrid.

Carlos:	**Karen, don't forget to check in your luggage.**
Karen:	**Don't worry, we're already at the Iberia counters.**
Employee:	**Which one is your suitcase?**
Karen:	**The one between the black and the grey suitcases.**
Employee:	**Is that all your luggage?**
Karen:	**Yes, except this bag, which I'll take as hand luggage.**
Employee:	**Please don't put it on the scales.**
Karen:	**Do I have to pay excess baggage?**
Employee:	**It does exceed the 20 kilograms, but don't worry. Gate number 9A. Next to passport control.**
Karen:	**This year with you guys was fantastic!**
Carmen:	**The time just flew by.**
Pedro:	**We'll miss you.**
Karen:	**Don't be sad. You guys are the best friends I have, and I'm grateful for everything you did for me.**
Carlos:	**Farewells are always sad…**
Karen:	**(to Lucía:) Don't forget to write to me.**
Lucía:	**Don't worry, I'll write to you and I'll send you a picture of Nicolás to put on your desk.**
Karen:	**I have to go now, they've called my flight… Don't look at me so sadly, Carmen.**
Carmen:	**Come here so that I can hug you. Best wishes to your mother!**
Karen:	**Bye, Pedro… Bye, Lucía… Bye, David… Bye Carlos.**
Carlos:	**Bye Karen. Have a safe trip!**
Carmen:	**Don't forget us! All the best!**

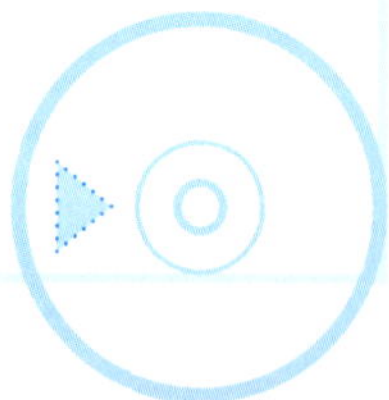

Grammar

Imperative (negative)

	tú	Ud.	vosotros	Uds.
compr*ar*	*no* compr*es*	compr*e*	compr*éis*	compr*en*
beb*er*	*no* beb*as*	beb*a*	beb*áis*	beb*an*
escrib*ir*	*no* escrib*as*	escrib*a*	escrib*áis*	escrib*an*

The negative imperative is formed from the subjunctive.

Position of pronouns with the negative imperative

Pronouns are positioned **between** no and the verb form.

The **indirect object precedes the direct object**:

¡*No se lo* compres!	Don't buy it for him!
¡*No os* lavéis!	Don't wash yourselves!

Relative pronouns

la que…	the one *(female)* who/which…
el que…	the one *(male)* who/which…
las que…	the ones *(female)* who/which…
los que…	the ones *(male)* who/which…
lo que…	that, which…

El/la/los/las + que represent **people and objects**. These forms are mainly used **after prepositions**:

el chico *con el que* te he visto	the boy with whom I saw you
la casa *de la que* ha salido	the house from which he came out

lo que is neutral:

Esto es *lo que* digo.	That is what I say.

If there is no preposition que follows:

Sois los mejores amigos *que* tengo.	You are the best friends I have.
La mesa *que* está en la cocina…	The table that is in the kitchen…

Defining locations

en las afueras de Madrid	**outside of** Madrid
delante de nuestra casa	**in front** of our house
detrás del árbol	**behind** the tree
entre las maletas	**between** the suitcases
en la mesa/*en* la maleta	**on** the table/**in** the suitcase
al lado de la mesa	**next** to the table
encima del escritorio	**on (top of)** the desk
sobre la mesa	**on** the table
debajo del puente	**under** the bridge
a la derecha de la iglesia	**to the right** of the church
a la izquierda de la cama	**to the left** of the bed

Exercises

Exercise 1

Put the verbs into the negative.

1 Cerrad ....

2 Ven ....

3 Haced ....

4 Recibidle ....

5 Sube ....

6 Vayan ....

7 Diga ....

8 Oigan ....

9 Pon ....

10 Piénsalo ....

Exercise 2

Rewrite the sentences following the example below.

e.g. **¿Vamos de campamento? No, no vayáis de campamento.**

1 ¿Toco la guitarra? No, ...

2 ¿Jugamos al fútbol? No, ...

3 ¿Compramos zumo de naranja? No, ...

4 ¿Pongo música? No, ...

5 ¿Salimos esta noche? No, ...

Exercise 3

Que or lo que? Fill in the correct form.

1 No quiero que hables de .... pasó el lunes.

2 Los niños comen un pastel .... está muy rico.

3 La cosa .... me contaste es muy importante.

4 Cuéntame todo .... has visto.

5 Las galletas .... he comprado están buenísimas.

6 ¿Viven aún en la casa .... está al otro lado de la calle?

Exercise 4

What are the opposites?

1 poco ....

2 delante ....

3 bien ....

4 lejos ....

5 también ....

6 siempre ....

7 sucio ....

8 encima ....

9 a la derecha ....

10 pequeño ....

Vocabulary

Below is a list of vocabulary encountered in this chapter.

abrazar	*to embrace, hug*
agradecer	*to be grateful*
alguna cosa a	*to somebody*
alguien	*for something*
al lado de	*next to*
báscula *f*	*scales*
colocar	*to put*
¿Cuál?	*Which one?*
debajo de	*under*
delante de	*in front of*
descuida	*not to worry*
despedida *f*	*departure; farewell*
detrás de	*behind*
echar a alguien	*to miss someone*
de menos	
en las afueras de	*outside of*
encima de	*on*
entonces	*then*
equipaje *m*	*hand luggage/*
de mano	*carry-on*
escritorio *m*	*desk*
excepto	*except, with the exception*
exceso *m*	*excess weight,*
de peso	*excess baggage*
facturar	*(here:) to check in*
foto *f*	*photo*
hacerse (-g-)	*to become*
inquietarse	*to worry, be concerned*
	about
marcharse	*to leave*
mostrador *m*	*counter*
mostrar	*to show*
pared *f*	*wall*
pasar	*to exceed*
ponerse triste	*to become sad*
preocuparse	*to worry*
puente *m*	*bridge*
¡Qué te vaya bien!	*All the best!*
silla *f*	*chair*
sobre	*on*
sofá *m*	*sofa*
vuelo *m*	*flight*

Key to exercises

Day 1

Exercise 1: 1. viaja 2. toma 3. hablan 4. estudia 5. hablamos 6. entras 7. toman
Exercise 2: 1. eres 2. es 3. es 4. es 5. sois 6. son 7. es
Exercise 3: 1. no viaja 2. no toma 3. no hablan 4. no estudia 5. no hablamos 6. no entras 7. no toman
Exercise 4: Es de Barcelona. Es español. Soy de Inglaterra. ¿Viaja Ud. como turista? ¿Viaja Ud. a España? ¿Toma Ud. leche y azúcar? No, sólo leche, gracias. Soy Paul. Soy profesor y estudio español. ¡Qué interesante!

Day 2

Exercise 1: 1. está 2. están 3. estáis 4. están 5. está 6. está
Exercise 2: 1. tomo el café 2. el avión es 3. el pasajero es 4. el bolso es 5. las maletas pesan 6. ¿Es Ud. -? 7. es un país 8. la señorita saluda
Exercise 3: los pasaportes; unas azafatas; los equipajes; unos pasajeros; las maletas; unas tarjetas; las aduanas; unos bolsos; los diccionarios; unos libros
Exercise 4: 1. sucias 2. grandes 3. simpáticos 4. interesante 5. blanca 6. amable
Exercise 5: una maleta pesada; un café dulce; un pasajero simpático; unos aviones grandes; un aduanero rubio.

Day 3

Exercise 1: 1. voy 2. vamos 3. va 4. van 5. vamos
Exercise 2: es; es ; es; es; está; es; es; están; son
Exercise 3: 1. son, somos 2. eres, soy 3. está, está
Exercise 4: mucha gente; la lengua francesa; los turistas franceses; tanto ruido; hoteles buenos; la última semana; pocas azafatas; tres pasajeros
Exercise 5: en autobús; a Granada; en tren; en barco; en avión; a Madrid
Exercise 6: Karen toma el equipaje y va al centro. Son 25 euros. Karen paga. En el Paseo de la Castellana n.º 6 baja. Hay mucha gente en el centro. Aquí está la dirección. ¿Dónde está la casa?

Day 4

Exercise 1: 1. habláis, habla, hablas, hablan 2. escribís, escribe, escribes, escriben 3. sois, es, eres, son 4. bailáis, baila, bailas, bailan 5. abrís, abre, abres, abren

Exercise 2: 1. se habla 2. se baila 3. se abre 4. se toma
Exercise 3: 1. tu 2. nuestros 3. mi 4. su 5. vuestros 6. vuestra, nuestro 7. sus 8. nuestros
Exercise 4: 1. más… que 2. más… que 3. más… que 4. las mejores 5. el… más
Exercise 5: catorce, veintinueve, quince, nueve, uno, cuatro, veinticinco, veintiuno, diecinueve, treinta
Exercise 6: 1. hija 2. marido 3. nieta 4. hijos 5. suegra 6. cuñada

Day 5

Exercise 1: 1. es or está 2. hay 3. hay 4. está 5. está 6. tiene 7. están 8. es 9. tiene 10. está 11. está 12. hay
Exercise 2: 1. hay 2. está 3. hay 4. está 5. hay 6. está 7. está 8. hay 9. está 10. hay
Exercise 3: 1. una 2. al 3. los 4. al, al 5. el, un 6. el del 7. unas 8. unos, del
Exercise 4: These are wrong: 1.a, 2.b, 3.a, 4.b, 5.a, 6.b
Exercise 5: 1. no 2. sí 3. no 4. sí 5. no 6. sí 7. no
Exercise 6: 1. toman 2. coméis 3. bebes 4. vivimos 5. tengo 6. pasa 7. abre 8. habla

Day 6

Exercise 1: 1. no 2. sí 3. no 4. no 5. no 6. no 7. sí 8. no 9. sí 10. sí
Exercise 2: 1. te… me 2. se 3. nos 4. se 5. os 6. te 7. se
Exercise 3: 1. todo el 2. todas las 3. todas las 4. todos los 5. todas las 6. toda la 7. todos los 8. todo el
Exercise 4: a) la una y media b) las cinco y cuarto de la tarde c) las cinco menos cuarto d) las siete en punto e) la una f) las doce menos cinco g) las diez y cinco h) la una menos veinticinco i) las tres y veinte de la tarde j) las diez de la noche
Exercise 5: 1. puedo 2. estoy 3. voy 4. suelo 5. tengo 6. me quedo 7. vengo 8. soy 9. como 10. arreglo
Exercise 6: ¿Puede ir a la agencia de viajes, por favor? – Sí, ¿puede decirme dónde está? – Tiene que ir hasta la esquina, cruza la calle y toma el paseo a la derecha. Y está allí enfrente. – Muy bien, gracias por su explicación.

Day 7

Exercise 1: 1. sabe 2. sé 3. sabéis 4. saben 5. sabe 6. sabes 7. saber 8. sabemos
Exercise 2: 1.a) 2.a) 3.c) 4.a) 5.c)
Exercise 3: 1. el 2. el 3. la 4. los 5. la 6. la 7. el 8. el 9. el 10. el
Exercise 4: 1. como, coméis, comes, comemos; 2. estoy, estáis, estás, estamos; 3. hago, hacéis, haces, hacemos; 4. voy, vais, vas, vamos; 5. soy, sois, eres, somos; 6. sé, sabéis, sabes, sabemos; 7. vengo, venís, vienes, venimos; 8. tengo, tenéis, tienes, tenemos; 9. preparo, preparáis,

preparas, preparamos; 10. abro, abrís, abres, abrimos

Exercise 5: hago, voy, alquilo, disfruto, me pongo, tengo, viene, bailan, cantan, son

Exercise 6: Buenos días, señora García. Vengo de Valencia. Estoy un poco cansado. Mis maletas son pesadas. ¿ Está su marido en casa? Muchas gracias por el café. ¿Qué, Ud. sabe cocinar paella? ¿A qué hora cenamos? ¿A las 10 de la noche? Voy un poco de paseo.

Day 8

Exercise 1: 1. queremos, quiere, quieres, quieren 2. almorzamos, almuerza, almuerzas, almuerzan 3. sentimos, siente, sientes, sienten 4. compramos, compra, compras, compran 5. empezamos, empieza, empiezas, empiezan 6. solemos, suele, sueles, suelen

Exercise 2: 1. 2.sg. 2. 3.pl. 3. 3.sg. 4. 1.sg. 5. 1.pl. 6. 3.sg. 7. 2.pl. 8. 2.sg. 9. 3.sg. 10. 3.pl.

Exercise 3: 1. Yo la abro. 2. Yo lo hago. 3. Yo las como. 4. Yo los escribo. 5. Yo os quiero. 6. Yo la compro. 7. Yo la pongo. 8. Yo los tomo.

Exercise 4: 1. lo 2. la 3. le 4. (saludar)la 5. preguntar(les) 6. lo 7. las 8. (poner) le 9. las 10. le

Exercise 5: 1. b 2. c. 3. a. 4. b.

Exercise 6: Medio kilo de tomates, por favor, dos litros de leche, una barra de pan, un cuarto de kilo de zanahorias, media docena de huevos, otra botella de leche y dos tarros de mermelada.

Day 9

Exercise 1: 1. No voy a hacerlo ahora. 2. Vas a tocar la guitarra. 3. Van a ir en coche a Madrid. 4. No lo vamos a escribir. 5. Vas a ir a la calle. 6. Vas a tener que llamarle. 7. Pilar no va a estudiar español. 8. No voy a encontrar el libro. 9. Vais a empezar temprano.

Exercise 2: 1. Para ir a Toledo. 2. Para comprar un billete. 3. Para ir al centro. 4. Para mañana. 5. Para Nicolás. 6. Para poder hablar español. 7. Para ir de paseo.

Exercise 3: 1. Dos mil trescientos cincuenta y tres. (2.353) 2. Diez mil doscientos siete. (10.207) 3. Ochocientos ocho. (808) 4. Mil quince. (1.015) 5. Treinta mil quinientos setenta y cinco. (30.575)

Exercise 4: 1. Alfonso trece, rey de España 2. Siempre llego el primero 3. Hoy es el tercer día de la semana 4. Quiero medio litro de leche 5. Juan Carlos primero de Borbón 6. Subimos a la décima planta 7. Compro un cuarto de kilo de tomates 8. Estamos en el séptimo mes del año

Exercise 5: 1. de 2. para/de 3. en 4. para 5. a 6. al 7. a 8. de 9. en 10. en

Day 10

Exercise 1: 1. parecen 2. puede 3. conozco 4. parece 5. quieres 6. trabajar 7. conoces

Exercise 2: 1. a mí 2. a nosotros 3. a ellos/ellas/Uds. 4. a vosotros 5. a ellas 6. a ellos/ellas/Uds. 7. a ti

Exercise 3: 1.usted 2. mí 3. nosotros 4. ellas 5. ti 6. ustedes

Exercise 4: 1. Quisiera un trozo de queso, por favor. Quisiera visitar la parte antigua de la ciudad. Quisiera probarlo. ¿Puedo ir? Quisiera estudiar español. Puedo hablar español.
Exercise 5: 1. por 2. para 3. por 4. para 5. para 6. para 7. por… para
Exercise 6: Inma es enfermera y Paco estudia informática. Los dos son buenos amigos. Se conocen bien. Se encuentran a menudo para ir al cine o al teatro. Inma trabaja cerca de la calle donde vive Paco. Por las tardes suelen ir de paseo. Estudian inglés porque quieren ir a Estados Unidos.

Day 11

Exercise 1: 1. c) 2. a) 3. b) 4. b) 5. a) 6. b)
Exercise 2: 1. a 2. – 3. – 4. a 5. a 6. – 7. – 8. a 9. a
Exercise 3: A nosotros los españoles nos gusta la vida. Nos gustan las fiestas y nos gusta el jerez. Nosotros los españoles somos así. ¿Conoce Ud. a los españoles?
Exercise 4: 1. conozco 2. hacéis 3. vamos 4. pongo 5. parece 6. salgo 7. están 8. tienen 9. doy 10. sé
Exercise 5: 1. ¿Puede esperar un poco? Sí, no hay ningún problema. 2. ¿De parte de quién? De Carlos Martini. 3. ¿Quién habla? Soy yo. 4. Hola, ¿cómo estás? Muy bien, gracias. 5. ¿A qué hora? A las 7.00 en punto. 6. ¿Te parece bien? Sí, está bien. 7. ¿Quieres salir conmigo? Sí, con gusto. 8. ¿Conoces el Café Triana? Sí, lo conozco.
Exercise 6: das, damos, dan; sales, salimos, salen; vas, vamos, van; pareces, parecemos, parecen; conoces, conocemos, conocen; duermes, dormimos, duermen; quieres, queremos, quieren; eres, somos, son

Day 12

Exercise 1: comido, querido, hablado, caminado, venido, trabajado, dormido, levantado, conocido, visitado
Exercise 2: 1. aburrido 2. afeitado 3. arregladas 4. prohibido 5. impresionada 6. cantadas
Exercise 3: 1. has hablado 2. no he tenido 3. has estado 4. has comprado 5. habéis arreglado 6. hemos desayunado
Exercise 4: En abril voy a estudiar español e inglés. Para ello voy a ir primero a España y luego a Alemania. He estudiado ya una vez estas lenguas y también el francés pero quiero mejorarlas. España e Alemania son países interesantes e importantes.
Exercise 5: 1. ¡Qué sed tengo! 2. ¡Qué rico es! 3. ¡Qué guapa es esta chica! 4. ¡Qué enferma está esta mujer! 5. ¡Qué impresionante es esta iglesia! 6. ¡Qué interesante es esta película! 7. ¡Qué caro está el jamón hoy! 8. ¡Qué hambre tengo!
Exercise 6: 1. tiene 2. hay 3. has 4. habéis 5. tiene 6. han 7. hay 8. tengo

Day 13

Exercise 1: 1. no 2. no 3. sí 4. no 5. sí 6. no 7. no 8. sí
Exercise 2: 1. veo, veis, ves, vemos; 2. pido, pedís, pides, pedimos; 3. salgo, salís, sales, sali-

mos; 4. sirvo, servís, sirves, servimos

Exercise 3: 1. algo 2. ningún 3. nada 4. algunos 5. algún 6. ninguna 7. alguien

Exercise 4: 1. No. 2. – 3. – 4. No. 5. No. 6. No.

Exercise 5: 1. bueno 2. bien 3. mala 4. mal

Day 14

Exercise 1: sido, visto, puesto, vuelto, ido, dado, hecho, escrito

Exercise 2: 1. inmediatamente 2. difícilmente 3. generalmente 4. rápidamente 5. normalmente 6. absolutamente

Exercise 3: 1. Sí, exactamente. 2. directamente. 3. difícilmente. 4. amablemente. 5. tranquilamente. 6. generalmente. 7. automáticamente. 8. cómodamente.

Exercise 4:

Fito es un perrito. Normalmente es un animalito pacífico. Tiene las patitas húmedas. Karen generalmente no tiene miedo a los perros. Fito saluda alegremente a la gente.

Exercise 5: 1. trabajar 2. levantado 3. practicar 4. comprar 5. vuelto

Exercise 6: 1. alegre 2. pequeño 3. poco 4. bueno 5. difícil 6. caliente 7. nuevos 8. abierta

Day 15

Exercise 1: 1. comiendo 2. tomando 3. cantando 4. esperando 5. haciendo

Exercise 2: 1. siguen viviendo 2. sigo esperando 3. siguen vendiendo 4. sigue durmiendo. 5. seguimos acostándonos

Exercise 3: 1. Entra en el bar pidiendo cerveza. 2. Marca los números repitiéndolos. 3. Vuelve a buscar el bolso no pudiendo encontrarlo. 4. Sale de la escuela corriendo. 5. Saluda haciendo una señal con la mano.

Exercise 4: 1. Estoy esperando 2. Estoy bailando 3. Estoy preguntando 4. Estoy yendo 5. Estoy llegando

Exercise 5: 1. charlar 2. llegado 3. esperando 4. repitiendo 5. llamar

Day 16

Exercise 1: 1. Iríamos de compras. 2. Acompañaríamos a los abuelos. 3. Comeríamos un helado. 4. Trabajaríamos poco. 5. Saldríamos al parque. 6. Subiríamos al tercer piso. 7. Nos ducharíamos.

Exercise 2: 1. podría 2. dirías 3. querríais 4. jugarían 5. irías 6. vendría 7. viviría

Exercise 3: 1. lo 2. la 3. lo 4. la 5. le, ella 6. te 7. las

Exercise 4: 1. se los 2. se lo 3. se lo 4. se las 5. se los 6. se las

Exercise 5: ¿Qué desea? Un vestido./ ¿Qué color desea? Algo en rojo./ ¿De qué material? No sé, de algodón o seda./ ¿Para quién es? Para mí./ ¿Qué talla tiene? La 44./ ¿Le gusta? Sí, me gusta mucho./ ¿Cómo le queda? Me resulta un poco estrecho./ ¿Se lo lleva? Sí, me lo llevo.

Exercise 6: Esta chica no está nunca en casa. Siempre está de viaje. Esta semana la he encontrado en Valencia y ahora está de nuevo en Madrid. Vive en esta calle grande que está al lado de esta iglesia famosa. No sé el nombre de esta iglesia que está en el centro.

Day 17

Exercise 1: 1. compré compraste comprarías compraríais 2. leí leiste leerías leeríais 3. canté cantaste cantarías cantaríais 4. abrí abriste abrirías abriríais 5. viví viviste vivirías viviríais 6. perdí perdiste perderías perderíais

Exercise 2: 1. visité 2. llamé 3. abrió 4. dejó, ofreció 5. tomamos 6. gustó 7. salí 8. ví 9. tomé, volví

Exercise 3: 1. de la 2. del 3. de la 4. de, de 5. del

Exercise 4: 1. Al salir de casa me quedé sin llaves. 2. Al ver esta película, nos reímos a carcajadas. 3. Al leer el periódico me puse triste.

Exercise 5: 1. Sin conocerlas no las voy a acompañar. 2. Sin ser muy listo sabe mucho. 3. Sin tener mucho dinero viajo mucho. 4. Sin ver a la chica no abro la puerta.

Day 18

Exercise 1: Ayer hice un viaje en tren. Me levanté muy temprano, me duché y me vestí. Luego tomé una tostada con café. Después cogí mi bocadillo para el almuerzo y lo metí en la mochila. Entonces salí de casa. Mi madre me llevó a la estación de autobuses y allí esperé media hora en vano. Entonces hice autostop. Tuve que esperar otros diez minutos y llegué a la estación justamente un minuto antes de de que saliera el tren. Lo cogí y ¡todo salió a pedir de boca!

Exercise 2: 1. No quiero ni salir. 2. No tengo tiempo ni para dar un paseo. 3. No puedo ni hablar.

Exercise 3: Nos encontramos ayer entre las siete u ocho de la tarde en un café. Tomamos un helado, uno o dos zumos y unas tapas. Nos sirvió un chico u hombre andaluz entre 18 o veinte años. A esto de las diez u once regresamos a casa.

Exercise 4: 1. hemos trabajado, estamos 2. voy 3. estuvimos 4. hicisteis 5. has comprado 6. queremos

Exercise 5: 1. No he entrado ni en la iglesia ni en la catedral. 2. No he visitado ni a los abuelos ni a los tíos. 3. No he comido ni huevos ni patatas. 4. No he comprado ni zumo ni galletas. 5. No he leído ni el libro ni el periódico. 6. No he ido ni de viaje ni de paseo. 7. No he visto ni como anda ni como baila. 8. No he oído ni a los perros ni a los ladrones.

Day 19

Exercise 1: El año pasado mis padres y yo hicimos un viaje a Madrid. Ellos no supieron nunca por qué no nos fuimos a Barcelona. Fue porque yo estuve antes en Madrid y esta ciudad me gustó mucho. Allí conocí la amabilidad de muchos. También mis padres se sintieron de maravilla cuando llegaron allí y me lo dijeron muchas veces.

Exercise 2: 1. durmió 2. supieron 3. hicieron 4. sintieron 5. quisimos, pudimos 6. fui 7. siguió

Exercise 3: 1. fuiste, fuimos, fueron 2. sentiste, sentimos, sintieron 3. te duchaste, nos duchamos, se ducharon 4. te afeitaste, nos afeitamos, se afeitaron 5. pusiste, pusimos, pusieron 6. dijiste, dijimos, dijeron

Exercise 4: Debe de haber un restaurante por aquí. El año pasado estuve aquí con unos amigos. El restaurante debe de estar abierto.

Exercise 5: 1. buen tiempo 2. gran alegría 3. mal amigo 4. cien kilómetros 5. primer mes 6. ningún hombre 7. algún hotel 8. mala noticia

Exercise 6: sentirse de maravilla; dormir como un tronco; hay que tener mucho ojo; reirse a carcajadas; quedarse con la boca abierta; descansar a pierna suelta; salir a pedir de boca; estar hecho polvo

Day 20

Exercise 1: 1. ponías, poníais, poníamos 2. saludabas, saludabais, saludábamos 3. te adelantabas, os adelantabais, nos adelantábamos 4. veías, veíais, veíamos 5. sabías, sabíais, sabíamos 6. ibas, ibais, íbamos 7. estabas, estabais, estábamos 8. eras, erais, éramos

Exercise 2: 1. iba 2. daba 3. mirábamos 4. eras, tocabas 5. no solíais

Exercise 3: 1. No puedo acompañarte hoy. ¡Qué pena! 2. Se sentó en nuestra mesa sin preguntar. ¡Qué cara! 3. No nos pasó nada en el accidente. ¡Gracias a Dios! 4. Los tomates están en oferta. ¿De verdad? 5. He olvidado el bolso en el metro. Lo siento. 6. Ha habido un fuerte huracán en Florida. ¡Qué horror!

Exercise 4: 1. ¿Qué es de tu tesis? 2. ¿Qué es de tus padres? 3. ¿Qué es de tu coche? 4. ¿Qué es de tu madre?

Day 21

Exercise 1: 1. comíamos, tomamos 2. cenaban, veían 3. cocinaba, arreglaba 4. fumaba 5. llegué, estaba 6. llegó, esperaba 7. se iban, se fueron 8. hacía, hizo

Exercise 2: 1. la 2. les/los 3. los 4. le/lo 5. lo

Exercise 3: 1. Este coche lo compró hace dos años. 2. ¡Qué hambre tenemos! 3. Preguntaremos a María si nos hace una Paella. 4. Este libro lo debes comprar de todos modos.

Exercise 4: A mí me gusta jugar al fútbol, pero a Juanita le gusta el alpinismo. A mí me gustan los churros, pero a mi madre le gustan más los pasteles. A mí me gusta la música clásica, pero a mi hermano le gusta el folklore.

Exercise 5: No me gusta mucho trabajar en esa oficina, porque pasan muchos coches y mucha gente por allí, el aire está muy sucio. Además tengo que escribir mucho. Antes me gustaba mucho, había muchos árboles y el aire estaba muy limpio, todos estábamos muy contentos, nos quedábamos más tiempo en la oficina.

Day 22

Exercise 1: 1.podrán, podréis, podré; 2. comerán, comeréis, comeré; 3. vivirán, viviréis, viviré; 4. harán, haréis, haré; 5. venderán, venderéis, venderé;
Exercise 2: 1. No pondrán música. 2. No sabrá la lección. 3. Estaré feliz. 4. Hará frío. 5. Volveremos pronto. 6. José estudiará español. 7. No querré ir al café.
Exercise 3: El próximo domingo organizaré una fiesta. Me pondré mi traje más bonito e invitaré a mucha gente. Tocaré la guitarra. Bailaremos y cantaremos hasta las cinco de la madrugada. Será muy divertido. Todos estaremos felices y diremos que es la mejor fiesta de todo el año.
Exercise 4: 1. En España uno se suele acostar tarde. 2. Uno se divierte mucho jugando al fútbol. 3. Los sábados uno no se aburre nunca. 4. Uno se alegra mucho de su suerte. 5. Cuando hace frío uno se pone el abrigo. 6. Uno se presenta al profesor. 7. Uno no se queda nunca en casa.
Exercise 5: 1. camarero 2. profesor 3. pintor 4. secretaria 5. azafata 6. enfermera
Exercise 6: 1. no 2. sí 3. sí 4. sí 5. no 6. no 7. no 8. sí
Exercise 7: 1. Buscar un nuevo trabajo. 2. Comprar el periódico todos los días. 3. Leer los anuncios de trabajo. 4. Escribir cartas y solicitar un puesto de trabajo. 5. Presentarse y tener una entrevista. 6. Empezar a trabajar.

Day 23

Exercise 1: No habrá venido. No estará. Se habrá ido. Habrá ido. Se quedará. Me llamará. Me comprará.
Exercise 2: 1. Le darán el coche. 2. Habrán terminado ya. 3. Irán a tu fiesta. 4. Sabrá inglés. 5. Hará buen tiempo. 6. Estará de acuerdo. 7. Habrá escrito la carta. 8. Llegará mañana.
Exercise 3: 1. a) de lo que 2. b) que 3. a) que 4. c) de las que 5. b) de la que 6. a) de la que
Exercise 4: 1. del que 2. de los que 3. de los que 4. de los que 5. de lo que 6. de lo que 7. del que 8. del que 9. que 10. que
Exercise 5: 1. b) 2. a) 3. c) 4.a) 5. b)
Exercise 6: 1. b) Muchísimas gracias. 2. b) Esto es más fácil de lo que se cree. 3. a) Con mucho gusto. 4. b) Le gusta más que cuidar a los niños. 5. a) El reloj parece antiquísimo. 6. b) ¿A cuánto estarán?

Day 24

Exercise 1: 1. El profesor fue buscado por la escuela de lenguas. 2. Toda la región ha sido destruida por el huracán. 3. El partido va a ser ganado por el Real Madrid. 4. El robo ha sido denunciado por la chica.
Exercise 2: 1. Mi hermano ganó el premio. 2. Yo he escrito las cartas. 3. Un ladrón robó el coche.
Exercise 3: 1. Pasado mañana se terminará/terminarán el trabajo. 2. Nunca se sabrá/sabrán la verdad. 3. Algún día se encontrará/encontrarán el bolso.
Exercise 4: 1. c) hay que 2. b) debe de 3. b) hay que 4. a) tienes que
Exercise 5: 1. hace 2. desde hace 3. desde 4. desde hace 5. desde hace

Exercise 6: Buenos días. Querría hablar con Carlos. Quería preguntarle si ha comprado entradas. Querría ver un partido de fútbol alguna vez.

Day 25

Exercise 1: 1. conduce, conduzca; 2. tiene, tenga; 3. lee, lea; 4. escribe, escriba; 5. sube, suba; 6. aprende, aprenda; 7. viene, venga
Exercise 2: Quiero que: 1. salgamos toda una noche. 2. visitemos un bar. 3. saques una entrada para el teatro. 4. veas una película.
Exercise 3: 1. salgan 2. salen 3. visitéis 4. visitáis 5. tomen 6. toman 7. ayudes
Exercise 4: ¿Me permite que: 1. abra la puerta? 2. fume un cigarrillo? 3. salga con su hija? 4. haga una pregunta? 5. visite a su familia? 6. entre en su casa?

Day 26

Exercise 1: 1. Dudo que estéis contentos. 2. Javier no cree que tenga suerte. 3.No creo que sepas cantar. 4. No creo que vayan a Granada este año. **Exercise 2:** 1. ¡Ojalá tengáis tiempo! 2. ¡Ojalá lleven abrigos! 3. ¡Ojalá haga sol! 4. ¡Ojalá hables español!
Exercise 3: 1. Es imposible que os acompañemos. 2. Es mejor que se quede en la cama. 3. Es preciso que salgamos. 4. Es probable que llegue hoy.
Exercise 4: 1. ¿Cuándo vas a venir a visitarnos? Cuando tenga tiempo. 2. ¿Cuándo va a invitar Karen a sus amigos? Cuando sea su cumpleaños. 3. ¿Cuándo van a ir tus padres de vacaciones? Cuando quieran. 4. ¿Cuándo va a terminar Pedro el cuadro? Cuando lo necesite.
Exercise 5: 1. es, está 2. está 3. está 4. es, está 5. es 6. está
Exercise 6: 1. haya 2. vuelve 3. tienes 4. hablan 5. descanséis 6. no te enfades

Day 27

Exercise 1: oiga, vaya, haya, venga, esté, empiece, diga, sienta, sea, dé, duerma, baile, quiera, salga, viva
Exercise 2: 1. quieras 2. vayamos 3. llegue 4. vayamos 5. estaba 6. digas 7. vea
Exercise 3: 1. Acabo de ponerla. 2. Acabo de encontrarla. 3. Acabo de comprarlo. 4. Acabo de verla. 5. Acabo de solicitarlo. 6. Acabo de reservarla.
Exercise 4: 1. a) habla 2. b) sepa 3. a) prestas 4. b) guste 5. b) están 6. b) visiten
Exercise 5: 1. cara 2. primer 3. cerrada 4. mucha 5. aburrido 6. temprano 7. nueva 8. pequeño
Exercise 6: 1. cuánto 2. cuántos 3. cuánta 4. cuántos 5. cuántas 6. cuánto

Day 28

Exercise 1: 1. conduce, conducid; 2. recibe, recibid; 3. vuelve, volved; 4. juega, jugad; 5. vende, vended;
Exercise 2: 1. Sí, fuma. 2. Sí, ábrala. 3. Sí, cantad y bailad. 4. Sí, ciérrala. 5. Sí, hablen español. 6. Sí, cómpralo. 7. Sí, conduzca. 8. Sí, acompañadla.
Exercise 3: 1. Mírela. 2. Preparadla. 3. Escríbela. 4. Arréglala. 5. Cómprelo. 6. Sáquenlas.
Exercise 4: 1. mías 2. suyo 3. vuestro 4. nuestra 5. tuyos 6. suya 7. mía
Exercise 5: 1. tanto 2. tan 3. tanta 4. tanto 5. tan
Exercise 6: 1. a 2. b 3. b 4. a

Day 29

Exercise 1: 1. habla, hable, hablad, hablen; 2. repite, repita, repetid, repitan; 3. empieza, empiece, empezad, empiecen; 4. haz, haga, haced, hagan; 5. pasa, pase, pasad, pasen; 6. di, diga, decid, digan;
Exercise 2: 1. tened 2. sé, haz 3. vayan 4. digan 5. pasa, compra 6. compruebe
Exercise 3: escribir, tener, decir, rellenar, trabajar, preguntar, mirar
Exercise 4: 1. solo 2. aquél, éste 3. mí, esto 4. están 5. sólo 6. aquel 7. el, él 8. sé 9. qué 10. qué
Exercise 5: 1. Tengo dolores de cabeza. 2. Me duele la garganta. 3. Creo que tengo fiebre. 4. No me siento bien. 5. Tengo tos. 6. ¡Qué te mejores!

Day 30

Exercise 1: 1. no cerréis 2. no vengas 3. no hagáis 4. no le recibáis 5. no subas 6. no vayan 7. no diga 8. no oigan 9. no pongas 10. no lo pienses
Exercise 2: 1. No, no toques la guitarra. 2. No, no juguéis al fútbol. 3. No, no compréis zumo de naranja. 4. No, no pongas música. 5. No, no salgáis esta noche.
Exercise 3: 1. lo que 2. que 3. que 4. lo que 5. que 6. que
Exercise 4: 1. mucho 2. detrás 3. mal 4. cerca 5. tampoco 6. nunca 7. limpio 8. debajo 9. a la izquierda 10. grande

Vocabulary

Here is a list of all the vocabulary that you have encountered throughout the book.

A

a rayas	*striped*
abanico *m*	*fan*
abierto	*open*
abonado *m*	*(telephone) subscriber*
abrazar	*to embrace, hug*
abrigo *m*	*coat*
abril *m*	*April*
abrir	*to open*
absolutamente	*absolutely*
abuela *f*	*grandmother*
abuelo *m*	*grandfather*
abuelos *m pl*	*grandparents*
aburrirse	*to be bored*
acabar	*to end, be finished*
accidente *m*	*accident*
aceite *m*	*oil*
aceite *m* de oliva	*olive oil*
aceitunas *f pl*	*olives*
acento *m*	*accent*
aceptar	*to agree*
acompañar	*to accompany*
acordarse	*to remember*
acordeón *m*	*accordion*
acostarse	*to go to bed, sleep*
acostumbrado, -a	*accustomed, used to*
acostumbrarse a alguna cosa	*to get used to something*
adelantarse	*overtake, (here:) to cut in (front)*
adelgazar	*to lose weight*
además	*furthermore*
adiós	*goodbye*
aduana *f*	*customs*
aduanero *m*	*customs officer*
aeropuerto *m*	*airport*
afeitar(se)	*to shave (oneself)*
a fuego lento	*on low heat*
agencia f de viajes	*travel agency*
agosto *m*	*August*
agradecer alguna cosa a alguien	*to be grateful to somebody for something*
agua (el) *f*	*water*
agua (el) *f* potable	*drinking water*
ahora	*now*
ahora mismo	*right now*
aire *m*	*air*
ajo *m*	*garlic*
al ajillo	*roasted with garlic*
a la derecha	*to/on the right*
al lado de	*next to*
a la izquierda	*to/on the left*
alegrar	*to cheer up*
alegrarse	*to be happy*
alegre	*joyful, happy; (here:) enthusiastic*
alegría *f*	*joy*
al fondo	*at the back*
algo	*something*
algo es un rollo	*something is boring*
algodón *m*	*cotton*
alguien	*someone*
alguno, -a	*some(one)*
allí	*there*
almuerzo *m*	*snack*
alojarse	*to stay (at s.o.'s place)*
Alpes *m pl*	*the Alps*
alpinismo *m*	*mountain climbing*

alquilar	*to let/rent*
alrededor de	*at, around*
alto, -a	*big, tall, high*
alumno *m*	*pupil/student*
ama (el) f de casa	*housewife*
amabilidad *f*	*friendliness*
amable	*friendly*
amarillo, -a	*yellow*
ambos, -as	*both*
a menudo	*often*
América	*America*
americano, -a	*American*
amiga *f*	*(female) friend*
amigo *m*	*friend*
amueblado, -a	*furnished*
Andalucía *f*	*Andalusia*
andar	*to walk (around), go*
andén *m*	*platform*
ángel *m*	*angel*
año *m*	*year*
anoche	*last night*
anorak *m*	*anorak (waterproof jacket)*
a no ser que	*unless, except*
anotar	*to write down*
anteayer	*day before yesterday*
antes	*before*
antiguo, -a	*old*
anual	*annually*
a nuestro lado	*next to us*
anuncio m de trabajo	*job advertisement*
apagar	*to switch/turn off*
a partir de	*from*
a pedir de boca	*exactly as one wants it (literally as the mouth desires)*
apellido *m*	*surname*
apetecer (-zc-)	*to want to*
a pierna suelta	*carefree (literally: with a dangling leg)*
aprender	*to learn*
a propósito	*by the way*
aproximadamente	*approximately*
aquello	*that (thing)*
aquí	*here*
árbol *m*	*tree*
armario *m*	*cupboard*
arquitecto *m*	*architect*
arreglado, -a	*repaired*
arreglar	*to order*
arreglarse	*to get by, manage*
arreglo *m*	*repair*
arriba	*on top, above*
arroz *m*	*rice*
artefacto *m*	*appliance, device, tool*
ascensor *m*	*lift/elevator*
aseo *m*	*toilet*
así como	*as well as*
asiento *m*	*seat*
aspecto *m*	*look*
atención *f*	*attention*
atender a alguien	*to care for someone*
a tiempo	*on time*
atraer	*to put on*
auricular *m*	*(telephone) receiver*
autobús *m*	*bus*
autocaravana *f*	*RV, mobile home*
automáticamente	*automatically*
autopista *f*	*motorway*
a veces	*sometimes*
a ver	*we'll see*
averiado, -a	*broken, defect*
avión *m*	*airplane*
avisar a alguien	*to inform someone*
ayuda *f*	*help*
azafata *f*	*flight attendant*
azafrán *m*	*saffron*
azúcar *m*	*sugar*
azul	*blue*

B

bailar	*to dance*
bajar	*to get off*
bañarse	*to bathe, swim*
banco *m*	*bank*
baño *m*	*bathroom*
bar *m*	*bar*
barato, -a	*cheap*
barco *m*	*boat, ship*
barra *f*	*loaf of*
barril *m*	*barrel*
barrio *m*	*neighborhood/district*
báscula *f*	*scale*
bastante	*rather*
batido *m*	*milkshake*
baúl *m*	*trunk*
beber	*to drink*
bebida *f*	*drink*
bicicleta *f*	*bicycle*
bien	*good, fine*
bienvenido, -a	*welcome*
billete *m*	*ticket*
billete *m* de tren	*train ticket*
bistec *m*	*(beef) steak*
blanco, -a	*white*
blusa *f*	*blouse*
boca *f*	*mouth*
bocadillo *m*	*sandwich*
bolsa *f*	*shopping bag*
bolso *m*	*bag, purse*
bonito, -a	*pretty, beautiful*
botella *f*	*bottle*
bravo	*great*
bueno, -a	*good*
buenas noches	*good evening/night*
buenas tardes	*good afternoon (until 8 p.m.)*
buenos días	*good morning*
bufanda *f*	*scarf*
buscar	*to search, look for*

C

cabeza *f*	*head*
cabina *f* telefónica	*phone booth*
cada	*every*
cada dos horas	*every two hours*
caer	*to fall*
café *m*	*coffee, café*
cafetería *f*	*cafeteria*
(una) caja de cerillas *f*	*a box of matches*
calamares *m pl* a la romana	*squid rings, battered and fried*
calefacción *f*	*heating*
calidad *f*	*quality*
calle *f*	*street*
calor *m*	*heat*
calzada *f*	*lane*
cama *f*	*bed*
camarero m, -a *f*	*waiter, waitress*
cambiar	*to change*
caminar	*to go, walk*
camino *m*	*way, path*
camino a	*on the way to*
camión *m*	*lorry/truck*
cámping *m*	*campsite/campground*
campamento	*campsite/campground*
campo *m*	*country(side)*
campo *m* de fútbol	*football pitch/soccer field*
canción *f*	*song*
cansado, -a	*tired*
cantar	*to sing*
cara *f*	*face*
caramba	*damn, (here:) wow*
cariñoso, -a	*affectionate*
carne *f*	*meat*

carne *f* de pollo *chicken meat*
carne *f* picada *ground [minced] meat*
carnicería *f* *butcher's (shop)*
caro, -a *expensive*
carretera *f* *street*
carta *f* *menu, letter*
casa *f* *house*
casa *f* de comidas *a place to eat*
casi *nearly, almost*
casi nunca *almost never*
caso *m* *case*
castañuelas *f pl* *castanets*
castellano *m* *Castilian (Spanish)*
catedral *f* *cathedral*
caza *f* *hunt*
cazuela *f* *casserole (dish)*
cebolla *f* *onion*
celebrar *to celebrate*
cena *f* *supper/dinner*
cenar *to have supper/dinner*
céntimo *m* *cent*
centro *m* *(city) centre/downtown*
cerca *close*
cerrar (-ie-) *to close*
cerveza *f* *beer*
cerveza *f* de barril *draught beer*
chalet *m* *detached house*
chaqueta *f* *jacket*
charlar *to chat*
chequeo *m* *check*
chico *m* *boy, guy*
chiflar *to go crazy*
chocar *to crash*
choque *m* *crash*
chorizo *m* *spicy sausage*
churro *m* *fritter*
cielo *m* *sky*
cigarrillo *m* *cigarette*
cine *m* *cinema*
cinta *f* *belt*
cinta f de equipaje *baggage claim*
cintura *f* *waist(line)*
cinturón *m* de seguridad *safety belt/seat belt*
cita *f* *date*
ciudad *f* *city, town*
claro *of course*
clase *f* *class*
clases *f pl* de tenis *tennis lessons*
clínica *f* *clinic*
club *m* nocturno *nightclub*
coche *m* *car, train compartment*
cocina *f* *kitchen*
cocinar *to cook*
coger (-j-) *to take*
colegio *m* *school*
colgar (-ue-) *to hang (up)*
colocar *to put*
comenzar (-ie-) *to start, begin*
comer *to eat*
comercio *m* *business, store*
comida *f* *lunch*
comisaría *f* *police station*
como *as, like*
¿Cómo? *How?*
cómo no *why not*
como para *as for*
como siempre *as always*
cómodo, -a *comfortable*
compasión *f* *compassion*
completo, -a *complete*
complicado, -a *complicated*
comportarse *to behave*
compra *f* *shopping*
comprar *to buy*
comprender *to understand*

comprobar (-ue-)	*to check, examine*
comunicar con	*to connect/communicate with*
con gusto	*with pleasure*
con mucho gusto	*I'd like (that) very much*
coñac *m*	*brandy*
concertar (-ie-)	*to arrange*
concreto, -a	*concrete*
conducir (-zc-)	*to drive*
conductor *m*	*driver*
conejo *m*	*rabbit*
confortable	*comfortable*
conocer (-zc-)	*to know, get to know*
conocimientos *m pl* generales	*general education*
conseguir (-i-)	*to obtain*
consistir de	*to consist of*
consulado *m*	*consulate*
consulta *f*	*GP's practice/doctor's office*
contagiar	*to infect*
contar (-ue-)	*to tell*
contener (-g-)	*to contain*
contento, -a	*content*
contestar	*to answer*
control *m*	*control*
control *m* de pasaportes	*passport control*
copa *f*	*(wine) glass*
copia *f*	*copy*
corral *m*	*chicken farm*
correr	*to run, flow*
cosa *f*	*thing*
cosas *f pl* dignas de ver	*sight (sights/objects) worth seeing*
costa *f*	*coast*
costar (-ue-)	*to cost*
creer	*to believe*
crema *f*	*cream soup*
cruzar	*to cross*
cuadro *m*	*picture*
¿Cuál?	*Which one?*
¿Cuánto, -a?	*How much?*
¿Cuánto es?	*How much does it cost?*
cuarto *m*	*quarter*
cubierto *m*	*cutlery*
cucaracha *f*	*cockroach*
cuchara *f*	*spoon*
cucharada *f*	*tablespoonful*
cuchillo *m*	*knife*
cuenta *f*	*account, bill/check (in a restaurant)*
cuero *m*	*leather*
cuidar a alguien	*to look after someone*
culpa *f*	*fault, guilt*
culpable	*guilty, at fault*
cumpleaños *m*	*birthday*
cuñada *f*	*sister-in-law*
cuñado *m*	*brother-in-law*
curioso, -a	*curious, interested*

D

dar	*to give*
dar gritos	*to scream*
dar un frenazo	*to brake*
darle tiempo al tiempo	*to take one's time*
de	*from*
¿De acuerdo?	*OK?*
de atrás	*from behind*
¿De dónde?	*From where?*
de maravilla	*wonderful, great*
de memoria	*by heart*
de nada	*you're welcome*
de noche	*at night*
de paso	*on the way*
de prisa	*fast*
de pura cepa	*genuine, true, pure*

de todos modos *in any case*
de verdad *really*
de vez en cuando *from time to time*
debajo de *under*
deber *to have to, must*
deber de *should, ought to be*
decir *to say*
declaración *f* *explanation, (here:) statement*
declaración *f* de los hechos *(here:) accident report*
declarar *to declare*
decorado *m* *decoration*
dejar *to leave*
delante de *in front of*
denuncia *f* *report*
denunciar *to report*
departamento *m* *department*
depende *it depends*
dependiente m/f *shop assistant/salesperson*
deporte *m* *(type of) sport*
depósito *m* *(petrol/gas) tank*
derecha *f* *right side, the right*
desagradable *embarrassing, unpleasant*
desastre *m* *disaster*
desayunar *to have breakfast*
desayuno *m* *breakfast*
descansar *to rest*
descolgar (-ue-) *to pick up (the phone)*
describir *to describe*
descuidar *not to worry*
desde *since*
desde hace *since… ago, for*
desear *to want, wish*
desgracia *f* *misfortune*
despedida *f* *farewell*
despedirse (-i-) *to say goodbye*
despedir a alguien *to lay someone off*
después *afterwards*
después de *after*
desvergonzado, -a *shameless, (here:) bad dog*
detallado, -a *detailed*
detrás de *behind*
deuda *f* *debt (money)*
día *m* *day*
día *m* de la salida *departure day*
día *m* del santo *name day*
diciembre *m* *December*
diferente *different*
difícil *difficult*
dígame *literally: "tell me" (when answering the phone)*
digno, -a *worthy*
dinero *m* *money*
dirección *f* *address, direction*
directo, -a *direct*
discoteca *f* *disco*
disfrutar de *to savour*
divertido, -a *funny, entertaining*
divertirse (-ie-) *to enjoy oneself*
docena de *f* *a dozen*
doler (-ue-) *to hurt*
dolor *m* *pain*
domingo *m* *Sunday*
donde *where*
¿Dónde? *Where?*
dormir (-ue-) *to sleep*
dormir como un tronco *to sleep like a log*
dormitorio *m* *bedroom*
ducha *f* *shower*
duchar *to shower*
dudar *to doubt*
dulce *sweet*
dulce *m* *sweet(s), pastry*
duro, -a *hard, firm*

E

echar	*to pour*
echar a alguien de menos	*to miss someone*
ejercicio *m*	*exercise*
electricidad *f*	*electricity*
electrizar	*to electrify*
elegante	*elegant*
el invierno	*winter*
el otoño	*autumn*
el verano	*summer*
empanadas *f pl*	*pies with different fillings*
empaquetar	*to wrap up*
empezar (-ie-)	*to start*
empleada *f*	*employee (female)*
emplear	*to employ*
en	*in*
en absoluto	*not at all*
en casa de	*at home with*
en caso de que	*in case of*
en las afueras de	*outside of*
en oferta *f*	*on special offer, on sale*
en plena calle	*right in the middle of the street*
en principio	*in principle, actually*
en un abrir y cerrar de ojos	*in the blink of an eye*
en vano	*in vain*
enamorado, -a	*in love*
encantado, -a	*nice to meet you*
encantar	*to enjoy, like*
encantar a alguien	*to appeal to someone*
encima de	*on*
encontrar (-ue-)	*to find*
encontrarse (-ue-)	*to meet*
encuentro *m*	*meeting*
enero *m*	*January*
enfadarse	*to be angry*
enfermera *f*	*nurse*
enfermo *m*	*sick person*
enfermo, -a	*ill, sick*
enfrente	*opposite*
¿En qué puedo servirle?	*What can I do for you?*
ensalada *f*	*salad*
enseñar	*to show*
¿En serio?	*Seriously?*
entonces	*then*
entrada *f*	*ticket*
entrar	*to enter*
entrar en	*to enter into*
entre	*between*
entrevista *f*	*(job) interview*
envuelto, -a	*wrapped up*
época *f*	*period, era*
época *f* del año	*season*
equipaje *m*	*luggage*
equipaje *m* de mano	*hand luggage, carry-on*
equipo *m*	*team*
escaparate *m*	*shop window*
escribir	*to write*
escritorio *m*	*desk*
escuchar	*to listen*
escuela *f*	*school*
escuela *f* de idiomas	*language school*
espalda *f*	*back*
España *f*	*Spain*
español, -a	*Spaniard/Spanish man/woman*
espárrago *m*	*asparagus*
especial	*special*
especializarse en	*to specialise in*
espectáculo *m*	*show*
esperar	*to wait*
esposa *f*	*wife*

esposo *m* — *husband*
esquí *m* — *skiing*
esquina *f* — *corner*
está bien — *OK*
estación *f* central — *main train station*
estación *f* de servicio — *(large) petrol/gas station*
estación *f* del metro — *underground/subway station*
estadio *m* — *stadium*
Estados Unidos — *United States*
estar — *to be*
estar acostumbrado a alguna cosa — *to be used to something*
estar de acuerdo — *to agree with*
estar de pie — *to stand*
estar hecho polvo — *to be destroyed, (literally: to be ground to dust)*
estómago *m* — *stomach*
estrecho, -a — *tight*
estropeado, -a — *broken*
estudiante m/f — *pupil/student*
estudiar — *to learn, study*
estudio *m* — *studio*
estupendo, -a — *excellent*
euro *m* — *euro*
evitar — *to prevent*
exactamente — *exactly*
exacto, -a — *exact*
excelente — *excellent*
excepcional — *exceptional*
excepto — *except, with the exception*
exceso m de peso — *excess weight*
excursión *f* — *excursion*
excusa *f* — *apology*
excusarse — *to excuse oneself*
exigir — *to request*
experiencia *f* — *experience*
experiencia *f* laboral — *work experience*
explicar — *to explain*
exposición *f* — *exhibition*
extranjero, -a — *foreigner m/f*
extravagante — *fancy, extravagant*

F

fabricar — *to produce*
fácil — *easy*
facturar — *(here:) to check in*
falda *f* — *skirt*
faltar — *to miss*
familia *f* — *family*
familiar — *family (adj.)*
famoso, -a — *famous*
fanático, -a de — *mad about*
fantástico, -a — *fantastic*
farmacia *f* — *pharmacy*
febrero *m* — *February*
feliz — *happy*
feliz cumpleaños — *happy birthday*
festejar — *to party, celebrate a feast*
festivo, -a — *festive*
fiebre *f* — *fever*
fiesta *f* — *feast, party*
fijo, -a — *firm, hard*
fin m de semana — *weekend*
finalmente — *finally*
flamenco *m* — *flamenco*
flan *m* — *caramel pudding*
flojo, -a — *light*
flor *f* — *flower*
fondo *m* — *back (of a room)*
footing *m* — *jogging*
formulario *m* — *form*
fotografía (foto) *f* — *photo*
frenazo *m* — *braking*

frenazo *m* de emergencia	*emergency stop*
frío *m*	*cold*
fruta *f*	*fruit*
fuego *m*	*fire*
fuera	*go away*
fuerte	*strong, (here:) substantial*
fumador *m*	*smoker*
fumar	*to smoke*
fútbol *m*	*football/soccer*

G

gafas *f pl*	*glasses, spectacles*
galante	*charming*
galleta *f*	*biscuit/cookie*
gallina *f*	*chicken*
gallinas *f pl* de corral	*free-range chickens*
gamba *f*	*prawn*
gana *f*	*wish, desire*
ganga *f*	*bargain*
garganta *f*	*throat*
gasolina *f*	*petrol/gas*
gasolinera *f*	*petrol/gas station*
gastar	*to consume, use (up)*
gato *m*	*cat*
generalmente	*generally*
genial	*genial, inspired*
gente *f*	*people*
gota *f*	*drop*
gracias	*thank you*
gracias a Dios	*thank God*
gramo *m*	*gram*
gran almacén *m*	*department store*
grande	*large, big*
grandeza *f*	*greatness*
grave	*serious*
gripe *f*	*flu, cold*
gris	*grey*
grito *m*	*scream*
grupo *m*	*group*
guapo, -a	*handsome, good-looking*
guay (coll.)	*great*
guía *m*	*(travel) guide*
guía *f* de teléfono	*telephone directory*
gustar	*to enjoy, like*

H

haber	*to have, be*
habitación *f*	*room*
habitación *f* doble	*double room*
habitación *f* individual	*single room*
hablar	*to speak*
hacer	*to do, make*
hace calor	*it's hot*
hace frío	*it's cold*
hace mucho calor	*it's very hot*
hace unos meses	*a few months ago*
hacer autostop	*to hitchhike*
hacer falta	*to be necessary*
hacer transbordo	*to change trains*
hacerse (-g-)	*to become*
hambre *f*	*hunger*
harina *f*	*flour*
hasta	*until*
¡Hasta la vista!	*Goodbye!*
¡Hasta luego!	*See you later!*
¡Hasta mañana!	*Until tomorrow!*
¡Hasta otro día!	*Until later! Bye for now!*
¡Hasta pronto!	*See you soon!*
hay	*there is/are*
helado *m*	*ice cream*
hermana *f*	*sister*
hermano *m*	*brother*
hija *f*	*daughter*

hijo *m*	*son*
hijos *m pl*	*children*
hinchado, -a	*swollen*
histórico, -a	*historical*
¡Hola!	*Hello!*
Hola, ¿qué hay?	*Hi, what's up?*
Hola, ¿qué tal?	*Hello, how are you?*
hombre *m*	*man, human being*
hombro *m*	*shoulder*
hora *f*	*hour*
horno *m*	*oven*
hospital *m*	*hospital*
hostería *f*	*casual restaurant serving local dishes*
hotel *m*	*hotel*
hoy	*today*
hubo (from haber)	*there was*
huella *f*	*track*
huevo *m*	*egg*
húmedo, -a	*damp, wet*
huracán *m*	*hurricane*

I

ida *f*	*one way*
ida y vuelta	*roundtrip*
idea *f*	*idea*
iglesia *f*	*church*
igual	*equal, the same*
imaginarse	*to imagine*
importancia *f*	*importance*
importante	*important*
importar	*to be important*
imposible	*impossible*
impresión *f*	*impression*
impresionante	*impressive*
impresionar	*to impress*
incluir	*to include*
incluso	*inclusive*
increíble	*incredible*
información *f*	*information*
informática *f*	*information technology*
ingeniero *m*	*engineer*
Inglaterra	*England*
Inglés, -a	*English, Englishman/ Englishwoman*
ingrediente *m*	*ingredient*
inhalación *f*	*inhalation*
inicial	*initially*
inmediato, -a	*immediately*
inofensivo	*harmless*
inquietarse	*to worry, be concerned about*
insaciable	*insatiable*
inspección *f*	*inspection*
inspiración *f*	*inspiration*
instalar	*to install*
instituto *m*	*institute*
interesado *m*	*applicant*
interesante	*interesting*
internacional	*international*
invitado *m*	*guest*
ir	*to go, drive*
ir de campamento	*to go camping*
ir de compras	*to go shopping*
irse	*to go away*
isla *f*	*island*
italiano, -a	*Italian*
izquierda *f*	*left*

J

jamón *m*	*ham*
jamón *m* serrano	*cured ham*
jardín *m*	*garden*
jerez *m*	*sherry*
jersey *m*	*sweater*
joven	*young*
judías *f pl* verdes	*green beans*

jueves *m*	*Thursday*
jugar	*to play*
julio *m*	*July*
junio *m*	*June*
junto, -a	*next to, together*

K

kilo *m*	*kilo(gram)*
kilómetro *m*	*kilometer*

L

laboral	*work-related*
ladrar	*to bark*
ladrón *m*	*thief*
lamentarse	*to regret, lament*
lámpara *f*	*lamp*
la primavera	*spring*
la primera vez	*(for) the first time*
largo, -a	*long*
lata *f*	*can, tin*
latino	*Latin*
lavabo *m*	*washroom*
lavado *m*	*laundry, wash*
lavadora *f*	*washing machine*
lavar en seco	*to dry-clean*
lavarse	*to wash oneself*
lección *f*	*lesson*
leche *f*	*milk*
leer	*to read*
lejos	*far*
lengua *f*	*language, tongue*
levantarse	*to get up*
libre	*free*
libro *m*	*book*
ligero, -a	*light*
limpio, -a	*clean*
líquido *m*	*liquid, fluid*
líquido *m* de frenos	*brake fluid*
lista *f*	*list*
listo, -a (estar)	*ready*
listo, -a (ser)	*clever, smart*
llamada *f*	*(phone) call*
llamada *f* a cobro revertido	*collect call*
llamar	*to phone/call*
llamarse	*to be called, to call oneself*
llave *f*	*key*
llegar	*to arrive*
llego tarde	*I am late*
llenar	*to fill (out)*
lleno, -a	*full*
llevar retraso	*to be delayed*
llevarse alguna cosa	*to take something along*
llover (-ue-)	*to rain*
lluvia *f*	*rain*
lo hago por mi cuenta	*I'll do it on my own*
lo siento	*I am sorry*
lo siento mucho	*I am really sorry*
lo siento, pero no es posible	*I'm sorry, but that's not possible*
local (adj.)	*local*
local *m*	*restaurant, pub*
loco *m*	*crazy person*
luego	*afterwards*
lugar *m*	*place*
luna *f*	*moon*
lunes *m*	*Monday*

M

madre *f*	*mother*
madrileño, -a	*inhabitant of Madrid, from Madrid*

madrugada *f*	*early morning*
magdalena *f*	*sponge cupcake*
maleta *f*	*suitcase*
malo, -a	*bad*
mañana *f*	*morning, tomorrow*
manchego	*Manchego (cheese)*
mandarina *f*	*tangerine*
mano *f*	*hand*
mantón *m*	*shawl*
marca *f*	*brand*
marcar	*to dial*
marcharse	*to leave*
marido *m*	*husband*
marrón	*brown*
martes *m*	*Tuesday*
marzo *m*	*March*
más	*more*
más o menos	*about, approximately*
más próximo, -a	*closest*
mascota *f*	*mascot*
matar	*to kill*
matar dos pájaros de un tiro	*to kill two birds with one stone*
mayo *m*	*May*
me	*me*
me encantan	*(here:) I love them*
media hora más	*another half hour*
medianoche *f*	*midnight*
medicamento *m*	*medication*
médico *m*	*GP/doctor*
medio, -a	*half*
mediodía *m*	*midday, noon*
mejorar	*to improve*
mejorarse	*to get well*
melancólico, -a	*melancholic*
menú m turístico	*tourist menu*
merecer (-zc-)	*to be worth*
merendar (-ie-)	*to have a snack in the evening*
merienda *f*	*evening meal*
mermelada *f*	*jam*
mes *m*	*month*
mesa *f*	*table*
meter	*to put into*
metro *m*	*underground/subway*
México *m*	*Mexico*
mi	*my*
miedo *m*	*fear*
mientras	*during, while*
mientras tanto	*during, while*
miércoles *m*	*Wednesday*
mil veces	*a thousand times*
mínimo, -a	*minimum*
mío	*mine*
mirar	*to see*
mismo, -a	*(the) same*
mochila *f*	*rucksack/backpack*
moda *f*	*fashion*
modelo *m*	*model*
moderno, -a	*modern*
molestar	*to disturb/bother*
momento *m*	*moment*
monedero *m*	*purse*
mono, -a	*cute*
monte *m*	*mountain*
(un) montón *m*	*lot*
un montón de	*a lot of*
morder (-ue-)	*to bite*
morir (-ue-)	*to die*
mostrador *m*	*counter*
mostrar (-ue-)	*to show*
motor *m*	*engine, motor*
mozo *m*	*attendant*
mucho, -a	*much, many*
muchas gracias	*many thanks*
muchedumbre *f*	*(packed) crowd*
mucho gusto	*nice to meet you, my pleasure*

mueble *m* *piece of furniture*
mujer *f* *woman*
museo *m* *museum*
música *f* *music*
muy *very*

N

nacional *national*
nadie *no one, nobody*
naipe *m* *playing card*
nata *f* *whipped cream*
natación *f* *swimming*
naturalmente *naturally*
Navidad *f* *Christmas*
necesario, -a *necessary*
necesitar *to need*
negro, -a *black*
nervioso, -a *nervous, anxious*
neumático *m* *tyre/tire*
nevar (-ie-) *to snow*
niebla *f* *fog, mist*
nieta *f* *granddaughter*
nieto *m* *grandson*
nietos *m pl* *grandchildren*
niña *f* *girl*
ninguno, -a *not one, nobody*
niño *m* *boy*
niños *m pl* *children*
no *no*
no es nada *it's alright, nothing happened*
no fumadores *non-smoking*
no hay de que *don't mention it*
¿No le parece? *Don't you think so?*
noche *f* *evening, night*
nombre *m* *name*
nórdico, -a *Nordic, from the north*
normalmente *normally*
nota *f* *note*
noticia *f* *message*
noviembre *m* *November*
nube *f* *cloud*
nuestro, -a *our*
nuevo, -a *new*
número *m* de teléfono *telephone number*
nunca *never*

O

o *or*
obra *f* *work*
ocasión *f* *occasion*
octubre *m* *October*
ocupado, -a *engaged/busy*
ocuparse de alguna cosa *to look into something*
ocurrir *to happen*
oferta *f* de trabajo *job offer*
oficina *f* *office*
oficina *f* de información *information bureau/office*
oficina *f* de la telefónica *telephone office*
ofrecer (-zc-) *to offer*
oír *to hear*
ojalá *hopefully*
olvidar *to forget*
operación *f* *operation*
oportunidad *f* *opportunity*
óptica *f* *optician*
organizar *to organize*
orgullo *m* *pride*
osito de peluche *teddybear*
oso *m* *bear*
oso *m* de felpa *teddybear*
otro, -a *other*

P

pacífico, -a	*peaceful, friendly; (here:) well-behaved*
padre *m*	*father*
padres *m pl*	*parents*
paella *f*	*paella (Spanish rice dish)*
paellera *f*	*paella pan*
pagar	*to pay*
país *m*	*country*
pájaro *m*	*bird*
palabra *f*	*word*
pálido, -a	*pale*
palmoteo *m*	*rhythmic clapping*
pan *m*	*bread*
pan *m* integral	*wholemeal/whole wheat bread*
panadería *f*	*bakery*
pantalones *m pl*	*trousers/pants*
papel *m*	*paper*
paquete *m*	*packet, bag*
un par de	*a few*
para	*for, to, therefore, so, in order to*
¿Para cuándo?	*For when?*
¿Para qué?	*For what?*
¿Para qué hora?	*For what time?*
¿Para quién?	*For who?*
para mayor seguridad	*for safety's sake*
parada *f*	*(bus) stop*
parecer (-zc-)	*to appear, seem*
pared *f*	*wall*
parque *m*	*park*
parrillada *f*	*grilled food*
parte *f*	*part*
parte f trasera	*rear (part)*
partido *m* de fútbol	*football/soccer game*
partir	*to depart, leave*
pasajero *m*	*passenger*
pasaporte *m*	*passport*
pasar	*to spend, to pass (by), drive (by)*
pasearse	*to go for a walk*
paseo *m*	*walk*
pasión *f*	*passion*
pastel *m*	*cake*
pastilla *f*	*tablet, pill*
pata *f*	*paw*
patata *f*	*potato*
patrón *m*	*patron saint*
pedir (-i-)	*to request*
pedir excusas	*to apologize*
pedir hora	*to make an appointment*
peinarse	*to comb one's hair*
película *f*	*film/ movie*
peligroso, -a	*dangerous*
pelo *m*	*hair*
pensión *f*	*B & B, guesthouse*
pequeño, -a	*small, little*
perder de vista	*to lose sight of*
perdiz *f*	*quail*
perdón	*sorry, excuse me*
perfectamente	*perfect*
periódico *m*	*newspaper*
permiso *m* de conducir	*driving licence/ driver's licence*
permitir	*to permit*
pero	*but*
perro *m*	*dog*
perseguir (-i-)	*to follow, pursue*
persona *f*	*person*
pesado,-a	*heavy*
pesar to	*weigh*
pescado *m*	*fish (dish)*
pie *m*	*foot*
pierna *f*	*leg*
pinta *f*	*look (appearance)*
pintar	*to paint*

pintor *m*	*painter*
Pirineos *m pl*	*the Pyrenees*
pisar	*to tread on*
piscina *f*	*swimming pool*
piso *m*	*flat Br/apartment Am*
piso *m*	*storey Br/floor Am*
planchar	*to iron*
planear	*to plan (ahead)*
plano *m* **de la ciudad**	*street map, map of the city*
planta *f*	*storey Br/floor Am*
plato *m*	*dish, course, plate*
playa *f*	*beach*
plaza *f*	*square*
plomo *m*	*lead (metal)*
pobrecito *m*	*poor thing*
poco, -a	*little*
poder (-ue-)	*to be able, can*
policía *m*	*policeman*
póliza *f* **del seguro**	*insurance policy*
pollo *m*	*chicken*
polvo *m*	*dust*
poner	*to place, put*
ponerse triste	*to become sad*
por	*for, through*
por aquí	*this way*
por ciento *m*	*percent*
por ejemplo	*for example*
por el momento no	*not at the moment*
por favor	*please*
por fin	*finally*
por lo menos	*at least*
por mucho que	*even if*
por si las moscas	*just in case*
porcelana *f*	*porcelain, china*
porque	*because*
porrón *m*	*decanter (for wine)*
portallaves *m*	*key rack*

postre *m*	*dessert*
(un) poquito *m*	*a little*
practicar	*to practice*
práctico, -a	*practical*
precio *m* **fijo**	*set price*
precioso, -a	*valuable, (here:) magnificent*
precisamente	*precisely*
predilecto	*favourite*
preferencia *f*	*right of way*
preferir (-ie-)	*to prefer*
pregunta *f*	*question*
preocuparse	*to worry*
preparar	*to prepare*
presentarse	*to present/introduce oneself*
presión *f*	*pressure*
prestar	*to borrow*
prever	*to plan ahead*
prima *f*	*cousin (female)*
primero, -a	*first*
primo *m*	*cousin (male)*
prisa *f*	*hurry*
probador *m*	*changing room*
probar (-ue-)	*to try out*
probarse (-ue-) alguna cosa	*to try something on*
problema *m*	*problem*
profesión *f*	*profession*
profesor *m*	*teacher*
profundamente	*deeply, profoundly*
prohibido, -a	*forbidden*
pronto	*immediately*
propina *f*	*tip*
proponer	*to suggest*
provincia *f*	*province*
próximo, -a	*next*
puente *m*	*bridge*
puerta *f*	*door*

puesto *m* de trabajo	*job position*
puro, -a	*pure*

Q

qué	*how, which*
¿Qué?	*What?*
qué barbaridad	*that's exorbitant/outrageous*
qué cara	*such nerve (literally: what a face)*
qué horror	*how awful*
qué interesante	*how interesting*
qué lástima	*what a shame*
qué marea de	*what a lot of*
qué pena	*what a pity*
¿Qué tal has comido?	*How did you like the food?*
qué te mejores	*get better soon*
qué te vaya bien	*all the best*
quedar	*to stay/remain*
quedarse	*to stay*
querer (-ie-)	*to want, like, love*
queso *m*	*cheese*
¿Quién?	*Who?*
quisiera	*I'd like to*
quizá(s)	*maybe, perhaps*

R

rápidamente	*quickly, fast*
(un) ramo *m*	*a bunch of*
rara vez	*seldom, rarely*
raro, -a	*rare, strange*
rato *m*	*moment*
realmente	*really, in fact*
rebanada de *f*	*slice of*
rebaja *f*	*discount*
recado *m*	*message*
recados *m pl*	*errands*
recepcionista *m/f*	*receptionist*
receta *f*	*prescription*
recetar	*to prescribe*
recibir	*to receive*
recoger	*to pick up, collect*
recomendar (-ie-)	*to recommend*
reconocer (-zc-)	*to admit*
reflejar	*to reflect*
regalar	*to give as a present*
regalo *m*	*gift, present*
regatear	*to barter*
región *f*	*region*
regla *f*	*rule*
regresar	*to come back, return*
reirse a carcajadas	*to laugh loudly*
rellenar	*to fill out*
reloj *m*	*watch, clock*
relojería *f*	*watch/clock maker's/shop*
remolcar	*to tow away*
RENFE *f* (Red Nacional de Ferrocarriles Españoles)	*State-run Spanish railway company*
reparaciones	*service*
reparar	*to repair*
repetir (-i-)	*to repeat*
requerir (-ie-)	*to request*
reserva *f*	*reservation*
reservar	*to book, make a reservation*
respetar	*to pay attention to*
respiración *f*	*breathing*
respirar	*to breathe*
resto *m*	*rest*
resultar	*to turn out*
retrato *m*	*portrait*
rey *m*	*king*
rico, -a	*tasty, rich, delicious*
río *m*	*river*

robar *to steal*
robo *m* *theft*
roedor *m* *rodent*
rojo, -a *red*
romper *to break, damage*
ropa *f* *clothing*
rubio, -a *blond*
ruido *m* *noise*

S

sábado *m* *Saturday*
saber *to know how, be able*
sabroso, -a *tasty*
sacar *to take out, to stick out*
saco *m* de dormir *sleeping bag*
sal *f* *salt*
sala *f* de espera *waiting room*
sala *f* de estar/comedor *living room/dining room*
salchicha *f* *sausage*
salir (-g-) *to depart, go out, leave*
saltar *to jump, leap*
saludar *to greet*
sangría *f* *sangria*
sano, -a *healthy*
sardina *f* *sardine*
sartén *f* *frying pan*
sé *I can, know how*
se quedaron con la boca abierta *they were left speechless*
secretaria *f* *secretary*
sed *f* *thirst*
sediento *thirsty*
seda *f* *silk*
seguir (-i-) *to continue, to follow*
según *according to*
segundo, -a *second*
seguramente *surely; (here:) no doubt*
seguridad *f* *safety*
sello *m* *stamp*
semana *f* *week*
semana *f* que viene *next week*
señal *f* *signal*
sencillo, -a *simple, plain*
sentarse (-ie-) *to sit down*
sentimiento *m* *sentiment, feeling*
sentir (-ie-) *to regret*
sentirse de maravilla *f* *to feel wonderful*
septiembre *m* *September*
ser *to be*
ser aficionado/a a alguna cosa *to be enthusiastic about something*
ser preciso *to be necessary*
ser probable *to be likely*
serie de *f*, una *a series of*
servicios *m pl* *toilets, bathrooms*
servir (-i-) *to serve*
servirse (-i-) *to help oneself*
sí *yes*
siempre *always*
siglo *m* *century*
silla *f* *chair*
simpático, -a *nice*
sin plomo *unleaded*
sino *but, otherwise*
situación *f* *situation*
sobre *on, over*
sobrina *f*, sobrino *m* *niece, nephew*
sofá *m* *sofa*
sol *m* *sun*
solamente *only*
soleado, -a *sunny*
soler (-ue-) *(to) usually (do)*

solicitar	*to order, apply for*
solicitar alguna cosa	*to ask for something*
sólo	*only*
solo, -a	*alone*
sonar (-ue-)	*to ring, sound*
sopa *f*	*soup*
sorpresa *f*	*surprise*
sótano *m*	*basement, cellar*
su	*your (formal)*
subir	*to board*
sucio, -a	*dirty*
sudado, -a	*sweaty*
suegra *f*	*mother-in-law*
suegro *m*	*father-in-law*
suela *f* (de zapatos)	*(shoe) sole*
sueldo *m*	*salary*
sueño *m*	*sleep*
suerte *f*	*luck, happiness*
sugerencia *f*	*suggestion*
sur *m*	*south*
susto *m*	*scare, fright*
suyo, -a	*yours (formal)*

T

taberna *f*	*(wine) bar*
tablao *m* de flamenco	*Flamenco stage*
tableta *f*	*chocolate*
tacón *m*	*heel*
taconeo *m*	*tap dancing*
talla *f*	*(clothes) size*
taller *m*	*garage, repair shop*
tamaño *m*	*size*
tambíen	*also, too, as well*
tampoco	*neither, not either*
tanto, -a	*so much*
tapa *f*	*tapa (snack in Spain)*
taquilla *f*	*ticket counter*
tardar	*to last, to need (time)*
tardar un rato	*to take a little longer*
tarde *f*	*afternoon*
tarjeta *f*	*business card*
tarjeta *f* telefónica	*phone card*
tarta *f*	*tart*
tasca *f*	*pub*
taxi *m*	*taxi*
taza *f*	*cup*
te importaría	*would you mind*
teatro *m*	*theater*
técnica *f*	*technology*
tele(visión) *f*	*TV*
teléfono *m*	*telephone*
temprano, -a	*early*
tenedor *m*	*fork*
tener	*to have*
tener a disposición	*to have at one's disposal*
tener ganas de	*to want to*
tener lugar	*to happen, occur*
tener mala cara	*to look bad*
tener miedo a alguna cosa	*to be afraid of something*
tener mucho ojo	*to keep one's eyes open*
tener razón	*to be right*
tener tos	*to have a cough*
tenis *m*	*tennis*
terminar	*to end*
tesis *f*	*thesis*
testigo *m*	*witness*
tía *f*, tío *m*	*aunt, uncle*
tiempo *m*	*time*
tiempo m libre	*spare/leisure time*
tienda *f*	*shop, tent*
tienda *f* de ropa	*clothing store*

tierra *f*	*earth*
timbre *m*	*doorbell*
tintorería *f*	*dry-cleaner's*
tíos *m pl*	*uncles and aunts*
típico, -a	*typical*
tipo *m*	*type, kind*
tirar	*to throw away*
tiro *m*	*shot*
tocar	*to play (an instrument)*
tocar el timbre	*to ring the doorbell*
toda una noche	*all through the night*
todavía	*still*
todavía no	*not yet*
todo	*everything*
todo el día	*the whole day*
todo está patas arriba	*everything is upside down*
todo recto	*straight ahead*
todos, -as	*all, whole*
tomar	*to take, drink*
tomar el sol	*to sunbathe*
tomar fotografías	*to take pictures*
tomar nota	*to note, write down*
tomate *m*	*tomato*
tortilla *f*	*Spanish omelet*
tos *f*	*cough*
toser	*to cough*
tostada *f*	*toast*
trabajar	*to work*
trabajo *m*	*work*
traducir (-zc-)	*to translate*
traer (-g-)	*to bring*
tráfico *m*	*traffic*
traje *m*	*suit*
tranquilo, -a	*calm, quiet*
transcurrir	*to go by, pass*
tratar de (+ inf.)	*to try to*
tren *m*	*train*
triste	*sad*
tristeza *f*	*sadness*
trozo *m*	*piece*
turista *m/f*	*tourist*
turístico, -a	*touristic*
tutearse	*to say "tú", to address with the informal "tú"*
tuyo, -a	*yours*

U

último, -a	*last*
un, -a	*one*
un, -a	*one*
universidad *f*	*university*
urgente	*urgent*
usar	*to use*
usted	*you (formal)*
utilizar	*to use*

V

vacaciones *f pl*	*holiday/vacation*
vale	*OK*
valer	*to be of use, worth*
valorar	*to value*
variado, -a	*various*
variedad *f*	*variety*
vaso *m*	*glass*
vaya	*well*
vecino *m*	*neighbour*
vendedor *m*	*vendor*
vender	*to sell*
venir	*to come*
venta *f*	*sale*
ventana *f*	*window*
ventanilla *f* de venta de billetes	*ticket counter*
ver	*to see*
verdad *f*	*truth*
verdadero, -a	*really, truly*

verde	*green*
verduras *f pl*	*vegetables*
vestíbulo *m*	*hallway*
vestirse (-i-)	*to get dressed*
vía *f* aérea	*by air*
viajar	*to travel*
viaje *m*	*journey*
vida *f*	*life*
vida *f* nocturna	*night life*
viernes *m*	*Friday*
vigilado, -a	*guarded*
vino *m*	*wine*
visita *f*	*visit*
visitar	*to visit*
viva	*(long) live*
vivir	*to live*
volante *m* del seguro	*insurance card*
volver (-ue-)	*to return*
vuelo *m*	*flight*
vuelta *f*	*return journey*

Y

y	*and*
ya	*already*

Z

zanahoria *f*	*carrot*
zapatería *f*	*shoemaker's*
zapato *m*	*shoe*
zumo *m* de naranja	*orange juice*

speaking your language

phrase book & dictionary
phrase book & CD

Available in: Arabic, Brazilian Portuguese*, Burmese*, Cantonese Chinese, Croatian, Czech*, Danish*, Dutch, English, Filipino, Finnish*, French, German, Greek, Hebrew*, Hindi*, Hungarian*, Indonesian, Italian, Japanese, Korean, Latin American Spanish, Malay, Mandarin Chinese, Mexican Spanish, Norwegian, Polish, Portuguese, Romanian*, Russian, Spanish, Swedish, Thai, Turkish, Vietnamese

*Book only

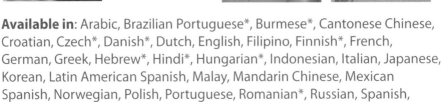

www.berlitzpublishing.com